# Once Upon a
# Time in China

# Once Upon a Time in China

## A Guide to Hong Kong, Taiwanese, and Mainland Chinese Cinema

## Jeff Yang

**Senior Contributors:**
Art Black, Grady Hendrix, Ric Meyers, Peter Nepstad,
Darryl Pestilence

**Contributors:**
John Charles, Andrew Grossman, Linn Haynes, Matt Levie,
Gary Morris, Yvonne Teh, Curtis Tsui, Caroline Vie-Toussaint

**ATRIA** BOOKS

NEW YORK   LONDON   TORONTO   SYDNEY

**ATRIA** BOOKS
1230 Avenue of the Americas
New York, NY 10020

Copyright © 2003 by Jeff Yang

Library of Congress Cataloging-in-Publication Data

Yang, Jeff.
    Once upon a time in China: a guide to Hong Kong, Taiwanese, and
mainland Chinese cinema / Jeff Yang; senior contributors, Art Black . . .
[et al.]; contributors, John Charles . . . [et al.].
        p. cm
        1. Motion pictures—China. 2. Motion pictures—China—Hong Kong.
    3. Motion pictures—Taiwan. I. Black, Art. II. Title
    PN1993.5.C4Y37 2003
    791.43'0951—dc22

                                                              2003066272


ISBN 0-7434-4817-0

First Atria Books Trade paperback edition December 2003

10  9  8  7  6  5  4  3  2  1

**ATRIA** BOOKS is a trademark of Simon & Schuster, Inc.

Manufactured in the United States of America

For information regarding special discounts for bulk purchases,
please contact Simon & Schuster Special Sales at 1-800-456-6798 or
business@simonandschuster.com

For Heather, my wife and the love of my life;
and for Hudson, who moved up his release date
to meet his parents early.

# Contents

Yang-yang reveals the unseen in *Yi Yi (A One and a Two)*.
*Courtesy of Sony Pictures Classics.*

# Preface

*I want to show them what they've never seen before.*

—*Yang-yang, Edward Yang's* Yi Yi (A One and a Two), *when asked why he takes pictures of the backs of people's heads*

Throughout my childhood, I thought of Chinese movies as a private treat—a guilty pleasure, not to be discussed or shared. That's because my youngest uncle, the one assigned to watch over me and my cousins on weekends when our parents were busy, had no clue what to do with a half-dozen unruly kids. To keep us quiet and out of trouble (or unsupervised trouble, anyway), he'd bring us down to Chinatown, to the crowded, smoky halls where the Chinese double-features played.

There, among audiences of napping retirees and adolescent thugs, we'd sit quietly mesmerized as epic tales of blood, thunder, and magic unspooled; as slapstick geniuses in bell-bottom pants tumbled wildly across the screen; even, with gritted teeth, as sloe-eyed Romeos stared soulfully at their tragic, terminal girlfriends.

Afterward, he'd take us all out to the Chinatown Ice Cream Factory, bribing us with mango ice cream to swear we'd been at the park. (God forbid that my parents ever put together the clues about where we'd really been; after all, pasty complexions and clothes that smelled like dried squid hardly spoke of sunny afternoons in a healthy outdoors environment.)

That's why, to me, Chinese films were secrets, to be mentioned only in whispers, out of earshot of adults and other polite company. And why no one was more shocked when, as the eighties drew to a close, they became the stuff of headlines, homage, and hysteria.

Suddenly, Jackie Chan—my own private childhood hero, the man who laughed at fear and made us laugh along with him—was joking along with Letterman and Leno on late-night TV. Chow Yun Fat, Hong Kong's most magnificent badass, was being heralded as the coolest actor in the world by the likes of *Los Angeles Times* and *Entertainment Weekly*. And American film critics were gingerly stepping around the unfamiliar territory of names that sounded like "Zang Ee Moe" (or dodging the issue entirely by simply referring to "the acclaimed director of *Ju Dou*").

As far as the eye could see was evidence that the films of Greater China—from the electric dreams of Hong Kong, to the post-Mao musings of the Mainland, to the angst-ridden urban dramas of Taiwan—had captured the American imagination. But it was also clear that most of the filmgoing public had been exposed to just a fraction of the proverbial iceberg. Chinese cinema represented over a century of achievement in three discrete yet interdependent industries; the works of Zhang Yimou and Jackie Chan, John Woo and Chen Kaige, Wong Kar Wai and Edward Yang were merely brilliant samples of a rich and complex canon.

And so, this book. *Once Upon a Time in China* is a comprehensive guide to the unique cinemas of Hong Kong, Taiwan, and the Mainland, and the first to explore these three incredible moviemaking industries as intertwined traditions. Each of *Once Upon a Time in China*'s six sections covers a different age in Greater Chinese cinematic history, from the dawn of the motion picture in turn-of-the-century Shanghai to today's alienated postboom generation. Chapter introductions provide context about the era, followed by capsule reviews of each period's most important and interesting films; interspersed throughout are short essays on Chinese cinema's most significant individuals, institutions, and phenomena, contributed by those who know them best. The material that could be included in this book was limited by its size. For those who want to read and see more, the reviews and essays found here and hundreds more are available in searchable form at www.OUATIC.com, a free website created to transform *Once Upon a Time in China* into a continuing, interactive dialogue about the world's most dynamic movie industries.

This book is a labor of love, by people who've become infatuated with extraordinary visions from half a world away, for moviegoers everywhere who've fallen in love with Chinese cinema . . . or who would, if they had the chance. It hopes to educate, to entertain, and to provide a handy reference for further exploration.

But most of all, it hopes to do what Yang-yang did: to show people what they've never seen before.

—*Jeff Yang*

# 1

# The Dawn of Chinese Film: 1896–1949

> After seeing these shadow plays, I thereupon sighed with the feeling that every change in the world is just like a mirage. There is no difference between life and shadow play . . . suddenly hidden from the view, suddenly reappearing. Life is really like dreams and bubbles, and all lives can be seen this way.
>
> *—A line from the earliest known*
> *Chinese movie review[1]*

In the spring of 1905, an ambitious photographer named Ren Qingtai hit upon a way to boost business at his thriving portrait studio: He decided to turn a large, unused side room into a theater where his friends could put on opera performances. The idea was less jaw-droppingly implausible than it might seem; Ren counted some of Shanghai's most popular actors and musicians among his acquaintances, and they readily agreed to put on impromptu concerts in his makeshift venue—the Fengtai Photography Shop performance hall and gallery.

What turned heads was Ren's *other* idea for the space. On nights when his friends weren't available, he wanted to use it to showcase the fancy new technology known as *dian ying xi*, "electric shadow plays"—or, as they were known in the West, "movies."

By that time, motion pictures had been shown in China for nearly a decade. In 1895, the Lumière brothers launched the industry known as cinema by displaying their primitive vignettes in a Paris café; a year later, on August 11, 1896, a Spanish entrepreneur known as Galen Bocca brought the new medium to Shanghai, screening a series of one-reel wonders to crowds who gathered at an "entertainment center" called Xu Garden. These entertainment centers offered a somewhat lowbrow alternative to Chinese opera, the most popular diversion of the time. Often located on the rooftop levels of department stores, they featured storytellers, jugglers, acrobats, and other performers who might otherwise be plying their trade on the streets.

But the miracle of the movies drew audiences of all types, from the elite to the working classes, to gawk at recordings of the exotic and the mundane—foreigners dancing, wrestling, and cavorting on beaches; faraway cities and sights, with their unusual architecture and the quirky customs of their residents. Bocca's movie festival packed the house. The following year, an American impresario came to Shanghai and began showing films to similar crowds in teahouses throughout the city. Despite the instant appeal of the medium, until Ren, no one had ever created a venue where movies were shown strictly for the sake of showing movies. There were no tickets sold for performances at teahouses and department stores; the exhibitions were there to lure paying customers into the building. Ren had hit upon the concept of the movie theater.

In a matter of months, the motion picture side of the Fengtai Photography Shop gallery quietly but surely squeezed out the live performance side. People who rarely went to operas were turning out for movies in droves, and it dawned upon Ren that his offbeat idea just might make him more money than he'd ever seen in his life. Unfortunately, the demand for motion pictures was beginning to outstrip the available supply of foreign imports, and Ren was reluctant to disappoint crowds with reruns. Like many a practical innovator, he resolved to take matters into his own hands. Through his stage acquaintances, he recruited Tan Xinpei, then known as the "King of Beijing Opera," to perform one of his most celebrated roles, the warrior-king in *Dangjun Mountain*, at the gallery. Then he borrowed a movie camera and invested in a reel of celluloid filmstock. The result, a crude piece of work shot in one take with a fixed camera (Ren was, after all, only familiar with still photography), nevertheless captured a thrilling performance by one of the era's biggest stars.

Upon its release in Ren's gallery, *Dangjun Mountain* (1905) proved to be a giant hit. People loved the opera, and people loved the movies. The "opera movie" provided the best of both worlds . . . while making it possible for anyone who could afford a ticket to see a performance often limited to the elite. Ren and his assistants at Fengtai would crank out other opera films for the next few years, and were rapidly beginning to believe they'd acquired a license to print money. Owners of the established opera theaters were, to say the least, discomfited by the idea that an upstart photo shop owner could, if he wanted, feature the great Tan Xinpei 365 days a year using this foreign technology (and without paying a dime of Tan's exorbitant fee). Ren deflected criticism with a shrug and a reference to the march of progress, no doubt while mentally counting his receipts.

In 1909, the Fengtai Photography Shop mysteriously burned to the ground. Perhaps taking the hint, Ren decided to get out of the film business altogether.

But the world had changed, and the movies were in China to stay. Beginning in 1907, permanent, film-only theaters were being built in Beijing and Shanghai, and had already begun popping up in Taiwan and Hong Kong. Then, in 1910, an American filmmaker named Benjamin Brodsky set up shop in Shanghai under the banner of the Asia Film Company—China's first film studio.

**CHINESE OPERA**

功夫

Scene from *The Love Eterne,* one of the
most popular opera stories ever put to film.
*Courtesy of Celestial Pictures. All rights reserved.*

In 1790, the reigning Emperor Qianlong celebrated his eightieth birthday in style, inviting opera troupes from all over China to come to the capital and perform. The troupes were a hit, and many stayed on to earn fame and fortune playing for the court. Slowly they began to blend together, as songs or dances that proved popular in one were quickly adopted by another, until at last a new style emerged that combined the best from each tradition. Today we know it as Beijing opera.

In those early days, opera was performed strictly for the pleasure of the emperor's court. But opera troupes needed a place to rehearse, and it was found that teahouses often had adequate space for that purpose. Soon, commoners began congregating in teahouses just to see the performances, and before long, some teahouses turned over completely to become the first opera theaters, charging admission. The court, however, was jealous of their entertainment, and often, heavy bribes had to be paid to keep this lucrative side business going.

Though Beijing opera is the dominant form of Chinese opera, even today, hundreds of regional styles remain in existence. Each has its own specialty: Beijing opera favors epic historical, mythological, or military plays, filled with acrobatics, while Cantonese opera, the style most popular around Hong Kong, emphasizes singing and often features love stories. What they have in common are elaborate costumes, dramatic makeup, and stylized movement, music, and song. Sets are nearly nonexistent; instead, actors use gestures or props to indicate that they are riding a horse or fighting an army. Players trained in acrobatics flip through the air in tightly choreographed combat sequences, while bearded generals in full armor, pennants fluttering, lumber through the chaos, spear in hand, flipping opponents to and fro. The prize for which the warriors contend? Usually, the hand of a beautiful woman—played, in most cases, by a man.

During opera's heyday in the 1930s, opera players were celebrities whose every move was followed by the public. It was only natural that opera stars would make the transition to the silver screen. In postwar Hong Kong, audiences who could ill afford the cost of live opera flocked to watch their favorite players on film. But by the end of the sixties, opera had lost much of its box office appeal, and by the seventies, Chinese opera had all but faded away. Opera students who spent countless twelve-hour days learning acrobatic, singing, and fighting skills graduated to find that opportunities to practice their art had disappeared. Their only recourse: joining the industry that had replaced it. The golden age of Chinese opera is gone, but—for fans of opera-trained stars like Jackie Chan, Lam Ching Ying, and fight choreographer Yuen Woo Ping—the soul of Chinese opera lives on.

*—Peter Nepstad*

## THE SHOWMAN

The story of Brodsky, the Russian Jewish émigré whose enterprising character would spark a cinematic explosion both on the Chinese mainland and in Hong Kong, is marked by some of the gaps and inconsistencies expected from a relentlessly successful promoter. According to an interview he later granted the *New York Tribune*'s George S. Kaufman—who would one day become a successful Broadway writer and producer himself— Brodsky brought in his first movie audience by "paying it to attend . . . surely a procedure unique in the annals of showdom. . . . In this manner several dozen theatres were put on their feet, in cities all over China."[2]

Brodsky's account notably overlooks the fact that motion pictures were already quite popular by the time of his arrival, and that movie theaters had been in place in major cities for years. But even if Brodsky wasn't the "father" of the Chinese film industry, he was certainly a key factor in its growth—at one point controlling a chain of eighty-one theaters, which needed to be fed with product. "There sprang up a demand for the Chinese photoplay," wrote Kaufman, "and Mr. Brodsky saw that he would have to satisfy it. Then and there was founded the Chinese Cinema Company [sic]. Mr. Brodsky is the only American connected with this enterprise. The consulting committee [includes] Kim Louey O'Hoy, Ma Yat Chiu, Fong Fu Gam and the like. At their two studios, they are turning out a picture a week."[3]

Asia Film Company's output was somewhat less prolific than Kaufman reported, with its single largest work being a mammoth ten-reel documentary entitled *Brodsky's Trip to China*, which was released in the United States to some acclaim. Despite the studio's moderate successes, it didn't turn out to be the powerhouse of profit that Brodsky hoped, and within a few years, he sold the business to an American insurance executive named Yashell and left for Hong Kong. Yashell recognized that, despite the studio's all-Chinese "consulting committee," Brodsky's unwillingness to give up the spotlight hampered the company's ability to work with the natives. Yashell decided that he had to find a Chinese frontman—someone who knew the local audiences and their tastes, and could hire and work with local performers.[4]

Yashell's answer came in the form of Zhang Shichuan, a trader and merchant who had no previous experience in the arts. He did, however, have a shrewd business sense, as well as the friendship of Zheng Zhengqiu, a leading light of Shanghai theater. "My friend Zheng centered all his interest on drama at the time. He was in and out of theaters every day," Zhang would later recall.[5] Like Ren Qingtai before him, Zhang drew his talent pool from the opera, and Zheng Zhengqiu's connections made it possible.

Under Zhang's supervision, Asia Film Company would make nearly five films a year over the next four years, including China's first fictional feature that wasn't simply a recording of an opera performance—1913's

*The Difficult Couple,* codirected by Zhang and Zheng. After the success of that film, Zhang began entertaining thoughts of striking out on his own, and in 1916, left to form the Huanxian Film Company, which produced just one film—the obscure *Wronged Ghosts in Opium Den* (1916)—before going bankrupt.

## HELLO, HONG KONG

By this time, the industry was becoming increasingly competitive. Other production companies had appeared on the scene, both in Shanghai and in the nascent economic powerhouse, the British colony of Hong Kong. Indeed, Benjamin Brodsky himself had invested in a new studio located in the colony, funding the cinematic efforts of a pair of brothers—Li Beihai and Li Minwei. Brodsky had met Li Beihai earlier on the set of Liang Shaopo's *Stealing the Roast Duck* (1909), a short comedy that is generally regarded as the first film produced in Hong Kong. *Roast Duck* was simplistic at best, featuring just three characters—Fatty, Skinny Thief, and Cop—but Skinny Thief was portrayed by the director, who would play a major role in the development of feature filmmaking in Hong Kong, while Li Beihai was cast as the cop.

The Li brothers proposed the creation of a production company called Hua Mei, or "China America" Films. After Brodsky and another American put up the necessary funds, the Li brothers made their debut film: the pioneering *Zhuangzi Tests His Wife* (1913). This film is notable not only for being just the second feature-length picture to be produced in the greater China region, but also for being the first to have a female cast member. Li Beihai played the philosopher Zhuangzi, while Li Minwei played as the sage's pretty young wife; Minwei's real-life wife, Yan Shanshan, took a supporting role as a serving girl.

Unfortunately, circumstances would then conspire to freeze the development of cinema in Hong Kong for nearly a decade. The colony had come to depend on Germany as its sole source of film stock, and the outbreak of the First World War in 1914 essentially made such goods unavailable. Films would not be made in Hong Kong again until the early twenties.

Li Minwei, the Father of Hong Kong Cinema, as the sage Zhuangzi's wife.
*Courtesy of the Hong Kong Film Archive.*

## SHANGHAI TRIAD

Meanwhile, in Shanghai, film production was booming. The same war that suffocated Hong Kong studios liberated companies operating in Shanghai, since the European studios that provided much of the product to Chinese theater chains were mostly shuttered.

As a result, local studios proliferated. In 1917, a printing and publishing company, Commercial Press, jumped into the movie game by trading the price of a return ticket home to an American filmmaker in exchange for all of his equipment. Not only did they emerge as an early industry leader, they also owned the lab that provided most of the other studios with film-developing services. In 1920 and 1921, the first full-length feature films were produced by Shanghai studios, the most notable of these being the Shanghai Film Company's *Sea Oath* (1921). But the Shanghai cinema landscape experienced its biggest upheaval with the reemergence of impresario Zhang Shichuan on the scene, announcing that he, Zheng Zhengqiu, and other partners were launching what would be the first of the major Shanghai studios: Mingxing Film Company.

The complementary talents and resources of Mingxing's founders gave it tremendous clout in the emerging industry, allowing the company to hire the most prominent early stars and filmmakers. However, the studio quickly faced a challenge from the very thing that made it a force to reckon with: the contrasting personalities and priorities of Zhang and Zheng. Business-minded Zhang was convinced the company should be focused on light entertainments that weren't burdened by a heavy moral tone. Zheng, on the other hand, was dedicated to the principle that film should uplift society, providing guidance and ethical example. Mingxing's early projects—comedies, newsreels, and a true-crime murder story—followed Zhang's commercial dictum. Ironically, they were profoundly unsuccessful, and as a result, Zhang gave way to his partner's wish to make *Orphan Rescues Grandfather* (1923), a somewhat maudlin drama whose underlying theme celebrated the value of education. *Orphan* ended up rescuing the studio, while convincing Zhang that it was possible to be both socially responsible *and* fiscally successful. Mingxing soon became famous for developing the cinematic genre known as "social problem" films—dramas that illuminated the ills of the modern world; when the Kuomintang's Nanjing government came into power, Mingxing subsequently became a magnet for leftist filmmakers whose work subtly (and not-so-subtly) criticized the Nationalist regime.

Another major studio of the time, and the one that, after many incarnations, would become the dominant film studio in all of Asia, was Tianyi Film Company, founded in 1925 by the Shaw brothers, led by eldest sibling Runjie. In sharp contrast to Mingxing, which was avowedly progressive in its politics and product, Tianyi was dedicated to preserving what it saw as "authentic Chinese culture"—incorporating in its works period settings and the stories of classic literature. As a result, leftist social critics generally dismissed its output, suggesting that its films celebrated backward ideas, superstitious beliefs, and reactionary attitudes; nevertheless, its films were extremely popular with working-class audiences.

Tianyi was largely responsible for the development of the other three predominant genres of early Chinese cinema: *baishi pian,* dramas that purported to record historical events and occurrences; *guzhuang pian,* costume dramas set in classical Chinese times; and *wuxia pian,* wandering-swordsman epics that were the ancestor of modern martial arts cinema.[6]

The last category became particularly popular in the latter half of the decade, prompted by the success of Tianyi's pioneering *Swordswoman Li Feifei* (1925), which set the prerequisites for the genre: fast action, gaudy costumes, and the thrilling acrobatics of Beijing opera. (Although ironically, socially conscious Mingxing benefited the most from the late-twenties dominance of *wuxia pian,* when Zhang Shichuan chimed in with one of his infrequent directorial turns, 1928's *The Burning of Red Lotus Temple,* which was so popular that it launched eighteen sequels.) From 1928 to 1930, over 250 *wuxia pian* were produced—nearly 60 percent of the industry's total film output.[7]

But the end of the decade saw the rise of the Nationalist Nanjing regime, and a resultant shakeup in the film industry, including the establishment of the National Film Censorship Committee in 1931, which formalized harsh controls on the content and tone of cinematic works, banning or restricting works that it saw as promoting superstition, immorality, or social unrest. At the same time, the industry's leading studios recognized that with over 170 film companies in production (146 in Shanghai alone), Chinese film was operating at a vast overcapacity, one that had driven the price paid by theater owners for a film print down almost 90 percent over the course of just a few years.[8]

Their solution was Machiavellian, but probably one that saved the industry: Six top studios came together to form a single corporation, called Liuhe (the "Joined Six"), including Mingxing, Minxin (the new studio founded by Li Minwei and his brothers Beihai and Haishan, which had transplanted itself from Hong Kong to Shanghai during the "Great Strike" of 1925), Great China-Lily, Shanghai Film Company, China Theater Company, and Youlian Film Company.

The partners' objective was to eliminate the competition with sheer economies of scale. Their plan proved successful; by the end of the decade, the number of studios still operating had dwindled to about a dozen.

Tianyi, which had always produced films on the cheap, scoffed at the cartel and stayed independent throughout the twenties; by the turn of the decade, there was no longer any real rationale for collusion, and the studios unwound their association. In 1929, two of them, Minxin and Great China-Lily, engaged in a formal merger to create Lianhua Film Company—the largest and most important studio of the thirties. (Lianhua would grow even larger in 1931, when it subsumed another Liuhe refugee, Shanghai Film Company.) The trinity of Lianhua, Mingxing, and Tianyi, along with two upstarts, Xinhua and Yihua, would dominate the golden age of Chinese cinema until the formal declaration of the Sino-Japanese War in 1937.

## LIANHUA AND THE GOLDEN AGE

Of the five major studios of the golden age, Lianhua enjoyed a privileged position, due in large part to its close ties with the KMT (Kuomintang) regime. Its high-minded, overtly moralist corporate mission was applauded by the Nanjing government, which was engaged in an aggressive campaign to root out "base culture." Much of its attention was focused on the crowd-pleasing but retrograde films being made by Tianyi, which—after the invasion of Manchuria by Japan in 1931—was subsequently coerced by the KMT into shifting its output toward propaganda in service of the war effort. By contrast, a number of politically powerful KMT officials actually joined Lianhua's board of directors, making the company virtually untouchable.

Given this freedom, Lianhua proceeded to make some of the most brilliant and popular films of the decade, implementing for the first time in Chinese film history a rich cinematic language (featuring complex camera movement and sophisticated editing and lighting) and naturalistic acting and directing techniques that broke away from the expressionistic legacy of traditional Chinese opera. Some of Lianhua's classics are Sun Yu's *Big Road* (1934), Cai Chusheng's *Song of the Fisherman* (1934), and Wu Yonggang's *Little Angel* (1935), all of which presented social issues with heretofore unseen subtlety and complexity.

As Lianhua's novel techniques were emulated by its rivals, these wholesale changes in the industry had an unexpected side effect: For the first time, screen stars, as opposed to transplanted opera performers, emerged—and in an upset of tradition, the biggest draws were not male but female. Top actresses had enormous fan followings, and were exhaustively and sensationally reported on by the press. No detail of romantic or sexual exploit was off limits. (Since the word "actress," before the silver screen, was generally synonymous with "prostitute," the unspoken media rationale seems to have been that female performers didn't need or deserve social privacy.)

Studios clamored to hire the most popular names and faces, knowing that the right lead actress could make a film instantly successful. Two performers in particular stood out as the reigning screen goddesses of this era, and while they occupied similarly tender places in the hearts of their fans, in all other ways, they were as different as night and day.

One was Ruan Lingyu, a mistress of melodrama who specialized in playing "broken blossoms," and whose life emulated her art. In 1935, she committed suicide at the peak of her stardom, driven by tragic circumstances that bore an eerie similarity to the melodramas that made her famous.

Born Ruan Fenggen in Shanghai on April 26, 1910 ("Lingyu" was an adopted stage name), Ruan witnessed the death of her father when she was five. His death precipitated a disastrous drop in the family's social standing. Forced to work to support her children, Ruan's mother became a maid to the wealthy Zhang clan. Young Ruan's budding beauty attracted the attention of the Zhang heir, Zhang Damin, and the two began a surreptitious affair, culminating in their secret marriage. The Zhangs were horrified when they discovered this serious breach of class propriety, and immediately hushed up their son's indiscretion.

But Ruan's overnight success while still a teenager soon turned the tables; as Ruan's star rose, her relationship with her nominal husband devolved into sheer economics, with Ruan paying Zhang simply to leave her alone.

Ruan's acting career began when the Mingxing ("Star") Film Company hired her at age sixteen to act in *Marriage in Name* (aka *The Fake Couple*), directed by leading filmmaker Bu Wancang. After making several more films for Mingxing, she jumped ship to the rival Great China-Lily Film Company, where she made another half-dozen films. By 1930,

The tragic Ruan Lingyu.
*Courtesy of the Hong Kong Film Archive.*

she was already well known, but Great China-Lily's merger that year with the rival Minxin ("People's Heart") Film Company, to create the Lianhua Film Company, made her the biggest name in the business. There she would find her greatest success in a series of intense, female-centered melodramas, many of them engaged with such pressing social issues as poverty, class conflict, prostitution, childbirth out of wedlock, women's rights, and, poignantly, suicide.

A scan of the titles of her films indicates something of their varied content—*Reminiscence of Peking* (1930), *Love and Duty* (1933), *Suicide Contract* (1930), *Goddess* (1934), *New Woman* (1934)—but fails to impart the subtlety of Ruan's performances, which were far more sophisticated than the tortured grimaces and flailings that marked much early silent cinema. Comparisons made by modern critics between Ruan and Greta Garbo are more than mere conceit; like the famous Swede, Ruan brought to her roles an unmannered directness and a sense of emotional authenticity that set her apart from her peers. Equally credible in the role of suicidal mother

(*Love and Duty*), career woman (*New Woman*), murderous prostitute (*Goddess*), even patriot (*Little Toys*, 1933), Ruan was a luminous presence whose cinematic collaborators well understood her appeal, showcasing her fragile, fleeting beauty through the use of trademark closeups.

At the height of her career, Ruan became romantically involved with a Shanghai businessman; Ruan's vengeful ex-husband, Zhang, no longer satisfied with extortion, exposed the affair and sued her for divorce. The resulting scandal incited an early tabloid feeding frenzy, as the local press churned the story into a sensation. Ruan, in shame and despair, killed herself on March 8, 1935, leaving behind a note that read: "The words of people are fearful." Her funeral, with crowds of mourners estimated in the tens of thousands, was noticed even by *The New York Times*.

The other goddess of the early Chinese screen has been nearly lost in the passage of time, though her career was five times longer and her fame, at its peak, at least as great. If Ruan was a beauty touched with sadness, her counterpart was a beauty touched by fire. She was unabashedly flirtatious with the camera, embracing her sensuality without shame or fear. Her name was Hu Die, the Butterfly, and for nearly a decade in old Shanghai, she ruled the silver screen.

The story goes that one day early in her childhood, Hu Die was taken

Screen queen Hu Die.
*Courtesy of the Hong Kong Film Archive.*

to see the Forbidden City by her father. As might be expected of a young child, she was full of questions: Who lived in the palace? Could she live there if she wanted to? And as they approached the throne in the old palace's great hall, her father told her that only the emperor could live in the City. Could she become the emperor when she grew up? she asked. And her father smiled and shook his head no.

Hu Die pulled away from him and scrambled up onto the throne. "If I can't become emperor in the future," she declared, "then I will become the queen."[9]

By the time she was twenty-five years old, she had made true her vow, winning the title of "Queen of Film" in the first magazine poll to select China's cinema royalty.

Unlike many of her fellow performers, Hu Die always knew that she wanted to be a movie star. Although she was born in Shanghai to a Cantonese family in 1908, she was raised in Northern China in the area around Beijing. She moved to Shanghai to join the screen trade immediately upon graduating from Zhonghua Film School in 1924. Over the next four years, she would make twenty films (sixteen of them for the Tianyi Film Company), gaining recognition for both her striking looks and the passion she brought even to minor supporting roles.

In 1928, Mingxing signed her to an exclusive contract, making her their signature star, and Chinese cinema's best-paid performer, paying her two thousand yuan a month—about twenty times what a standard repertory actress made at the time, and about eight times what a top *male* performer, like Lianhua hunk Jin Yan, made. The classic films in which she appeared included the early *wuxia* epic *Burning of Red Lotus Temple* (1928), as well as China's first "talkie," *Sing Song Girl Red Peony* (1930), and the leftist masterpiece *Twin Sisters* (1933). Although her friend and rival Ruan Lingyu was considered to be by far the more talented actress, Hu Die was prettier and more versatile: She could sing and dance, she could cry on cue, and she could speak both Mandarin and Cantonese fluently. The latter skill would prove an undeniable asset after sound became a standard feature in motion pictures.

While Hu's life was not as tragic as that of Ruan, she faced her own share of personal challenges. Although she was happily married, she was coerced into a sexual relationship with the head of the KMT secret police, which ended only when the official was killed in a plane disaster. The 1937 Japanese invasion led her, like many other industry lights, to flee to Hong Kong; there, her language skills enabled her to appear in Mandarin and Cantonese-language films, including the first "two-way" picture—*Rouge Tears* (1938), which was made in both Mandarin and Cantonese versions.

As Shanghai rebuilt its industry after the war, the Chinese film market increasingly became divided between those two dialects, and Hu Die's flexibility gave her unprecedented career resilience. Even after she grew out of ingenue roles, she was still in great demand for more mature parts, dividing her time between the Mandarin and Cantonese film industries. She retired from the movies in 1967, after a career that spanned five decades, and emigrated to Canada, where she lived until her death on April 23, 1989—a rare example of a female star whose career boasted both incredible success and unprecedented longevity.

## UNDERCURRENTS OF UNREST

The decadence and flash of twenties Shanghai was merely a glittery surface, hiding social divisions that would eventually tear Chinese society apart. Most filmmakers had a progressive bent to their politics, even if, as was the case with twenties directors like Zheng Zhengqiu and Bu Wancang, this was primarily expressed in their preoccupation with moral instruction. A younger cohort of directors and screenwriters was more radical in its beliefs, wholeheartedly embracing left politics—and increasingly, the Communist party, which had barely survived a bloody purge by the KMT in 1927. The League of Leftist Performing Artists, secretly organized by Communist party leaders, counted among its members many of the most prominent talents in the business. Three of the big five studios had key creative personnel who were closet Communists—including Lianhua, despite its strong ties to the KMT.

The increasingly leftist tone of film production at the major studios was at first tolerated by the government, because the KMT initially saw the moral content of leftist film as aligned with its own social uplift programs, such as the so-called "New Life" Movement. But hard-right members of the KMT became increasingly discontented; finally, in 1933, they organized a riot at the production headquarters of the prominently progressive Yihua Film Company, shattering windows, beating personnel, and destroying machinery—assigning credit for the action to the "Anti-Communist Squad of the Shanghai Film Industry."

The stage was set for China's two diametrically opposed ideologies to erupt in open combat—but with the invasion of Shanghai by Japan in 1937, another war would delay that inevitable showdown for nearly a decade.

## DODGING THE BULLET

Fears of war had shattered Shanghai's economy; now Japanese bombs were doing the same to its infrastructure. The Shanghai film industry was paralyzed, with some studios, like Mingxing, closing their doors forever, and others attempting to ride out the storm in the city's British- and French-controlled "foreign concession" areas (Shanghai's so-called "Orphan Island"). The bulk of Shanghai's cinematic talent chose a third option: relocating to Hong Kong.

After the end of World War I, Hong Kong's film industry had gradually risen from the ashes, largely due to the efforts of the intrepid Li brothers Minwei and Beihai, whose successful founding of Minxin Film Company opened the way for the launch of a profusion of other studios. But when the Great Strike of 1925 precipitated a wholesale shutdown of Hong Kong's businesses, Minxin evacuated to Shanghai, eventually merging into the Lianhua giant, while other, smaller studios simply disappeared. (The exception to this rule was Grandview, the unique "transpacific" studio founded by U.S.-trained partners Moon Kwan Man Ching and Joe Chiu Shu Sun; Grandview, affiliated with Lianhua and headquartered in San Francisco, survived and thrived as a major cinematic force from its founding in 1935 until the mid to late forties.)

But after the Japanese invasion of Shanghai, a vast train of cinematic refugees took up residence in the temporary safe harbor of the colony—some just until the war's inevitable end, others for good. The subsequent half-decade, in which the island was insulated from the growing chaos of the Mainland, became a first golden age for Hong Kong's motion picture industry. By the end of the thirties, the colony's industry had grown to such a point that there were more theaters per capita on the island than anywhere in Greater China.

Then, in 1941, the false security offered by British rule disappeared, when the Japanese staged an all-out invasion of Hong Kong.

## BETWEEN WORLD WAR AND CIVIL WAR

In 1945, after nearly a decade of devastating conflict, Japan retreated from China's territories, leaving behind a nation in disarray. Although the Nationalists attempted to launch a rebuilding campaign from their wartime capital of Chongqing, they faced growing tension with the Communists, who had served as uneasy partners against the common Japanese enemy during the war. Still, before the two parties began to engage in open combat, there was a brief period in which China, and its film industry, had the opportunity to regroup. The Japanese had hit Shanghai hard, but a core of returning talent and some scattered production facilities remained. During the war, both Japan and the Nationalists had recognized the value of the film industry as a propaganda resource, and created centralized production and distribution facilities to handle their limited cinematic output. Upon declaring victory over the Japanese, the KMT co-opted the motion picture infrastructure the enemy had built and added it to the system under its existing control. The resulting Central Film Studio produced a wide range of films, ranging from pro-Nationalist propaganda to romantic fluff.

But there were independent voices in China as well. Cai Chusheng, returning from sanctuary in Hong Kong, recruited a group of fellow former Lianhua peers to create the "Lianhua Film Society," an autonomous studio that managed to produce two masterpieces in less than a year— *Eight Thousand Li of Cloud and Moon* and the first installment of the two-part epic *Spring River Flows East* (both 1947). The following year, the society merged into another free-standing studio, Kunlun Film Company, creating an institution that served as the linchpin of leftist cinema for the remainder of the pre-Communist era. Among the classic works produced by Kunlun were *Myriad of Lights* (1948), *An Orphan on the Streets* (1949), and *Crows and Sparrows* (1949), perhaps the greatest work of the postwar period. Another, less ideologically motivated autonomous studio was Wenhua Film Company, whose productions—comedies such as *Phony Phoenixes* (1947) and melodramas like the brilliant *Spring in a Small Town* (1948)—were driven primarily by commercial concerns and artistic objectives.

In some ways, the four years between the end of the war and the beginning of the Revolution represented the apex of pre–Communist era cinema. Despite the challenges filmmakers of the period faced—including runaway inflation that raised the prices of some everyday objects by over a *million* percent in the final years of the decade—they were making movies of unprecedented sophistication, beauty, and creative diversity. For Chinese cinema, it was the calm before the storm.

—*Jeff Yang, with Gary Morris (Ruan Lingyu)*

# 2

# Swordsmen and Revolutionaries: The Fifties and Sixties

Pay Serious Attention to the Discussion of the Film *The Life of Wu Xun.* The question raised by *The Life of Wu Xun* is fundamental in nature. A fellow like Wu Xun . . . strove fanatically to spread feudal culture and . . . fawned in every way on the reactionary feudal rulers—ought we to praise such disgusting behaviour? The appearance of the film *The Life of Wu Xun,* and particularly the spate of praise lavished on Wu Xun and the film, show how ideologically confused our country's cultural circles have become!

—*Editorial by Mao Zedong,* People's Daily, *May 20, 1951*[10]

**B**y mid-1949, the Chinese civil war had entered its endgame. The Nationalist Army had lost over one and a half million soldiers in the previous year alone, and all pretense of its ability to hold China had begun to collapse, with the Red Army prevailing in key battles throughout the north. By December 8, 1949, the KMT had launched a "strategic retreat" to the island of Taiwan, where they established a new seat of government in the city of Taipei. Indeed, the retreat was a foregone conclusion. Mao Zedong, architect of the Great People's Revolution, had already announced the establishment of the People's Republic of China two months earlier, on October 1, 1949.

Where cinema was concerned, the result was a cleaving of the Chinese motion picture industry into three separate and ideologically disparate entities. Cinema in Mainland China fell under the pall of the Communist party, which slammed shut China's largest market to "foreign" producers (with the notable exception of the Soviet Union), and increasingly required filmmakers to abide by rigid political standards. In Taiwan, after the chaos and destruction invoked by the Chinese civil war, the film industry underwent a slow period of rebuilding; there, too, output was initially shaped by government censorship and control, although the relatively free flow of talent and product between Taiwan, Hong Kong, and the West inoculated the region against the creative isolation suffered by the Mainland. Finally, Hong Kong—whose cinematic influence in the region had historically been eclipsed by sophisticated, cosmopolitan Shanghai—came into its own, experiencing an unprecedented flowering of artistic achievement and commercial success and evolving into Asia's most important motion picture industry.

## LOWERING THE BAMBOO CURTAIN

Movies had long been seen by Chinese Communists as a strategic political resource. Because film was a broadly accessible popular medium whose means of production were easily centralized and controlled, it was recognized as having overwhelming advantages as a tool for propaganda. Indeed, seven months *before* the founding of the People's Republic, the CCP (Chinese Communist Party) had already established a ministry to oversee all film production, exhibition, distribution, and education: the Central Film Bureau. By November 1949, the gathering of cinematic resources under the bureau's supervision was well underway, with three of China's largest studios falling under the direct operational control of the bureau. These were the Northeast, Beijing, and Shanghai film studios; together, they accounted for more than three-quarters of China's total film output. Although private film companies would continue to exist for the next few years, their ability to produce work independent of the CCP's strict constraints was severely curtailed.

A key example of the consequences of party-line deviation came with the release of 1950's *The Life of Wu Xun,* a decidedly leftist film by a decidedly leftist filmmaker, Sun Yu. Although it was initially praised for its proeducation message, criticism of the film from the very top—Mao himself—soon triggered a broad public campaign denouncing it as counterrevolutionary, since it praised a figure who "toadied" to feudal overlords, instead of taking up arms and overthrowing society's oppressors.[11] This wholesale shifting of public opinion proved deadly to independent film companies, who were never certain when they would suffer political attack, and whose box office results now depended as much on their adherence to ideology as on their ability to deliver entertaining product. Accepting their fate, in 1952, the remaining private studios allowed themselves to be absorbed into the central film system, eliminating independent film on the Mainland for much of the next half-century. After this, the Central Film Bureau came into its own. It oversaw admissions and curricula at the Beijing Film School (later the Beijing Film Academy); it established strict quotas for subject matter (funding a set number of films about agriculture, a set number about worker productivity, and so forth); it approved project proposals, scripts, and directors; it censored final product; it decided whether, when, and how films would be released; and it controlled film criticism in party organs such as the *People's Daily* newspaper.

In short, the bureau had near-absolute control over cinema, and used it to enforce an aesthetic philosophy it referred to as "socialist realism." This required artists to represent "deep truths" rather than "surface truths," which is to say, strict party doctrine, rather than individual interpretation or opinion.[12] As a result, cinematic innovation on the Mainland was essentially put into a state of suspended animation, until 1956, when the Hundred Flowers period—Mao's short-lived and ultimately tragic experiment with cultural openness—allowed the creation of works that diverged from, or even criticized, government doctrine.

## "ORPHAN ISLAND" REDUX

Meanwhile, the great current of change occurring on the Mainland smashed down over the tiny island on its eastern coast with the force of a tidal wave.

Taiwan had long had a disproportionate prominence in the political history of Greater China. Ceded to Japan as part of the settlement that ended the first Sino-Japanese War in 1895, Taiwan was ruled as a Japanese colony for most of the first half of the twentieth century. Its people were second-class citizens in their own homeland: The Fukienese dialect spoken by most natives was banned in schools and other public forums, while Japanese was established as the official language of law, commerce, and government. Non-Japanese were restricted from holding most positions of power and influence; and the educational system was restructured in order to indoctrinate Taiwanese children as loyal Japanese subjects.

When the island was finally returned to China in 1945, nearly half a million Japanese nationals, representing virtually the entire ranks of Taiwan's business and civil leadership, were forcibly deported. A society whose native culture and identity had been suppressed—sometimes violently— for half a century braced itself for reassimilation into the Chinese mainstream. But the KMT, locked in bloody civil war with the Communists, hardly had the resources to fill the void left behind by the departing Japanese. Social services collapsed. Many local businesses, battered by the war and in most cases missing key management, went bankrupt or were taken over by unscrupulous profiteers. Inflation spiraled out of control: Prices went up by as much as 2,500 percent a year for staple goods, rendering paper currency virtually worthless. When the KMT moved to fill available political positions with Mainland transplants, hopes on the island for some kind of self-determination were squelched.

Facing the worst of both worlds—continued oppression, without the economic and social stability of the old colonial regime—native Taiwanese became increasingly bitter. On February 28, 1947, the situation came to a bloody head, as an incident of police brutality triggered spontaneous unrest that swept the island. The riots were put down by KMT forces in a crackdown still referred to by Taiwanese as the *Er Er Ba* ("two-two-eight") Incident. By the time the violence wound down, some twenty thousand Taiwanese had been killed.

Ironically, it was just two years later that Taiwan became involuntary host to 1.6 million Nationalist soldiers and their families, retreating from the CCP takeover of the Mainland. In 1948, the population of Taiwan was around 7 million, meaning that this flood of refugees represented some 20 percent of the total population—many of them unemployed, some of them homeless, and all of them promised a better life and brighter future in Taiwan than the one they'd left behind. Instead, the Mainland arrivistes found an island in total economic disarray, with residents whose memory of the Er Er Ba massacre still remained fresh.

To prevent the outbreak of open revolt, the Nationalists—referred to by natives as *wai sheng ren* ("born-elsewhere people")—imposed strict martial law. During the decade that followed, a series of ruthless purges was launched, ostensibly to root out communist collaborators, resulting in a chilling climate of widespread and peremptory persecution, arrests, and executions that came to be called the "White Terror." Although its worst abuses were gradually eliminated, martial law was not formally lifted until 1987.

That a unique national cinema managed to grow out of this turmoil is a small wonder; that the Taiwanese motion picture industry eventually emerged as one of Asia's most influential and vibrant over the next few decades is nothing short of a miracle. Buoyed by subsidies from the government's Central Motion Picture Corporation (which was seeking to promote "healthy realism") and by surging demand from Mandarin-language film circuits in Hong Kong for (neither healthy nor realistic) period swordfighting flicks, Taiwanese cinema entered into the beginnings of a golden age in the mid-sixties. Indeed, by 1966, the Taiwanese film industry had ramped up to a point where only Japan and the prolific "Bollywood" studios of India exceeded it in feature film production in Asia.

The sizzling days of Shanghai as a capital of the silver screen were gone, perhaps never to return. The center of cinematic gravity had shifted outward, to Taiwan and its island cousin to the south, Hong Kong.

## HONG KONG STEPS INTO THE SPOTLIGHT

Colonial Hong Kong had been the bolt-hole of choice for movie people fleeing the Japanese occupation, and then, after World War II, for leftist filmmakers and performers taking refuge from Nationalist crackdowns on suspected communist sympathizers. As the CCP solidified its hold over the Mainland, a new flood of artists and moguls established themselves on the island, fearing that the Communist takeover threatened both their creative freedom and their personal safety (quite rightly, as it turned out, since many left-leaning artists who returned to the Mainland in triumph after the Revolution ironically ended up being purged during the CCP's "Anti-Rightist" Movement of 1957).

Postwar Hong Kong cinema teemed with talented and colorful characters, such as the enterprising Zhang Shankun, a film mogul who'd parlayed gangland roots into a position as chief of Shanghai's Xinhua Studios. After Shanghai's foreign concessions (China's so-called "orphan island") were overrun, Zhang was pressed into service as general manager of Japan's propaganda factory, the United China Film Production Company. Japan's World War II defeat led to Zhang's indictment as a collaborator, whereupon he promptly "relocated" to Hong Kong. There he was instrumental in launching both Yonghua Studios and its biggest competitor, the Great Wall Film Company, before reviving Xinhua as a Hong Kong–based concern. These, along with Jiang Boying's Da Zhonghua Film Company and the leftist Fenghuang Studios, were among the most active motion picture producers in the decade immediately following the war.

As the fifties wound on, however, the story of Hong Kong cinema distilled itself into the tale of a colossal war between two great studios—a cinematic arms race that advanced the quality and popularity of Hong Kong motion pictures by leaps and bounds, while affirming the region's status as the new "Eastern Hollywood."

## SHOWDOWN IN HONG KONG

If there was a "challenger" in this contest, it was the Cathay Organization—one of Malaysia's most successful and far-ranging business conglomerates, with diverse interests in banking, mining, agriculture, and manufacturing. In the thirties, its legendary founder, the orphan-turned-entrepreneur Loke Wan, had moved Cathay into the lucrative Southeast

Dato Loke Wan Tho.
*Courtesy of the Cathay
Organization.*

Asian film distribution business. But it was his son, Loke Wan Tho, who transformed the company into a cinematic force to reckon with. Aggressively expanding the company's chain of theaters, Dato Loke ("Dato" being a Malay honorific equivalent to "Sir") also moved to ensure a steady flow of product for his screens, shooting Malay-language films in Singapore, and establishing an Asian distribution deal with England's Rank Organization.

In 1949, Cathay partnered with Hong Kong's ambitious and high-minded Yonghua Studios—the same studio cofounded by Zhang Shankun—and began distributing its product throughout Southeast Asia. A few years later, Cathay launched its own Hong Kong–based production subsidiary, the International Films Distributing Agency, which made its first film in 1953.

Locked in fierce competition with Great Wall and other left-leaning studios, Yonghua suffered numerous financial losses over the years, in each case prompting Dato Loke to bail it out with loans. Finally, in 1955, as the studio continued to flounder, he took it over and merged it into IFDA, establishing MP&GI—the Motion Pictures and General Investment Corporation—for the first time putting a major, full-scale production company under the same roof as his chain of fifty-odd Hong Kong theaters.

Loke brought more than deep pockets to MP&GI. A man of refined tastes and cosmopolitan sensibilities, he endowed the studio with a unique, Hollywood-inspired aesthetic—aiming to produce intelligent, modern stories for a new generation of Chinese sophisticates. To ramp up the studio's standards, Dato Loke aggressively signed promising young actors and directors to exclusive contracts. He also spent heavily to recruit established talent, even luring Eileen Chang, Shanghai's most popular author and perhaps the most prominent female novelist in Chinese history, into MP&GI's fold as a screenwriter.

Meanwhile, across town, another company was making its move to dominate the nascent Hong Kong film market. MP&GI was a newcomer

The illustrious Run Run Shaw.
*Courtesy of Shaw Brothers.*

on the cinematic landscape, a veritable upstart; this player was a sea-soned, cunning veteran of China's bitterly competitive prewar industry—none other than Shaw and Sons, the latest incarnation of the studio helmed by the extraordinary brothers Shaw.

The Shaws had begun their illustrious motion picture career in Shang-hai in 1923. Shao Zuiweng, better known to the world as Runjie Shaw, was a wealthy textile heir who'd graduated from Shenzhou University, only to flit through a number of professions, including lawyer, banker, and theater manager. Shaw had had the fortune of serving as a curious bystander at the early days of the Mingxing Film Company, founded by three men who'd worked for him or with him on past drama projects: dealmaker Zhang Shichuan, critic and writer Zheng Zhengqiu, and top theatrical producer Zhou Jianyun.

When Mingxing's *Orphan Rescues Grandfather*, released that same year, took Chinese box offices by storm, Shaw recognized that the film industry offered fiscal opportunities that the theater world did not. Like textiles, and unlike stage plays, films could be distributed broadly, with tremendous economies of scale. Also like textiles, a successful pattern (whether developed by your company or a competitor's) could be used as a template for a dozen new ones, saving considerably on creative costs. These precepts would guide the Shaws' motion picture production strategy for the next seventy-five years.

In 1925, Runjie launched Shanghai's seminal Tianyi Film Company, bringing his brothers Runde, Runme, and Run Run on as junior partners. The brothers used their business savvy and populist instincts to corner the market on genre entertainment—horror stories, magical fantasies, and swashbuckling swordplay epics.

Unfortunately, Tianyi's output soon ran afoul of the ruling Nationalist party, which was attempting to squelch occult ideas, superstitious cus-toms, and other forms of "backward thinking." The Kuomintang's launch of a campaign of official harassment against Tianyi, combined with the start of the Sino-Japanese War, prompted the Shaws to flee to Singapore, bringing the most valuable parts of Tianyi with them. (This reportedly included an enormous cache of buried gold that the Shaws had stashed in case of just such an emergency.)

Once ensconced there, under the new name of the Nanyang (or "South Seas") Film Company, the Shaws began to diversify their interests, establishing a new production arm in Hong Kong, while building a vast distribution network of theaters throughout Southeast Asia. Second brother Runde served as general manager of the new outfit, while third brother Runme produced many of the early Nanyang films; during World War II, as the Shaws' presence in Singapore and Malaysia grew, he shifted the studio's focus toward films made locally in Singapore, using Indian "Bollywood" directors to shoot Malay dramas, horror films, fantasies, and romances, all well spiced with musical numbers. All told, Nanyang made over half of the three hundred films that make up the golden age of Malay cinema, which lasted from the mid-forties through the late sixties. In the meantime, Nanyang leased its darkened Hong Kong–based production facilities to Da Zhonghua Film Company, which, through wholesale import of Shanghai talent, became the first major studio to launch in postwar Hong Kong.

But in 1949, after making some forty-odd movies, Da Zhonghua collapsed under the weight of massive debt and brutal competition. For the Shaws, this was a stroke of unexpected fortune. Despite their extensive success in Southeast Asia, the Shaws had cannily deduced that the future of commercial cinema in the region lay in Hong Kong, and were determined to spare no expense in ensuring that this future would be synonymous with the name Shaw. Da Zhonghua's demise allowed them to reoccupy their Hong Kong studios and resume producing Chinese-language films under the fresh corporate banner of Shaw and Sons. But this was merely a prelude to their unveiling of a new chapter in the Shaw story—one that would change the landscape of Chinese cinema forever.

For most of the early fifties, the youngest Shaw brother, Run Run, had been tasked with overseeing the family's far-flung theater properties. When he expressed his eagerness for a larger challenge, his brothers handed him the biggest one they had: the building of a state-of-the-art, full-service production studio that would stand as China's largest.

In 1957, a proud Run Run unveiled the fruit of his labors: Movie Town, a full forty-nine acres of permanent sets and sound stages, dubbing facilities, printing labs, and dormitories for contract performers and artists; it even boasted an in-house film school. All told, Movie Town was a marvel

Li Lihua, in seductive repose.
*Courtesy of the Hong Kong Film Archive.*

of the modern filmmaking craft, and it gave notice to the world that the studio now known simply as "Shaw Brothers" was deadly serious about being the emergent Hong Kong cinema world's two-thousand-pound gorilla.

And so the stage was set for an era marked by remarkable acts of skullduggery, vengeance, and double- and triple-dealing. As in the earlier Shanghai era of Chinese film, the strict studio system made marquee names—particularly leading ladies—simultaneously the most potent of weapons and the most prized of spoils. And in this high-gloss, high-stakes tabloid world, a trinity of stars stood out, though the three could hardly have been more different.

Li Lihua was the oldest and perhaps the greatest of the threesome: In an era where careers were often measured in heartbeats, she was a seemingly ageless icon whose career dated back to prewar Shanghai and lasted into the early seventies. Born in 1924, the daughter of famed Beijing Opera actress Li Guifan, Li underwent opera training at an early age, and entered the film industry at age sixteen. Her first film, *Three Smiles* (1940), made her an instant star. She continued working in Shanghai during the Japanese occupation, prompting accusations of collaboration after the war; this led her to move in the late forties to Hong Kong, where she enjoyed great popular and critical success in over 120 films, mostly for the Shaw Brothers studio, lending her uniquely regal presence to musicals, comedies, and tragedies alike, both period and contemporary. Her collaborations with director Li Hanxiang were particularly well-received, including *Empress Wu Tse Tien* and *Yang Kwei Fei* (1963), although the commercial failure of 1965's ornate two-part epic *Beauty of Beauties* led directly to the bankruptcy of Li Hanxiang's studio. Rare among Hong Kong actresses of the era, she has a Hollywood film to her credit: the admittedly forgettable *China Doll* (1958). Often referred to as Chinese cinema's foremost "sour" beauty (sexy and imperious, in contrast to cute, wholesome, "sweet" beauties), Li retired in 1973, making her swan song in King Hu's extraordinary *The Fate of Lee Khan*.

Grace Chang Ge Lan and Peter Chen Hou, in sync, in MP&GI publicity shot. *Courtesy of the Hong Kong Film Archive.*

It was an appearance opposite Li in Li Hanxiang's romantic melo-drama *Red Bloom in the Snow* (1956) that launched the career of the sec-ond great screen queen of fifties Mandarin cinema—Grace Chang Ge Lan, who became MP&GI's first and perhaps brightest homegrown star, as a singing, dancing sensation who provided the soundtrack for a gener-ation of young swingers. Born Zhang Yuying in Nanjing in 1934, the opera-trained Chang relocated to Hong Kong with her family in 1949, and debuted in Bu Wancang's *Seven Sisters* in 1953. In 1955, Chang signed a contract with International Films Distributing Agency, MP&GI's corporate predecessor. After *Red Bloom* marked her as a rising ingenue, Chang made her star breakthrough in *Mambo Girl* (1957), the picture that launched the era of the modern Hong Kong movie musical. She fol-lowed that up with a torrid performance in *The Wild, Wild Rose* (1960), an update of Bizet's *Carmen* set in a Hong Kong cabaret, directed by Wong Tin Lam (father of lowbrow box office king Wong Jing) and featur-ing the monster soundtrack hit "Ja Jambo," penned by Japanese com-poser Ryoichi Hattori. In 1959, Chang became the first Hong Kong per-former to appear on American TV, performing on *The Dinah Shore Show* in support of her first and only U.S. album, entitled *Hong Kong's Grace Chang: The Nightingale of the Orient*. Although Chang is best remem-bered for her musical roles, she starred in all manner of films, from the grand anti-Japanese war classic *Sun, Moon, and Star* (1961) to the cos-tume fantasy *The Magic Lamp* (1964). Marriage led to her final retire-ment from the screen in 1964 at the age of thirty, after having appeared in about thirty films; even then, she continued her singing career via her first love, the opera stage.

But it was the third member of the trio who cast the greatest shadow over the era: Linda Lin Dai, Li Lihua's greatest rival and the first and most prominent of the era's many tragic cases of self-destruction. Born Cheng Yueru in Guangxi Province in 1934, the daughter of a Nationalist official named Cheng Siyuan, Lin fled with her family to Hong Kong in 1948, where her portrait was seen by a producer in a photo gallery; the producer quickly signed her to a contract with leftist studio Great Wall. After several years in which Lin did little more than pose for publicity snapshots—her career in stasis due to her father's KMT background—

Linda Lin Dai, in happier times. *Courtesy of the Hong Kong Film Archive.*

Lin left Great Wall to make *Cui Cui* (aka *Singing Under the Moon,* 1953), directed by and costarring her then-lover Yan Jun. The film won great acclaim, launching a glorious career that ended, all too typically, in disaster. Highlights of her career include the hugely popular romantic melodrama *Love Without End* (1961), costarring Kwan Shan (father of contemporary star Rosamund Kwan Chi Lam); the trendsetting folk opera *Diau Charn of the Three Kingdoms* (1958), the first of her many highly regarded collaborations with director Li Hanxiang; and Li's stunning historical epic *The Kingdom and the Beauty* (1963). Though Lin's professional life glittered, her personal life was marked by heartbreak; her first love Yan Jun would go on to marry her nemesis Li Lihua in 1957, prompting Lin to flee to New York, where she took classes at Columbia University, and in 1959, met L. Shing, the wealthy son of a prominent forties warlord. In 1961, the pair married in Hong Kong, where Lin gave birth to a boy. But her delicate personality was unable to sustain the combined pressures of stardom and a spouse given to infidelity; after

Publicity stills for Betty Le Di and Kitty Ting Hao, two more tabloid victims. *Courtesy of the Hong Kong Film Archive.*

repeated attempts at suicide, she succeeded in taking her life in 1964. She left behind a canon of some fifty films as well as two unfinished works, the magical fantasy *The Lotus Lamp* and the three-and-a-half-hour, two-part epic romance *The Blue and the Black*. Both films were ultimately completed using stand-ins, and released to tremendous success, their box office take inflated by the star's sad and untimely end.

Lin's example set off a horrifying trend among starlets of her day: Kitty Ting Hao, who specialized in "culture clash" romantic comedies, committed suicide in 1967, at the tender age of twenty-seven; "Classic Beauty" Betty Le Di took her life in 1968, a year after her divorce from male comic star Peter Chen Hou; and "Wild Girl" Margaret Tu Chuan overdosed on sleeping pills in 1969 in a double suicide with a female roommate, after the failure of her marriage to a wealthy Hong Kong tycoon. Though not all of Mandarin cinema's leading ladies ended their careers (and lives) in so catastrophic a manner, this string of tragedies was emblematic of the pressures faced by the era's stars; fragile souls like Lin, Ting, Le, and Tu were collateral casualties in MP&GI and Shaw's ugly and bitter war for cinematic supremacy.

## CLASH OF THE TITANS

The first blow was struck in 1956, when MP&GI hired top writer/director Tao Qin away from Shaws, which had convinced him to migrate from Shanghai, and which had come to depend on his prolific, extremely popular output. MP&GI's move paid immediate dividends when Tao's seminal family comedy *Our Sister Hedy* (1957) became a huge critical and box office hit. But it was just the tip of the iceberg Dato Loke was planting in the path of the Shaws' *Titanic;* that same year, the studio also scored major successes with Yueh Feng's Linda Lin Dai vehicle *Golden Lotus,* and Evan Yang Yi Wen's *Mambo Girl,* featuring electric performances by Grace Chang and popular hunk Peter Chen Hou.

Run Run's counterattack was swift and devastating. Shortly after collecting his Best Picture award for *Our Sister Hedy,* Tao Qin announced his intention to *return* to Shaw Brothers—bringing along with him Yueh Feng, Linda Lin Dai, and Peter Chen Hou.

The battle then began in earnest. In 1962, the rumor hit the streets that MP&GI was planning to make *Liang Shanbo and Zhu Yingtai*, a star-studded adaptation of a beloved folktale. The story, sometimes referred to as the "Butterfly Lovers," concerns a girl from a wealthy family named Zhu Yingtai, who journeys into the world disguised as a man in order to gain an education—which, at that time, was forbidden for women. At school, she meets an impoverished but honest boy named Liang Shanbo. With all of the other rooms at the school already filled, Zhu and Liang end up as roommates. Over the course of their studies, Zhu falls in love with Liang, and Liang begins to have feelings for Zhu as well—although he is confused by his feelings for what he believes to be another man. When at last her true identity is revealed, they agree to marry, but Zhu's parents forbid the match on account of Liang's family background, and promise her hand to someone else instead. Liang sinks into despair, falls ill, and dies. On her wedding day, Zhu insists that her marriage procession pass by Liang's grave. As it does, she leaps from the palanquin, Liang's tomb opens up, and she plunges into the yawning crevasse. Suddenly, two beautiful butterflies flutter up from the earth, and dance away in the breeze together. (Since the butterflies are the liberated spirits of Zhu and Liang, this passes for a happy ending.) The star-studded adaptation would feature statuesque Li Lihua as leading "man" Liang and lovely Lucilla Yu Ming, a beloved screen beauty making her final screen appearance, as the doomed Zhu.

Upon catching wind of these plans, Shaws immediately tasked their top filmmaker, Li Hanxiang, to create their own adaptation of the "Butterfly Lovers" story, vowing to beat MP&GI's production to theaters. Ever the team player, Li shot his version in record time, casting journeyman period-piece ingenue Betty Le Di and then-obscure Ivy Ling Po as the romantic leads. Upon its release, *The Love Eterne* (1963) was an unexpected smash—one that quickly burgeoned into a phenomenon, drawing packed crowds and inspiring multiple repeat viewings by swooning fans. By the time *Liang Shanbo* came out a year later, it was seen as a pale effort in comparison and mostly ignored.

A few years later, it was MP&GI's turn; after learning of Shaws' intent to make the period fantasy *The Lotus Lamp* (1965), they announced their decision to film the same story as *The Magic Lamp* (1964), rush-shooting it in black and white to get it out ahead of their hated rival. This time, MP&GI won, despite the fact that Shaws engaged virtually its entire roster of directors in an effort to win the race. The pattern was repeated time and again, with the studios announcing parallel productions derived from familiar operas, novels, or folkloric tradition. Publicly, they blamed coincidence and bad timing, but everyone knew the real truth: Shaws and MP&GI were locked in mortal combat, and neither empire had any intention of giving the slightest bit of ground.

Though both of the giant studios made films in Mandarin, their philosophies and output were as different as the men who ran them. Dato Loke was a wispy intellectual who had studied history and ornithology at Cambridge University. Revered by his employees, he set high standards but allowed artists untold creative freedom. Under his helmsmanship, MP&GI gained fame for smart urban comedies and superbly mounted musical extravaganzas. The company's epic ambitions were also obvious in such productions as the award-winning two-part blockbuster, *Sun, Moon, and Star* (1961), an expensive romance featuring top stars Lucilla Yu Ming, Grace Chang, and Julie Yeh Feng playing female soldiers in love with the same man and united against a common enemy, the Japanese.

By contrast, Run Run Shaw (eventually to be known as *Sir* Run Run, after twice being decorated by the queen for his services to world cinema) was a shrewd pragmatist who shared his family's business sense and populist sensibility. Although himself a devoted movie fan (who, according to noted film critic Stephen Teo, boasted that he watched more pictures in a day than most reviewers saw in a week), he had no truck with either MP&GI's urbane elitism or the overt political bent of smaller rivals like Great Wall. To him, the cinema industry was all about providing entertainment; movies were leisure goods that should be made efficiently and well, and distributed as widely and as profitably as possible. The bread and butter of Shaw Brothers was the crowd-pleasing genre film: *wuxia* movies, ghost stories, opulent period epics like Li Hanxiang's *The Kingdom and the Beauty* (1961) and *Empress Wu Tse Tien* (1963), and the occasional mawkish melodrama, like Tao Qin's classic Linda Lin Dai starrer *Love Without End* (1961).

The Shaw textile heritage probably contributed to Sir Run Run's propensity to see cinematic talent—particularly performers—as workers rather than artists, and to pay them accordingly, while providing them with such manufacturing-industry amenities as room and board at Movie Town dormitories and mess halls. Where the pictures themselves were concerned, however, Shaw set a standard that few others could match, migrating to new technologies as soon as they were available (from synch sound to color to the widescreen aspect ratio the studio eventually popularized as "ShawScope"), and spending upward of HK$800,000 per picture—in an era when some producers were regularly making films for one-twentieth that amount.

The battle seemed evenly matched, with the only winners being audiences and the only losers being small, independent production companies. But on June 20, 1964, everything changed, with the shocking death of Dato Loke in a plane crash. The following year, MP&GI reorganized as the Cathay Organization Hong Kong, but along with its name and guiding light, the studio had lost its focus. The number of productions at the renamed Cathay began to dwindle, and its box office successes became fewer and further between; by the waning years of the sixties, it became clear that Shaws was becoming Hong Kong's sole cinematic superpower, and by extension, the dominant filmmaking force in all of East and Southeast Asia. But even as it achieved supremacy, Shaws, in its hard-nosed attitude toward artists and employees, was sowing the seeds of its own destruction. The giant studio began to hemorrhage talent, from leading actors to top directors—and most critically, its executive in charge of production, Raymond Chow, the man who would soon serve as David to the Shaws' Goliath.

## A TALE OF TWO TONGUES: MANDARIN VS. CANTONESE

Epic as it might have been, the truth is that the Shaws–MP&GI death-match was, to a certain extent, an intramural skirmish. The industry as a whole was embroiled in a larger and more subtle conflict, one that had begun in 1931, with the release of the first Chinese "talkie." This was the tug of war between two broadly spoken Chinese dialects: Mandarin, the northern dialect also known as *putonghua*, or "common language," and Cantonese, the dialect spoken by most of China's south, including the residents of Hong Kong.

With the advent of motion picture sound, studios were forced to make a choice between two mutually unintelligible tongues. Mandarin's status as the formal language of government and scholarship gave it an aura of sophistication that Shanghai's upmarket studio heads preferred; the broad reach of Cantonese among blue-collar workers and farmers made it the language of choice for more populist producers, such as the Shaws' Tianyi Film Company.

When the arrival of the Sino-Japanese War led Tianyi to abandon the Chinese market, it was left to smaller, independent companies to carry the Canto-cinema torch. Like Tianyi, these Hong Kong–based independents churned out cheap, visceral thrills for the working masses, in the form of ghost stories, opera films, and most especially martial arts epics; for a brief, shining period, Cantonese cinema thrived, until the Japanese occupation brought film production to a sudden halt.

The war's end didn't immediately revive Canto-film's fortunes. Hong Kong's devastated economy, complicated by the arrival of seemingly endless trains of refugees as the Communists pressed their advantage on the Mainland, meant that the industry remained depressed through the end of the forties.

But in 1949, Canto-cinema was saved, appropriately, by a legendary martial arts hero. That was the year when an intrepid filmmaker named Wu Pang, questing about for subject matter to inspire demoralized Hong Kong audiences, hit upon the story of Wong Fei Hung (1847–1924), a Cantonese physician and martial artist renowned for his patriotism and virtue. Wu convinced Yong Yao Film Company to underwrite his vision, and recruited a stellar cast, including veteran opera player Shek Kin as the story's arrogant villain; top leading man Tso Tat Wah as Leung Foon, Wong's most famous disciple; and Li Lan—the very first winner of the Miss Hong Kong Pageant—as the ingenue. The pièce de résistance was Wu's choice as Master Wong: Kwan Tak Hing, an opera star and martial arts master who had acquired the nickname "The Patriotic Entertainer" due to his avid fundraising activities during the war. An able fighter and expert lion dancer, Kwan embodied many of the skills and values represented by Wong himself, lending an uncanny verisimilitude to his performance.[13]

Wu's two-part *The True Story of Wong Fei Hung* showcased the avuncular Kwan as he dispensed Confucian wisdom and used his dazzling combat abilities to save a young woman from the clutches of a local bully. It was an astonishing commercial success, not just in Hong Kong, but throughout Southeast Asia—spawning a barrage of sequels that approached the status of cottage industry. In 1956 alone, at the height of the Master Wong mania, twenty-five Wong Fei Hung films were made and released; by the end of the sixties, the episode count had reached a grand total of sixty-seven, all featuring Kwan, Shek, and Tso, making the trio one of the most prolific screen teams in Chinese cinematic history. (The only serious competition may have come from the beloved "Yam-Pak" duo—Yam Kim Fai and Pak Suet Sin, two women who played opposite each other in fifty-nine Cantonese opera films, including 1959's classic *The Purple Hairpin*. Yam invariably took the role of "male" lead, and, like Mandarin-language gender-bender Ivy Ling Po, became something of a romantic idol to her considerable female following.)

## WONG FEI HUNG

Every great civilization has its cultural heroes. America has Davy Crockett; the British have Robin Hood. The Chinese have Wong Fei Hung, master of the martial and healing arts. Born in Guangdong in 1847, Wong was the son of a renowned fighter and herbalist named Wong Kai Ying, one of the famous "Ten Tigers of Guangdong." When his father, hoping for a more peaceful life for his son, refused to teach him martial arts, Fei Hung sought out his father's teacher, Luk Ah Choy, instead. Fei Hung subsequently mastered an arsenal of techniques, including the legendary "No-Shadow Kick." Upon coming of age, Fei Hung built a martial arts school around his father's Po Chi Lam clinic, was married four times, and had ten sons. He died in 1924 at the age of seventy-seven, survived by his children and a legion of students who kept his legacy alive.

Just a few decades later, in 1949, Hong Kong cinema needed a jumpstart. The decision was made to produce a film on a subject that would be sure to bring audiences back to the theaters—Wong Fei Hung. Veteran opera star Kwan Tak Hing was picked to portray the hero, and *The True Story of Wong Fei Hung* hit theaters later that year. The film was an enormous success, spawning an incredible chain of sequels; dozens of directors and stars learned their craft working on the series, including celebrated director Lau Kar Leung (ironically, the student of a student of a student of the *real* Wong Fei Hung). Lau went on to try his own hand at the Wong Fei Hung legend with *Challenge of the Masters* (1976). Lau's novel concept was to show Wong as an awkward young man rather than a mature elder statesman; the film proved to be a key influence for one of the greatest kung fu movies of all time, *Drunken Master* (1978), directed by Yuen Woo Ping and starring Jackie Chan at the dawn of his stardom. Yuen and Chan's insight was to push Lau's "awkward young man" idea as far as it could go, into outright comedy; they also added the conceit that Wong was a master of "Drunken Style" boxing, for which there is no historical evidence. (It does, however, look terrific on screen.)

Yuen and Chan's comic interpretation transformed kung fu cinema, and prompted a major revival in Hong Kong film. But Wong's legacy was far from done; in 1991, Tsui Hark—ever one to embrace and extend the past—tackled the great hero's legend with a new spectacle, starring Mainland *wushu* star Jet Li. Tsui's twists were a bolder take on combat, a romantic backstory between Wong and his young "Aunt 13," and a new focus on Wong's patriotism in the face of outsiders. Given the uncertainty surrounding the approach of 1997, the subtle political edge of the *Once Upon a Time in China* series (six episodes, 1991 through 1997) struck a chord with audiences, proving again Wong Fei Hung's status as a hero for all generations.

*—Linn Haynes*

---

Although the fifties and sixties saw the rise to dominance of the Mandarin-language cinema among "sophisticated" audiences, Cantonese film held its own as a populist, largely blue-collar entertainment, devel-

oping its own parallel constellation of stars—which, unlike the all-female ranks of Mandarin idols, featured a trio of standout leading men, due in large part to Canto-film's generally grittier, action-oriented genre fare.

The first of these was Walter Tso Tat Wah, who began his screen career as an extra in early thirties silent films, surged to stardom in the role of chief disciple Leung Foon in Kwan Tak Hing's long-running Wong Fei Hung series, and continued his martial expoits as the heroic swordsman Lung Kim Fei in the *Buddha's Palm* quartet of martial arts fantasies. Over the next decade and a half, he subsequently established himself as Hong Kong's foremost cinematic detective, appearing in more than fifty features as a trench-coated, fedora-wearing private eye, including the first two installments of the popular "999" films.

His replacement in the series, Patrick Tse Yin, was a stark contrast to the earthy, grizzled Tso—a suave, unreconstructed playboy who regularly made headlines with his flashy, fast-paced personal life. Tse's standout films include Lung Kong's bleak *Story of a Discharged Prisoner* (1967)—later remade by action auteur John Woo as the gunslinging classic *A Better Tomorrow* (1986)—and Chor Yuen's campy cat-burglar actioner *The Black Rose* (1965) and its sequels.

The third major Canto-hunk of the era was teen idol Lui Kei, who began his career at Shaw Brothers' Cantonese film unit, but moved on to

Clockwise from top left: Patrick Tse Yin, with frequent costar Patsy Kar Ling; teen idol Lui Kei and Connie Chan Po Chu; "Hong Kong's Shirley Temple" Fung Bo Bo (with Linda Lin Dai); Josephine Siao, in her child-star days. *Courtesy of the Hong Kong Film Archive.*

smaller studios when Shaws went Mandarin, becoming the de facto leading man of the Cantonese "youth film," frequently playing alongside Josephine Siao Fong Fong and, particularly, Connie Chan Po Chu; in 1967 and 1968 alone, he appeared in six films with Siao and twenty with Chan. Later in his career, he moved from acting to filmmaking, becoming a well-known director in the soft-core pornography genre known as *fengyue*.

Lui Kei's frequent costars were a band of youthful girl performers popularly known as the "Seven Cantonese Princesses," who even starred together in a 1967 movie of the same name. The youngst of the septet, Fung Bo Bo, began her career at age seven as "Hong Kong's Shirley Temple," rising to fame as the downtrodden waif in tearjerkers like *Sorrowful Orphans* (1961). Three others—Josephine Siao Fong Fong, Connie Chan Po Chu, and Nancy Sit Ka Ying—established enduring careers as adolescents that continued through their teens and beyond, with Siao and Chan emerging as the most popular actresses of the era (the two frequently worked together, with Chan sometimes playing male roles and becoming, like other cross-dressers before her, the romantic idol of schoolgirls throughout Asia). The last three "princesses," Sum Chi Wah, Fung So Po, and Wong Oi Ming, retired soon after coming of age.

The golden era of Canto-film continued through the mid-sixties, with romantic melodramas, slapstick comedies, juvenile-delinquent films, and detective thrillers vying for popularity alongside the industry's bread and butter, martial arts pictures. But all the while, Shaw Brothers and MP&GI were pushing the creative and budgetary envelope in their battle for control over Mandarin-language cinema; as the sixties drew to a close, even the venerable Wong Fei Hung couldn't prevent the Cantonese film industry from becoming totally eclipsed.

—*Jeff Yang, with Grady Hendrix (Shaw Brothers),*
*Art Black (Cathay/MP&GI; Cantonese Stars),*
*and Linn Haynes (Wong Fei Hung)*

# 3

## Martial Arts and Melodrama: The Seventies

An amusing yet fiscally serious slant on international films is the current world "boomlet" in Hong Kong–made "chop-socky" or Kung Fu action.
—Variety's Art Murphy, May 9, 1973[14]

**A**s the seventies began, the Shaw brothers were in an uncommonly powerful position. They were the undisputed kings of Hong Kong cinema, a status sealed by Cathay's decision in 1970 to cease film production entirely. Smaller independents, who had scuttled into the Canto-film niche to avoid competing directly with the Shaws juggernaut, found their air supply dwindling, as Shaw Brothers shifted its resources away from its struggle with Cathay and toward absolute vertical dominance of the local movie industry.

Shaws was already a controlling stakeholder in the Mandarin-language film market, through ownership of the largest domestic Mandarin theater circuits; monopoly of relationships with Southeast Asian Mandarin-language distributors; and production of the lion's share of Mandarin-language pictures. By exerting their profound market leverage, Shaw Brothers effectively, if temporarily, killed off Cantonese as a cinematic language, squashing the indies. In 1971, only one Cantonese-language film was released in Hong Kong, down from 211 in a decade before; for the next two years, none were released at all.

Tactically, the elimination of the Canto-film industry seemed like a sound maneuver; strategically, it would prove to be an error in judgment. Though Shaws was synonymous with Mandarin-language film production in Hong Kong, Hong Kong was not the only player in Mandarin-language film production. The studio now faced a head-to-head, one-against-many battle with an entire motion picture industry—that of Mandarin-speaking Taiwan, whose movie output had surged in the preceding decade. This new phase of commercial warfare would eventually lead to a kind of mass-extinction event, in which both the Taiwanese motion picture industry and Shaw Brothers Studios met their demise, having extended themselves too far and spread themselves too thin to survive the changing consumer tastes and market conditions that emerged by decade's end.

But until then, there was jubilee. With the Mainland embroiled in Mao's Cultural Revolution, Taiwan and the Shaws had free license to explore beyond the borders of Greater China, turning their attention toward other Asian markets, and then, eventually, the rest of the world. The secret weapon they used in these efforts was one wrested away from the corpse of the deceased Canto-film industry: the martial arts movie.

## WUXIA RISING: THE SWORDS COME OUT

The great duel of Shaws and MP&GI was fought on battlegrounds largely defined by Hollywood; aside from the occasional period costume drama, the stuff of Mando-film dreams was contemporary musicals, comedies, and romantic melodramas inspired by Western counterparts. But as Hong Kong emerged from its postwar funk, audiences began to crave more aggressive—and more quintessentially Chinese—entertainment. Sir Run Run Shaw, who, even as his studio thrived on bubbly confections like Tao Qin's *The Love Parade* (1963) and *The Dancing Millionairess* (1964), was privately dismissive of such "women's movies," was typically early to recognize this trend.

Taking as his cue the rising popularity of Japanese *chambara* pictures (samurai films, whose name derived from the Japanese sound for clashing blades—"chan-chan-bara-bara"), Shaw commissioned several of his younger directors to reintroduce the traditional swordsman genre known as *wuxia* to Mandarin-speaking audiences. The first of these was a man whose technical innovations and breathtaking visual creativity would reshape Chinese cinema as a whole: Hu Jinquan, better known to Western audiences as King Hu.

Born in Beijing in 1931, Hu moved to Hong Kong in 1949 to attend college. Left stranded there by the Communist Revolution, he found employment doing odd jobs for Voice of America and then at a series of small film studios, including Great Wall, before being hired by Shaw Brothers in 1958 as a set designer and character player. After acting in over thirty films, Hu was asked by Li Hanxiang to assistant direct the blockbuster opera hit *The Love Eterne* (1963), and made his solo debut two years later with the war film *Sons of the Good Earth*. When Shaw decided the time was ripe to reinvent the *wuxia* genre, Li's endorsement led the studio to give the task to the relatively untested Hu.

A longtime opera fan, Hu took as his inspiration the obscure opera *The Drunken Beggar,* transferring its rhythm and aesthetics to the screen, while incorporating into its narrative the traditional operatic character of the *dao ma dan,* or "woman warrior." He also inaugurated an innovation that would eventually be a hallmark of Hong Kong action cinema: the crediting of a "martial arts director," whose sole responsibility was to coordinate the film's high-flying combat spectacles. This novelty was necessitated by the demanding physicality of Hu's vision. His swordsmen existed midway between the earthbound bladesmen of early *wuxia* epics and the mystical,

King Hu's groundbreaking
*Come Drink With Me.*

energy blast–wielding Cantonese warriors of the then-popular *Buddha's Palm* series; they were suprahuman, but not *super*human, able to leap vast, trampoline-assisted distances, dodge blows at camera-blurring speeds, and run up walls and across the surface of water. Eschewing wires and optical effects, Hu pushed his dance- and opera-trained performers to the limits of their corporeal abilities, framing them with artful camerawork to make their feats appear stunning, but just at the edge of the credible.

## JIANG HU—THE "MARTIAL WORLD"

American moviegoers who flocked to see *Crouching Tiger, Hidden Dragon* (2001) may have thought translators were asleep at the wheel, when the otherwise-English subtitles repeatedly included the Chinese phrase *"jiang hu."*

Jiang *who?* Whatever this jiang hu thing was, Li Mu-bai (Chow Yun Fat) knew it intimately and wanted to leave it behind, while Jen (Zhang Ziyi) fantasized about it, but in truth didn't understand it at all. So what is it, and why did translators allow the term to slide past untouched?

The fact is, there's no exact English translation for the concept. *Jiang hu* literally means "rivers and lakes," as in the wild, unsettled regions on the fringes of civilization; metaphorically, however, it has a much more complex connotation. Centralized government had little reach into the world of *jiang hu;* even if it did, its residents, many of whom are society's exiles and renegades, would refuse to submit to common law. What prevents the residents of *jiang hu* from descending into mere anarchy is an unwritten code of ethics—a chivalry of the outlaw brotherhood. It is ultimately this code that is being invoked when the phrase *jiang hu* is used.

The term has been around at least since the twelfth century, when it was one of the central themes of the classic Chinese novel *Shuihu zhuan* (variously translated into English as *The Water Margin* or *All Men Are Brothers*). *The Water Margin* is a story of 108 heroes who, one by one, are wronged by corrupt officials and branded as outlaws. They gather in the marshlands—the margin where wood and waters meet, where heavily armored imperial troops cannot penetrate—and form an army to wage war against the regime. It is an epic novel, in some versions 120 chapters long. The exploits of these legendary bandit heroes, such as Wu Song, Lin Chong, and Lu Zhishen the "Flowery Monk," are familiar in every Chinese household.

The heroes of *The Water Margin* embody the spirit of *jiang hu,* defining it by their example. All are honest and courageous, but quick to anger, and willing to avenge a wrong regardless of the personal cost. If they make a pledge, no matter how trivial, they honor it with their lives. When they meet as strangers, they may come to blows—but upon demonstrating that their skills are worthy of mutual respect, they pause to introduce themselves. The reputation of the fighters is usually so great that, upon recognizing the identity of his opponent, one or the other will call an end to the duel. Together they will enter a teahouse, and feast and drink enough for seven men.

This is the essence of *jiang hu*—fighting fair, respecting your opponent, and celebrating the shared bond that comes of living in the fraternity of the rivers and lakes. It is a recipe for a kind of honor among renegades; guideposts for living life the "martial way."

—*Peter Nepstad*

---

The result was *Come Drink With Me* (1966), a brilliant fusion of lavish set-pieces and intricate, acrobatic fight choreography, featuring young ballerina-turned-actress Cheng Pei Pei as heroine Golden Swallow and Yueh Hua as Drunken Cat, an intoxicated beggar who turns out to be much more than he appears. The film was a smash success—inaugurating a new era of Mandarin-language *wuxia* movies.

But while Hu's subsequent works *Dragon Gate Inn* (1967) and *A Touch of Zen* (1970) would establish him as Greater China's first internationally recognized director, he wouldn't make them for Shaws. Even early in his career, Hu was an auteur, at a time when producers had little patience for such types. He was intelligent, meticulous, and a bit of a perfectionist, traits that made him prone to budgetary excess and shooting-schedule disasters. After Run Run suggested that he should emulate veteran hack Xu Zheng-hong, an offended Hu left Shaw Brothers and Hong Kong, accepting an offer of employment from the Union Film Company—which, not coincidentally, was the Cathay Organization's primary partner in Taiwan.

It was left to another filmmaker to carry the banner of martial arts at Shaws—a journeyman director whose cinematic sensibility represented a polar opposite to that of refined perfectionist Hu. His name was Chang Cheh, and, to the delight of Shaws' accountants, he saw films as meals rather than feasts—churning out product at a lightning pace, while embracing the studio's edicts to sauce up storylines with wilder action and more visceral violence.

Born in 1923 in Qingtian, China, as an adult Chang moved to Shanghai, where he worked for the government's Ministry of Cultural Affairs. In 1947, he launched his screenwriting career by penning *The Girl with the Mask*, the first Mandarin-language film to be shot in Taiwan, following that up by writing and codirecting *Storm Cloud Over Alishan* (1949). In the late fifties, he moved to Hong Kong, where he worked briefly as a newspaperman and novelist before being hired to join the Shaw Brothers screenwriting team.

If Run Run Shaw was dismissive of "women's films," Chang was downright hostile toward them; he wrote his early scripts, like 1960's *Tender Trap of Espionage* and *Black Butterfly*, with gritted teeth, complaining to his peers that the cinematic spotlight should be put back on men—the kind of *real* men who'd tear off their own legs and gleefully use them to beat their enemies to death, if no other weapon were available.

In 1966, Chang would get his chance, when Shaws teamed him up with water-polo champion turned action star Jimmy Wang Yu for a low-budget swordplay film called *Tiger Boy*. King Hu had taken inspiration from the stylized, balletic aesthetics of Beijing opera; Chang drew his from the grim, blood-soaked epics of *chambara*, a genre where heads and limbs flew with abandon.

The response was limited, but promising enough for Shaw Brothers to give Chang and Wang the thumbs-up to take their vision to a whole new level, assigning them such top supporting talent as veteran scripter I Kuang and top action choreographer Lau Kar Leung. The result was *The One-Armed Swordsman* (1967), a muscular, angst-ridden epic of bloodthirsty masculinity that ushered in an entirely new sensibility for martial arts cinema. It became the first film to ring up $1 million at the Hong Kong box office. The following year, Chang and Wang teamed up once

Real men lose limbs. Chang Cheh's *The One-Armed Swordsman. Courtesy of Celestial Pictures. All rights reserved.*

more, to make a "sequel" to King Hu's breakthrough film *Come Drink With Me*, entitled *Golden Swallow*. Though it featured Cheng Pei Pei repeating her turn in the titular role, it was as much a Wang Yu vehicle as *The One-Armed Swordsman*.

By this time, Jimmy Wang Yu had become the island's biggest star, and knew it. As the sixties drew to a close, Wang demanded from Shaws the right to direct himself—a demand they had no choice but to accept.

## FISTS BREAK BLADES: DAWN OF THE KUNG FU ERA

Wang's notion was to distill macho violence down to its rock-hard core, tossing aside even the fancy swordplay that had made his Chang Cheh films such bloody good fun. The end product of his fevered imagination was *The Chinese Boxer* (1970), featuring Wang himself as stoic avenger Lei Ming—the first in a long line of kung fu students to undergo wildly masochistic "training" in order to avenge murdered teachers. It was another tremendous success, and it took martial arts cinema in a fertile new direction.

Bare-handed boxing—or, to use the Cantonese euphemism, "kung fu," meaning "skill acquired through training"—is perhaps the most quintessentially Chinese of disciplines, permeating Chinese art, religion, and history. Its basic skills are the underpinnings of Chinese operatic movement; its mystical foundations are intimately tied to traditional Taoist beliefs; and its practice was the preferred means for rallying revolutionaries to the patriotic cause through centuries of dynastic rule, culminating in the disastrous anti-foreigner "Boxer Rebellion" in 1900. Kung fu had seen its first flourishing in the long-running Wong Fei Hung series of the sixties, but even as it succeeded among Cantonese audiences, it was looked upon with distaste by the Mandarin-speaking elite.

But the success of *The Chinese Boxer* threw open the floodgates. Kung fu cinema dominated the remainder of the decade—not just in Greater China, but in the West as well, where dubbed Hong Kong and Taiwan exports found an unexpectedly eager following. The pillars of post-*Boxer* kung fu included Wang Yu's ex-partner Chang Cheh, who went on to launch the careers of such greats as David Chiang (*Vengeance,* 1970), Chen Kuan Tai (*Boxer from Shantung,* 1972), Ti Lung (*Five Masters of Death,* 1975), Alexander Fu Sheng (*The Chinatown Kid,* 1977), and the quintet known as the "Five Venoms" (Philip Kwok Choy, Chiang Sheng, Lo Mang, Lu Feng, and Sun Chien); and Lau Kar Leung, Chang's former action coordinator, who took up directing in 1975 and became the greatest master of "pure" kung fu cinema, supported by his blood brother Lau Kar Wing, his half-brother Lau Kar Yung, and his adopted brother Gordon Lau Kar Fai. Others who made key contributions to the canon included Cheng Chang Ho, whose *King Boxer* (aka *Five Fingers of Death,* 1972) became the first international kung fu hit, and Canto-cinema legend Chor Yuen, who directed another global success, 1972's *The Killer* (aka *Sacred Knives of Vengeance*).

But the one individual most responsible for kung fu's international invasion made just four films before his untimely death, and he himself was an import from the West. Though his given name was Lee Jun Fan, the world knew him by a nickname he received as a child. He was the man they called Dragon—the one and only Bruce Lee Siu Lung.

## THE YUEN CLAN

Jackie Chan. Jet Li. Donnie Yen. Good performers all. But when you're ready to get serious about onscreen martial arts, there's just one name you need to know: Yuen. As in Yuen Woo Ping (choreographer of 1993's *Iron Monkey;* 2000's *Crouching Tiger, Hidden Dragon;* and 1999's *The Matrix*). As in Yuen Cheung Yan (who gave 2000's *Charlie's Angels* their wings). As in veteran villain Sunny Yuen. Martial artist turned Buddhist monk Brandy Yuen. Eternal naïf Yuen Yat Chor. And, of course, their father and teacher Simon Yuen—the *original* drunken master.

The "Yuen Clan," as they're known in the business, have been in the Hong Kong stunt trade ever since Simon immigrated to the territory from Northern China. He was a home-schooling Beijing Opera teacher who trained his kids in wild acrobatics and kung fu, while employing them as stunt men on the numerous films he fight directed, including the legendary, long-running original Wong Fei Hung series starring Kwan Tak Hing.

There's a great tradition of immigrants coming to a new country and, through hard work and diligence, bettering themselves and realizing their dreams. Just as the likes of Billy Wilder and Douglas Sirk came to America and invented Hollywood's golden age, the Yuens came to Hong Kong, opened their imaginations, and pulled out a mind-bending new vision for movie martial arts. Raised in poverty, paid a pittance for their bone-breaking work as stuntmen, upon gaining a foothold in the industry, they unleashed displays of hair-raising high weirdness and surreal wirework onto an unsuspecting industry.

The glory days of the Clan came when they were given the opportunity to helm their own films in the early eighties. Each has since gone on to individual fame, but during this period, the five brothers combined forces to create one lean, mean, action machine. The fruits of their collaborative labor—*Dreadnaught* (1981), *The Miracle Fighters* (1982), *Drunken Tai Chi* (1984), and *The Buddhist Fist* (1979)—are pungent pulp creations whose frames are packed with dimestore wonders that overwhelm and astound the viewer; curiosities like robots, fighting jar monsters, music-controlled frogmen, fire-breathing marionettes, bong-smoking grannies and rat-faced drunks—all larded up with leering gags and toilet humor.

The Yuen Clan's achievement as the creators of this unique set of martial arts spectacles has since been overshadowed by their latter-day adoption by Hollywood as action choreographers to the stars. But fans of their high-gloss American efforts will find their early oeuvre a startling look at a truly unique absurdist vision, made by a set of talented performers who seem completely and totally thrilled to be doing their jobs.

—*Grady Hendrix*

## ENTER (AND EXIT) THE DRAGON

Even today, three decades after Bruce Lee's death, he is still, and likely always will be, the martial artist against whom all others are judged. His legacy stands in spite of his having left just a handful of pictures behind; his canon looms large because of the unprecedented impact of his work, not to mention the legions of imitators it inspired.

Lee was born in San Francisco, California, on November 27, 1940, the son of visiting Chinese actor Lee Hoi Chuen and his wife, Grace; it was reportedly the supervising doctor, Mary Glover, who suggested his English name for the hospital records. He officially became an actor at three months, a Hong Kong child actor at six, and was on the cusp of teen stardom before his penchant for getting into trouble forced his family to banish him back to America. There, his anger and attitude became tempered with passion and discipline; his readily apparent charisma and skill would soon lead him to minor success in Hollywood—playing the supporting role of Kato in *The Green Hornet* (1966–67), and guest roles on *Ironside* (1967–75), on *Longstreet* (1971–72), and in the James Garner movie *Marlowe* (1969).

But after Hollywood's standard-procedure racism and ignorance denied him the lead role in *Kung Fu*, the television series originally cre-

The one and only
Bruce Lee. *Courtesy
Jun Fan Jeet Kune Do.*

ated as a vehicle for his unique skills, a disappointed and angry Bruce returned to Hong Kong—where he discovered that he was considered a major star (by way of example, *The Green Hornet,* aired on Hong Kong TV, was referred to there as *The Kato Show*). The films he subsequently made there—*The Big Boss* (aka *Fists of Fury,* 1971), *Way of the Dragon* (aka *Return of the Dragon,* 1972), *Fist of Fury* (aka *The Chinese Connection,* 1973), and *Enter the Dragon* (1973), as well as the fragmentary *Game of Death* (1978)—set box office records in Hong Kong and throughout Southeast Asia.

Unfortunately, Lee never survived to see his greatest triumph: In 1973, just months before the release of his biggest hit, *Enter the Dragon,* he died of a cerebral edema under mysterious conditions. He was just thirty-two years old. Author and martial arts enthusiast Steven Barnes has suggested that Lee was pushing himself so hard that his body surrendered; that he essentially committed accidental suicide. But whatever the cause of his death, during his short life, he consecrated the genre of kung fu cinema and opened Hong Kong film up to the world.

Lee's passing left a tremendous void in the industry, one that others quickly raced to fill. Some studios released movies starring inferior Bruce

Lee impersonators—unrelated martial artists with names like Bruce Li, Bruce Lai, Bruce Le, and Dragon Lee. Others advanced "successors" to the Dragon's throne, of varying ability and popularity.

No one, however, felt the loss of Lee more deeply than the company whose fortunes were built upon his stardom: the upstart studio Golden Harvest, founded by ex–Shaw Brothers employees Raymond Chow and Leonard Ho.

## THE GOLDEN GUYS

Chow and Ho had taken over the former Yonghua Studios lot from MP&GI in 1970, vowing to challenge the near-monopoly of their former employer with an entirely new filmmaking paradigm. Rather than treating performers and filmmakers like contract laborers, Golden Harvest would make them business partners, giving them generous profit-sharing deals and an unprecedented amount of creative freedom.

The signing of Bruce Lee was a textbook example of the contrast between Golden Harvest and Shaw Brothers. After hearing that Shaws had offended Lee by offering him a standard player's contract worth just nine hundred dollars a month, Chow sent Lau Leung Wah, the lovely wife of top Golden Harvest director Lo Wei, to present Lee with a break-the-bank two-picture deal. Lee signed it, and in doing so, changed the course of cinematic history.

In the year or so it had existed, Golden Harvest had pooled a number of Shaw Brothers refugees under its banner, beginning with founders Chow and Ho, and including director Lo and actors Patrick Tse, Jimmy Wang Yu, and Cheng Pei Pei. More than anything else, however, it was the signing of Lee that transformed the studio from impertinent upstart into legitimate rival.

Riding Lee's stardom, Golden Harvest was able to accomplish in a handful of years what the Shaw Brothers had been trying to do for thirty: They brought mass recognition to Hong Kong film. Suddenly, international distributors besieged the colony looking for anything they could use to feed the craze for kung fu, and previously distant Hollywood giants like Warner Bros. were showing up, hat in hand, offering coproduction deals. Lee's star power also gave Golden Harvest a means of levering open distribution channels that had previously been controlled by Shaws. Dangling the prospect of the next Bruce Lee film before operators throughout Hong Kong, Taiwan, South Korea, Malaysia, Singapore, and Thailand, Golden Harvest was able to develop a theater network that competed head to head with the Shaws. In short, Lee made Golden Harvest a cinematic superpower, and his abrupt demise left them twisting in the wind, with domestic pundits and international partners wondering if they would recover from the blow.

As it turns out, Chow and Ho had learned a thing or two during their tenure at Shaw Brothers—particularly, the lesson that the best fruit sometimes grew on other people's trees. The duo promptly plucked a promising young star right from under Sir Run Run's nose: the man who would become the original king of Hong Kong comedy, Michael Hui Koon Man.

## MICHAEL HUI AND THE CANTO-RENAISSANCE

In 1973, Cantonese cinema had been in a coma for several years. This was in part due to the Shaw Brothers Mandarin monopoly on distribution channels. But there was another phenomenon that contributed greatly to the Canto-film collapse: the arrival in Hong Kong in 1967 of the first locally broadcast television channel, which offered Cantonese cinema's traditional blue-collar audiences a free alternative to the movies. Naturally, the owners of the new channel, TVB, were once again none other than the enterprising brothers Shaw.

Like the pay-cable station Rediffusion TV, which had been on the island since 1957, TVB initially ran programming imported from abroad. By the early seventies, however, the Shaws had begun to producing original Cantonese-language TV programming, such as the hugely successful variety series *Enjoy Yourself Tonight* (still around today, having long since become the longest-running show in Hong Kong history).

Soon, television evolved into a star factory with surprising clout; so much so that the Shaws decided to experiment with a little media cross-pollination. In 1973, Shaw Brothers produced Chor Yuen's *The House of*

Look, Ma, it's the neighbors! Shaws' *The House of 72 Tenants.*
*Courtesy of Celestial Pictures. All rights reserved.*

*72 Tenants,* the only Cantonese-language film to be released in Hong Kong that year, with a cast made up almost exclusively of talent groomed at TVB. It was an unexpected box office success, prompting Shaws to reexamine its television roster for possible breakout cinema stars. Chief among the prospects was a former high-school teacher named Michael Hui, who had rocketed to stardom alongside his pop-star brother Sam on the wings of their popular 1972 TV series *The Hui Brothers Variety Show.* That year, director Li Hanxiang had given Hui a cinematic podium for his comedy in the Mandarin-language farce *The Warlord,* but the film had merely scratched the surface of Hui's talents. On the heels of *72 Tenants,* Shaws gave the thumbs-up for three more pairings between Li and Hui, betting that the chemistry would eventually pay off.

Then Golden Harvest entered the picture, waving a paycheck that was considerably larger than any ever offered to a nonaction performer, while promising Hui broad creative license over his films—including the freedom to make them in Cantonese. Sweetening the deal was the fact that Golden Harvest had already signed Hui's brother Sam, giving the brothers the opportunity to revive their television team.

Hui made the leap, and Golden Harvest finally had a star capable of lifting the studio out of its post-Bruce funk. Beginning in 1974 with *Games Gamblers Play*, Michael, Sam, and their younger brothers Ricky and Stanley developed what would become the Hui Brothers formula: intelligent satire, sophisticated but never patronizing, that took no prisoners in puncturing hoary Chinese customs and popular Hong Kong trends. In 1977, the Hui Brothers had their biggest hit with *The Private Eyes*, which upon its release trounced Bruce Lee's Hong Kong box office record. Over the next fifteen years, Hui, both with his siblings and solo, would continue to be one of the studio's top draws.

But Chow and Ho had seen the liability of putting all of their eggs into one basket, and they heatedly continued to recruit up-and-coming talent. Actors like James Tien and Carter Hwang and actresses like Angela Mao Ying and Nora Miao were given vehicles that catered to their abilities and appeal, directed by top-tier filmmakers like Huang Feng. Relishing Golden Harvest's open and nurturing environment, these stars lured

Michael Hui does the Great Dictator, in *The Warlord*.
*Courtesy of Celestial Pictures. All rights reserved.*

other talent to the studio in their wake. Indeed, it was one of Huang's protégés who eventually emerged as one of the studios' most important players: Sammo Hung Kam Bo.

Initially signed as a stuntboy on the lowest rung of the studio ladder, Hung impressed Chow and Ho with his skill and drive. He was soon promoted to action coordinator, and then given the chance to direct, developing a reputation for working efficiently and coming in under budget. Throughout the seventies and eighties, Hung's productions were the backbone of Golden Harvest's extensive output. But it was Hung's relationship with an old opera academy classmate that would make its deepest mark on the studio's history. Hung gave a young "brother" his first stuntman gigs and helped recruit him to the studio after he evolved from B-movie washout to Hong Kong's biggest action hero. As a result, fresh from the success of the legendary *Drunken Master* (1978), Jackie Chan became the island's highest-paid performer—and Golden Harvest's latest secret weapon in its quest for international success.

## MR. HONG KONG

Born Chan Kong Sang on April 7, 1954—his name literally translates to "Born in Hong Kong" Chan—the young son of Charles and Lee Lee Chan was rambunctious and disinclined toward education; when Charles was forced to go overseas for work, the Chans signed the boy over to a traditional opera school for training, believing it to be the best place for a seven-year-old with Kong Sang's obvious physical talents.

But opera training was no picnic; the dozens of children enrolled at Master Yu Jim Yuen's China Drama Academy lived a Dickensian life of grueling practice and harsh, sometimes extreme punishments (the apprenticeship contract said that disobedient students could be beaten "even to death"). The end result of the discipline and training was that the best of the students, selected to join an elite performance troupe called the Seven Little Fortunes, were among the best martial artists, acrobats, and performers that the island had to offer.

Unfortunately, at the end of their apprenticeships, Chan and the other teenaged Fortunes found themselves rudely ejected into a world where

Jackie gets ready for mayhem in *Rumble in the Bronx. Courtesy of Jackie Chan and New Line Cinema.*

movies, particularly action movies, had replaced Chinese opera in the hearts of most Hong Kong audiences. Having little choice but to adapt to the times, they eventually emerged as some of the most important figures in the contemporary Cantonese motion picture industry.

Due to the group's rotating membership, there were actually over a dozen different performers who were at one or another time members of the "Seven" Little Fortunes; each adapted the "Yuen" moniker as a part of their stage name out of respect for their *sifu*—an age-old Beijing Opera tradition with its roots in Confucian hierarchies of respect. Some kept their Fortune names after graduation, while others adopted new monikers, or went back to their birthnames. (Note that the similarly named and equally influential "Yuen Clan," sons of *sifu* Simon Yuen, were not students at the Academy, but nevertheless had numerous ties to its graduates; Simon himself played Jackie Chan's teacher in *Drunken Master* [1978]—which was directed by Simon's son, master fight choreographer Yuen Woo Ping.)

Among the most prominent Fortunes is "Yuen Ting" (aka Ng Ming Choi), one of the earliest Fortunes to fly the nest. The story goes that as a senior member of the troupe, the kindhearted Ng was tasked with administering Sifu Yu's notoriously brutal punishments, a burden that eventually prompted him to flee the academy. He worked as a low-wage "stunt boy" before becoming a part of the Golden Harvest performing stable, appearing in films like *Fist of Fury* (1972) and *Enter the Dragon* (1973) and in a number of King Hu's later *wuxia* classics, such as *The Fate of Lee Khan* (1973) and *The Valiant Ones* (1975). In the early nineties, Ng ventured into producing, helping finance King Hu's official "comeback" film, *Painted Skin* (1993), before becoming a prolific producer of ultra-low-budget grindhouse fare. "Yuen Wah," a wiry, mustachioed fighting expert who was regarded as one of Sifu Yu's finest students, became part of Bruce Lee's inner circle at Golden Harvest, often stunt-doubling for Lee himself, and went on to a long career as a character acter specializing in wiry, mustachioed villains. (Bizarrely enough, in the late nineties, he made headlines when he was hired to be a public spokesman for safe sex!) The often-overlooked "Yuen Bun" has played stunt and supporting roles in hundreds of films, but achieved his greatest renown as director Johnnie To's action choreographer of choice in the late nineties. "Yuen Kwai" (aka Corey Yuen) was in his youth the troupe's resident comic book geek; he turned his childhood affection for fantasy into a career as one of Hong Kong's finest genre directors, and has worked with virtually all of his *sai lo* ("brothers") in his career. His finest films include *Yes Madam* (1985), *Righting Wrongs* (1986), *The Legend of Fong Sai Yuk* (1993), *The Bodyguard From Beijing* (1994), and *My Father Is a Hero* (1995). His work as a stunt choreographer has also yielded an impressive oeuvre, ranging from his collaboration with brother Jackie Chan and the Yuen Clan on *Drunken Master* (1978) to his recent Hollywood choreography for films like *Lethal Weapon 4* (1998), *X-Men* (2000), and *The One* (2001).

But the three most prominent members of the Fortune troupe are the trio nicknamed the Three Brothers, who displayed their easy fraternal dynamic in some of action cinema's great classics, while also creating canons of supremely distinguished solo work. "Yuen Biao" (aka Ha Ling Shan) was the youngest male member of the troupe (there were indeed women at the Academy, though none emerged with careers as distinguished as those of the men). Biao's unparalleled agility and acrobatic skill, as well as his status as Sifu Yu's favorite, led to his being named a Fortune faster than any of his peers. After the Academy shut down, Biao chose to follow his master to America, but returned some years later disillusioned with his prospects there. He was taken under the wing of Big Brother "Yuen Lung," better known as Sammo Hung Kam Bo, who helped him gain a foothold in the industry and eventually, his first starring role in *Knockabout* (1979). As one of the first of Sifu Yu's boys to rise to prominence in the film industry, rising from stunt coordinator and action choreographer to one of Golden Harvest's top directors and actors, Hung played a similar mentor role to many of his opera brothers, atoning for his reputation as one of the school's biggest bullies. Without Sammo's assistance, it's unlikely that the third of the Three Brothers, "Yuen Lo"—aka Jackie Chan—would have amounted to much of anything, as he was generally considered one of Sifu Yu's more mediocre and unmotivated students!

Hung plucked Chan from the pool of underpaid freelance stuntboys at Shaws and brought him to Golden Harvest, where he was employed regularly as a fight extra and double on such notable films as Bruce Lee's *Fist of Fury* and *Enter the Dragon*). This provided Chan with enough of a showcase that, in 1975, he was approached by Willie Chan—the former general manager of Cathay/MP&GI in its waning years, and now the general manager of the new production company founded by Lo Wei, the "millionaire director" who had directed Bruce Lee's earliest films. Willie would eventually become Chan's lifelong manager and business partner, but at the time, he offered the struggling youth the opportunity to become an action star, under the man who had launched the career of the biggest star in Hong Kong history. Chan accepted, and—under the new name of Chan Sing Lung (literally, "already a dragon")—made the first in a string of box office disasters with Lo, *New Fist of Fury* (1976).

It wasn't until 1978, when a disgusted Lo "loaned" Chan to Ng See Yuen's Seasonal Films, that he finally came into his own. Given creative license by Ng and director Yuen Woo Ping, Chan came up with a mischievous, clownish persona that was the exact opposite of Bruce Lee's vengeful, stone-faced killer. *Snake in the Eagle's Shadow* (1978) and its followup, *Drunken Master* (1978), became two of the biggest box office hits in Hong Kong history—prompting a bidding war for Chan's services that ended with Golden Harvest victorious.

# WILD STUNTS

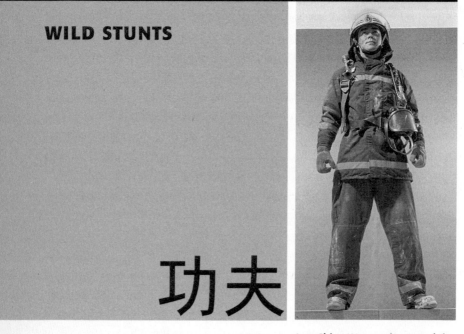

功夫

Lau Ching Wan carries a torch in *Lifeline*. *Courtesy of Celestial Pictures. All rights reserved.*

Given all of the bone-cracking, body-bruising, back-breaking feats of mayhem they try (and sometimes fail) to pull off, Hong Kong performers must be numbered among the bravest—and craziest—entertainers on the face of the planet. Think of Michelle Yeoh *vaulting a motorcycle* onto the roof of a speeding train, or Jackie Chan, *dangling from a helicopter's rope ladder* while its pilot weaves desperately through the turrets of the Kuala Lumpur skyline—feats performed by the actors themselves, without the use of digital technology or advanced safety equipment. Moreover, both of these stunts appeared in the same movie—*Police Story III: Supercop* (1992). By proving that they're willing to put their lives on the line to drag oohs, aahs, and ouches from the audience, Hong Kong talents have raised the art of action spectacle to a level Hollywood can't begin to approach. Do you think the Oscars will ever have a "Best Action Choreography" category, as the Hong Kong Film Awards have since their creation? Unlikely, to say the least.

No discussion of these stunning physical feats can begin without invoking the hallowed name of Jackie Chan, who's taken his opera-honed acrobatic ability, combined it with his martial arts savvy and love for silent movie talents like Buster Keaton and Harold Lloyd, and blended it all together into a whirlwind of grace and toughness. On the distaff front, Hong Kong action women like Michelle Yeoh and Cynthia Yang more than hold their own, becoming famous for doing their own "gags"—breaking glass, taking falls, and getting repeatedly thwacked, and (to paraphrase the famous quotation about Ginger Rogers), doing it all in high heels and a miniskirt. Yeoh, in particular, is well known for the Chanlike list of injuries she's sustained: a dislocated shoulder, cracked ribs, twisted vertebrae, and ruptured arteries. The end result of all of this pain and suffering is a true-to-life adrenaline jolt that no other industry in the world would dare to offer. But for all the thrills and wincing laughter audiences might enjoy as a result, don't forget that these are truly dangerous shenanigans. A tumble from a tree in 1986's *Armour of God* nearly killed Jackie Chan when his head hit a rock; Michelle Yeoh broke her neck when she made a twenty-foot fall from a highway overpass in Ann Hui's 1996 film *Ah Kam* (aka *The Stuntwoman*) and landed right on her head; Conan Lee wrecked himself (and it's all bone-crunchingly still in the movie) in the otherwise lackluster *Tiger on the Beat 2* (1990) when a thirty-five-foot jump went horribly awry; and most recently, hot ingenue Cecelia Cheung severely injured her spine in a motorcycle accident during a charity show for Hong Kong's TVB television station—risking permanent paralysis.

When it comes to Hong Kong stunts and action, the old adage holds especially true: Don't try this at home!

*—Curtis Tsui*

---

Meanwhile, Chan's personal life spun him into the orbit of another superstar, an actress who was as big in her world as he was in his. She was one of Taiwan's two most popular leading actresses (and, by many accounts, the more beloved of the two), but she would soon become Mrs. Jackie Chan. Her name was Joan Lin Feng-jiao, and as part of the quartet of performers dubbed the "Two Lins and Two Chins," she ruled the Taiwanese box office for most of the decade.

## LINS AND CHINS: TAIWAN'S CINEMATIC ROYALTY

Dewy-eyed damsels pining for wealthy older gentlemen; star-crossed lovers separated by parental disapproval, previous commitments, or incurable disease; soft-focus shots of solitary, heartbroken figures, posing teary-eyed at sunset. From these and a buffet of similar clichés were constructed the genre that made up nearly half of Taiwan's cinematic output in the seventies: the romantic melodrama.

Most of these movies were adaptations of works by romance novelist Qiong Yao, Taiwan's most popular female author. Nearly all of them starred some combination of the four top stars of the day—Charlie Chin Hsiang-lin, Chin Han, Brigitte Lin Ching-hsia, and Joan Lin Feng-jiao. Ironically, the not-so-private personal lives of the Lins and Chins were perhaps far steamier than the soapy storylines that made them famous. Although Joan Lin shocked the world with her secret 1983 marriage to Jackie Chan and her abrupt retirement from the screen, this indiscretion from Taiwan's favorite girl-next-door was nothing compared to the controversy surrounding her fellow Lin, Brigitte.

Lin had made her movie debut as a teenager, in a Qiong Yao tear-jerker entitled *Outside the Window* (1972), opposite the older and very married Chin Han. Chin and Lin would go on to star in dozens of other love stories, displaying a unique chemistry that prompted rumors about

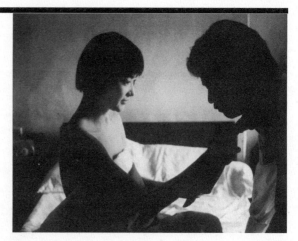

Beauteous Brigitte in Ann Hui's *Starry Is the Night.*
*Courtesy of Celestial Pictures.*

a real-life romance between the two—rumors rooted in fact. As the seventies ended, the whispers rose in volume, until, pursued by attack-dog journalists, Lin fled to the United States, hiding out in San Francisco in hopes that the furor would die down. Instead, a new complication developed: The other Chin, Charlie, pursued her to California, and asked for her hand in marriage. Desperately uncertain what to do, Lin called Chin Han and begged him to come join her; he was unable to leave his wife and family behind, and Lin finally accepted Charlie Chin's proposal.

The subsequent half-decade was a rocky one for all three points of the love triangle, as Brigitte and Charlie broke off their engagement and Chin Han's wife of twelve years filed for divorce. Over that period, Brigitte and Charlie shifted their careers to Hong Kong, and a broken Chin Han found plum leading man roles denied him, as conservative Taiwanese audiences faulted him for doing in life what he acted out on screen. With the retirement of Joan Lin, the ruling family of Taiwanese cinema was gone, and with it, it seemed, the heart of Taiwan's motion picture industry.

By the end of the seventies, the primary leverage Taiwan's producers had over Shaw Brothers and other Hong Kong competitors—their facility in Mandarin—had been rendered moot by the introduction of dubbing. Films shot in either of the dialects (with Cantonese increasingly becoming the preferred language of production) were simply relooped for release in the other. Since most films were still shot without sync sound, relatively little was lost through this process. As a result, the boundary between the Mandarin and Cantonese movie circuits evaporated, and the Asian cinema market became a free-fire zone, controlled by no single player and open to any competitor with the right money and the right star power.

## DUBBING AND SUBTITLING

With the arrival of 1997, the British relinquished their colony; the Union Jack came down in Hong Kong, and the yellow-stars-on-red-field flag of China came up. While some wondered whether human rights would be upheld, and freedoms of speech preserved, fans of Asian cinema in the West had another burning question: Would there still be English subtitles on Hong Kong movies?

The British first mandated English subtitles for all Hong Kong theatrical releases in 1963, as a means of keeping an eye on anticolonial propaganda. Producers had no objections, since even then the potential for Cantonese movies in foreign markets was apparent; by adding Chinese as well as English subtitles, Cantonese films were made suitable for export to Mandarin-speaking markets, without resorting to the more expensive technique of redubbing.

Now that the profile of Hong Kong cinema has risen in the West, subtitling is simply a matter of profit. Hong Kong's small local population is barely capable of sustaining a moderate-sized movie industry; subtitling in English and other languages allows Hong Kong movies to be exported all over the world.

Of course, any Anglophone who's watched a subtitled Hong Kong movie knows that the process is far from perfect. Often hastily produced based on half-completed (or nonexistent) scripts—and sometimes without even basic knowledge of the storyline—translations have ranged from amateurish to comical. Some problems are due to inherent linguistic differences: Spoken Chinese uses few gender-specific terms, so subtitlers often must make arbitrary pronoun choices based on context. Sometimes errors are due to poorly translated idioms, with curses and expressions of affection or lust the most frequent victims. For the most part, however, enthusiasts say that learning "subtitle English" is like picking up a specialized dialect. Experienced Hong Kong movie fans know that "How comfortable!" is an expression of sexual pleasure, while "How come?" is what people say when faced with something shocking and inexplicable.

But what about the other translation option, dubbing? In the wake of Bruce

Lee, cheap theaters and late-night TV were flooded with martial arts films dubbed in unusually harsh or nasal voices, in phrasing peppered with unnatural pauses, setting a low-water mark for English dubbing of Asian films. Despite the flagrant mediocrity of the results, distributors continued to argue that subtitling drastically limited audiences. But in 2000, the success of the subtitled *Crouching Tiger, Hidden Dragon* gave this assumption the lie. The following year, a more traditional Hong Kong martial arts epic—Yuen Woo Ping's *Iron Monkey* (1996)—was cleaned up and given a theatrical release in the United States . . . with subtitles.

*—Peter Nepstad*

----

Meanwhile, Hong Kong's motion picture industry was experiencing a spectacular new flood of creativity, as Golden Harvest and its equally freewheeling competitors gave a generation of young directors their first chance at feature filmmaking. Taiwan's conservative, hidebound industry, still shaped as much by government controls as the invisible hand of commerce, offered few such prospects. For these reasons and more, as the eighties began, Hong Kong reigned as Greater China's sole remaining center for commercial cinema. The colony would make the most of this opportunity.

*—Jeff Yang, with Peter Nepstad (King Hu),*
*Ric Meyers (Chang Cheh, The Five Venoms,*
*Bruce Lee, Lau Kar Leung),*
*Darryl Pestilence (Michael Hui, Golden Harvest),*
*Gary Morris (Brigitte Lin)*

# 4

# New Wave Dreams and Ballistic Kisses: The Eighties

As early as 1976 or 1977, I told my boss that the film I wanted to make most was a gangster movie . . . I wanted to make a lone killer film like [Jean-Paul] Melville's *Le Samouraï,* or a gangster movie like those in which Humphrey Bogart played . . . When I was in Taiwan, I talked with Tsui Hark one day about a film that we both wanted to remake: *Story of a Discharged Prisoner* (1967), because we both adored the director, Patrick Lung Kong, and we appreciated the spirit of the film. We hoped to present again the spirit of the swordsman. His ideal version was a feminist one with three female protagonists. I wanted to make a male version. The role [played by] Patsy Kar Ling would now be taken up by a male hero.

—Director John Woo, at a Hong Kong Film
Archives seminar on the film environment
that shaped him[15]

**T**hey were a bold new breed: educated in the West, shaped by the pop culture of the sixties and seventies, and steeped in the latest technological advances. They had no truck with time-honored traditions and standards, and even as they embraced hoary genres like the *wuxia* film, they redefined them. Neither did they have patience with the old "apprenticeship" system, in which novice filmmakers worked as assistants for years or even decades before getting their turn behind the camera.

Instead, upon returning to Hong Kong, film-school degrees in hand, they took jobs in what was then the most accessible forum available: Hong Kong public television.

Established in 1970, RTHK (Radio Television Hong Kong) was a government-subsidized channel that sought to offer an issues-oriented alternative to TVB's variety shows and soap operas. Its signature program was a series launched in 1972, entitled *Below the Lion Rock*. Originally presented as a series of five- to fifteen-minute shorts, featuring a working-class extended family facing myriad common everyday issues, the program was intended to illuminate governmental objectives in a warm and comical manner.

Under the progressive management of young turks like Ann Hui and Allen Fong, however, the spots took on a life of their own—growing in length and breaking away from the family format, and ultimately challenging and even criticizing government policies on important issues.

As these socially conscious programs became popular, the commercial stations TVB, CTV, and Rediffusion/ATV followed suit, launching realistic crime programs like TVB's *CID* and *ICAC* (presented by the government's Independent Commission Against Corruption), and a number of influential series, like *Ten Sensational Cases* and *Operation Manhunt*, from Johnny Mak, then ATV's head of production. The commercial stations also served as launchpads for fresh talent: Now-defunct CTV birthed Tsui Hark's first directorial effort, the *wuxia* mystery series *Gold Dagger Romance* (1978), while TVB gave Patrick Tam, perhaps the New Wave's most artful stylist, his first job as a production assistant.

But by the end of the seventies, the golden age of Hong Kong TV was ending. Programs were becoming stale, and viewership was dropping off. Meanwhile, the inauguration of the Hong Kong International Film Festival in 1977 offered a high-profile showcase for independent-minded foreign art films, piquing the interest of the New Wave's television babies. Small local film companies had also proliferated, and were actively seeking new, skilled talent. Searching for a new medium, TV writers and directors found themselves readily offered low-budget projects by these companies; sensing a trend, even the major studios, Shaw Brothers and Golden Harvest, began taking tentative steps to scout new directorial talent.

Tuo Zhonghua chills out in Yim Ho's *The Day the Sun Turned Cold.*

*Courtesy of Fortissimo Films. All rights reserved. Special thanks to Marnix van Wijk.*

Yim Ho's *The Extras* (1978) is often cited as the first film of what is now known as the Hong Kong New Wave, although aesthetic and conceptual precedents to the New Wave exist in the serious, issue-oriented films of Lung Kong (1967's *Story of a Discharged Prisoner,* 1974's *Hiroshima 28*) and Tang Shuxuan (1970's *The Arch;* 1974's *China Behind*), produced during the sixties and early seventies—as well as Josephine Siao and Leong Po Chih's unvarnished crime drama *Jumping Ash* (1976).

Still, the trickle of independent creativity of this earlier period was nothing compared to the results of the latter-day mass emigration of young talent from TV to film. The New Wavers brought a never-before-seen level of technical sophistication and topical sensibility to the cinematic medium. While the previous generation of filmmakers had been dominated largely by Mainland expatriates with a wistful nostalgia for the motherland and little interest in the contemporary Hong Kong experience, this fresh, idealistic, postwar generation was vitally concerned with issues of local identity. They were Hong Kongers born and bred; they spoke Cantonese as a native tongue, and their sensibilities were drawn from Hong Kong's unique context, as a colonized society suspended between East and West.

The debut of the New Wavers caused Cantonese cinema to revive, with a vengeance. Unlike many avant-garde movements, the New Wave actively sought to blend art with commerce, and politics with entertainment. The "hosts" they chose for their viral messages were by and large genre works like those that had long been the staple of Canto-cinema, only mutated in strange and subversive ways.

Crime stories were particularly popular; cheap to produce and box office friendly, they also lent themselves well to the discussion of social issues. Super-8-hobbyist-turned-TV director Alex Cheung made his feature debut in 1979 with *Cops and Robbers;* Peter Yung made *The System* (1979); Kirk Wong directed *The Club* (1981); and Terry Tong released *Coolie Killer* (1982).

Other directors embraced *wuxia* films as source material; Tsui Hark, who had already drawn from *wuxia* in his TV work, turned to film in 1978, creating a period martial arts fantasy that borrowed liberally from Chor Yuen's swordplay films for Shaw Brothers, but updated them with modern techniques and concepts, in *The Butterfly Murders* (1979). (His next two films, both released in 1980, demonstrated the kind of range Tsui would show throughout his illustrious career: The devastatingly bleak crime thriller *Dangerous Encounter–1st Kind* and the cannibal comedy *We're Going to Eat You.*)

Meanwhile, Patrick Tam reinvigorated the period martial arts film, with his brooding dissertation *The Sword* (1980); Dennis Yu, after making his brutal revenge shocker *The Beasts* (1980), created a whole new horror genre with his influential creature-feature *The Imp* (1981), set in the dingy urban jungle of Hong Kong public housing estates. And Ann Hui, who had made her debut with the socially conscious psycho-thriller *The Secret* (1979), updated the ghost story by investing it with unique local flavor in *The Spooky Bunch* (1980).

Hui, the New Wave's most prominent female member, evolved into a skillful tightrope walker, skirting the line between arthouse and mainstream for the next twenty years. Following the mainstream success of *The Spooky Bunch,* she made a pair of explicit sociopolitical allegories, 1981's *The Story of Woo Viet* and 1982's *Boat People,* the latter earning her her first Best Director trophy at the Hong Kong Film Awards.

## JIN YONG

If you've seen a Hong Kong sword-play picture produced any time in the last couple of decades, you've probably seen a story based on a novel by Jin Yong—the pseudonym for a remarkably prolific writer and publisher named Louis Cha Leung Yung. Born in Zhejiang Province in 1924, Cha adopted the moniker to pen works of heroic fiction without damaging his credibility in his day job as a serious writer. Ironically, both of Cha's personas attained the pinnacle of success in their respective fields; Louis Cha the journalist went on to found *Ming Pao Daily,* one of Hong Kong's best-read and most influential newspapers, while Jin Yong the writer of martial arts fantasies is perhaps the most popular Chinese writer ever, with some *one billion* books in print. (In fact, there's a common saying that "wherever people speak Chinese, you will find Jin Yong.")

Cha began writing his Jin Yong novels during Hong Kong's post–World War II pop-fiction renaissance. Among his innovations was the depiction of heroes as flawed—often fatally so. Though his champions were superhuman fighters, their personalities were all too mortal, and the keys to their destruction often lay in weakness of character rather than battlefield defeat.

Taiwanese writer Gu Long would go on to write many novels in the "Jin Yong style," most of which were turned into grand productions by Shaw Brothers, but Cha, the father of the genre, remained its shining star. A Buddhist scholar by hobby, Cha infused his works with mysticism, inventing an array of magical martial arts styles, while allowing his damaged heroes to grow and develop over the course of their endeavors, moving themselves toward perfection in the Buddhist karmic tradition. His epic novels typically ran to thousands of pages over multiple volumes, with meandering plots and huge casts of characters bound up in convoluted relationships, including romantic ones—previously taboo in martial arts literature. (Although, to be sure, these love affairs frequently turn out to be inadvertently incestuous, or to contain some other tragic and terrible obstacle. Readers weren't buying the books for the love stories anyway.)

Beginning in 1958, the Emei Film Company began producing self-contained story arcs from Jin Yong epics as movies, launching a tradition that continues to this day, despite Cha's decision to retire his "Jin Yong" identity when his day job as founder and publisher of *Ming Pao* required too much of his time and attention. Even though he sold the paper in 1993 to a media conglomerate, he refuses to revive his fictional writing. The media world is the richer for Cha's decision (not to mention Cha himself—he was estimated to be China's 64th-wealthiest man in 1991[16]), and the martial world the poorer.

*—Peter Nepstad*

---

But Hui would prove to be an anomaly. By 1982, most of her fellow New Wavers had either fallen into obscurity or moved on from their independent roots, hired by Golden Harvest or upstart mini-major studios like Cinema City and D&B Films. For these "graduates," commercial viability increasingly became a concern; it was left to a second wave of TV refugees to take up the creative slack. This Second Wave of directors— including such stalwarts as Wong Kar Wai, Jacob Cheung, Lawrence Ah Mon, Clara Law, and Mabel Cheung—would, over the next decade, become the burgeoning industry's nucleus.

As it turns out, Ann Hui was instrumental in launching the career of the filmmaker who would become the dean of this Second New Wave: Stanley Kwan. After graduating from Hong Kong's Baptist College with a degree in communications, Kwan applied to TVB's actor's training program, and was rejected. Hui, sensing in Kwan a fellow independent spirit, decided to take the thwarted performer under her wing, employing him as assistant director on three of her films, including the classic *Boat People.*

Kwan's first solo films after his apprenticeship, 1985's *Women* and 1986's *Love Unto Waste,* were flawed but interesting works that merely hinted at his promise. Although both garnered him Best Director nominations at the Hong Kong Film Awards, it was his third feature, the tragic romance-cum-ghost-story *Rouge* (1988), that would establish his unique voice and vision. Executives at Golden Harvest were flabbergasted when they saw the film: *This is a ghost story? Where are the special effects?* But, with the support of his superstar producer—Jackie Chan—Kwan's vision won out. *Rouge* was a huge hit in Taiwan, where it was released in its original form (the film was released in Hong Kong with minor cuts for length). It also won him Best Director and Best Picture at the Hong Kong Film Awards.

## CHINESE GHOST STORIES

Beautiful maidens who vanish at dawn. Hapless scholars ensnared by demonic trickery. White-browed priests whose rites are the sole defense against the massed forces of evil. The ghost story has a long and rich history in China, having developed in written form by the seventh century A.D. Early stories were anecdotal in nature, like contemporary urban legends—reports of weird phenomena that "really happened," albeit to far-off friends and distant relatives. To archive these extraordinary occurrences, scholars recorded them in the form of small essays that were distributed to acquaintances. The immense popularity of these tales soon led to formal publication, in compilations that were eagerly read and enjoyed by the literary elite.

The most famous of these compendiums was written by a scholar of the Qing Dynasty (1644 to 1911 A.D.) named Pu Songling, whose stories were compiled and released posthumously under the title *Liaozhai Zhiyi,* or "Strange Stories from a Chinese Studio." These stories, and stories like them, were eventually adapted as Chinese opera, and from there became the inspiration for an entire cinematic genre.

The heart of the Chinese ghost story is the "lady ghost," generally the spirit of a maiden who died young and unmarried. According to folk tradition, everyone becomes a ghost at death. The family of the deceased must burn offerings—incense and paper money—to ensure that the spirit can buy a proper place in the afterlife. A woman who dies before marriage has no husband or son to burn incense for her, preventing her from entering the underworld. As a result, ghost maidens haunt the living, looking for the romance and marriage that they never had in life. At the core of almost every ghost story, then, is a love story, between a man and a ghost.

But of course, there are inevitably complications to ghostly romance: demons who want the ghost woman for themselves. Meddling Taoists who want to save the man from his own foolishness. Whether the romance takes place in ancient China or modern Hong Kong, the result is almost always the same: No good can come from love between ghost and mortal.

*—Peter Nepstad*

Subsequently, the action hero would also produce Kwan's *Centre Stage* (aka *Actress*) in 1991, a biopic about the rise and subsequent persecution and suicide of thirties superstar Ruan Lingyu. Mixing interviews, archival footage, dramatic reenactment, and surreal interpretive sequences, the film places Ruan's tragic life within the context of contemporary analyses of her films and historical influence.

The film's jarring blend of nostalgic exploration and postmodern experimentation has led some critics to set it within a continuum of films shaped by 1984's Sino-British Joint Declaration on Hong Kong, which formalized Hong Kong's return to Mainland control in 1997. Its announcement, just as so many of the New and Second Wave filmmakers were coming into their own, meant that the sensibilities of the leading lights of nineties Hong Kong cinema were shaped by the figurative ticking of a clock.

## TVB TAKES FLIGHT; TAIWAN TUMBLES

In addition to launching dozens of celebrated careers, the rise of Hong Kong's New Wave had two important consequences.

The first related to the demise—or perhaps more correctly, the transformation—of one of Hong Kong cinema's most influential players. Unable to adapt its rigid "dream factory" system to the New Wave's auteurist whirlwind, an outgunned Shaw Brothers declared its intention to cease film production entirely. To punctuate its decision, it sold its storied Movie Town backlot to its own subsidiary, TVB, which promptly renamed it TVB City and put it to work cranking out episodic soaps and swordsman dramas, starring an interchangeable array of hopeful, mostly anonymous novices.

As usual, Sir Run Run's decision proved fiscally brilliant. Gone were the old stars, their ego-driven demands, and their escalating salaries. With no incentive to hire recognizable names to ensure box office dominance, Shaw set his sights instead on launching new talent, continuing his successful concept of an on-site school for actors. Now, however, the most promising "graduates" were automatically signed to long-term "management contracts" that guaranteed TVB a piece of future showbiz earnings. Meanwhile, much of the training consisted of time spent toiling on TVB's slate of weekly programs, for pay that amounted to a few dollars an hour. But then as now, there were few better ways for showbiz hopefuls to break into the industry, and most of these were also controlled by Shaws—including the phenomenon that has perhaps become the industry's most prolific source for new female talent: the Miss Hong Kong beauty pageant.

Established as an annual event on TVB in 1973, the pageant became a preferred stepping-stone to stardom when first runner-up Chiu Ah Tse was cast in the TVB series *Shanghai Beach* (aka *The Bund*), a runaway hit that helped establish the career of her costar, TVB training-school graduate Chow Yun Fat. Other contestants who went on to successful careers at TVB and in film include Cherie Chung (1979), Kathy Chau (1985), Suki Kwan, and Chingmy Yau (1987), as well as Miss Hong Kong winners Joyce Godenzi (1984), Michelle Reis (1988), Monica Chan (1989), and Anita Yuen (1990).

The pageant's greatest discovery may well be Maggie Cheung, perhaps the most acclaimed and versatile actress in contemporary Chinese cinema. Born September 20, 1964, in Hong Kong, Cheung moved to England with her family when she was eight, staying there until the age of seventeen. After she graduated from high school, her parents rewarded her with a trip to the city of her birth. While there, she was "discovered" on the street by a talent agent, who offered her a contract to be the face of a local retail chain—if she agreed to stay. After modeling for several years, she decided to enter the Miss Hong Kong pageant. While she didn't win, she was named runner-up, and given the title of "Miss Photogenic." Signed by Shaws immediately after the pageant, she debuted in the film *Prince Charming* (1984), and then appeared in the TVB serial *Police Cadet,* alongside TVB trainees and future stars Tony Leung Chiu Wai and Lau Ching Wan.

The list of notable TVB alumni goes on and on: Other training school grads include Simon Yam, Kent Cheng, Stephen Chiau, Louis Koo, Francis Ng, and director Ringo Lam. Even many pop-idols-turned-actors have TVB to thank for their careers: Three of the four "Heavenly Kings" of Canto-pop—Andy Lau, Leon Lai, and Aaron Kwok—went through the TVB training school while honing their musical chops, while singing competitions on the network first brought national exposure to divas like Anita Mui and Leslie Cheung.

The other secondary consequence of the Hong Kong New Wave was subtler, but equally important. In 1980, stung by the United States' decision to diplomatically recognize the Mainland at Taiwan's expense the year before, Taiwan was forced to use culture as its primary means of maintaining international relations. As more and more nations followed America's lead, Taiwan's embassies were converted into "overseas cultural centers," with a new mandate to engineer positive public relations through dissemination of Taiwanese traditional and contemporary arts. To this end, the Government Information Office sought to turn its Golden Horse Awards—the Taiwanese version of the Oscars—into an internationally recognized film event. In 1981, however, government ministers looked on in consternation as Hong Kong filmmakers walked off with prizes in major categories, with Tsui Hark winning Best Director for his light farce *All the Wrong Clues (for the Right Solution)* (1980).

This embarrassment led James Soong, then the head of the GIO, to announce an initiative to lift the "artistic" and "professional" standards of Taiwanese film—an initiative that led directly to the establishment of the movement known as New Taiwanese Cinema.

## DRINKS AT EDWARD'S

The group most identified with what became known as the "New Tai-wanese Cinema" was initially less an artistic school than a gang of drink-ing buddies. The gang's leader, if only because the parties took place at his house, was a computer programmer named Edward Yang.

Yang was Shanghainese, but had moved to Taipei with his family in 1949, at the tender age of two. While a teenager, he dabbled in cartoon-ing and comics—his only experience in the arts before his cinematic career. During his college years, he ended up traveling to the United States to study computer design and information sciences. Only after he completed his tech-related schooling was he bitten by the film bug; entering the University of Southern California's film school, he studied for one semester before dropping out after, in his words, "concluding I had no talent." Moving to Seattle, he worked in computers for nearly seven years.[17]

Then thirty years old, Yang—mired in a midlife crisis—saw Werner Herzog's *Aguirre: The Wrath of God,* his first brush with arthouse cinema. According to Yang, it was the first time he realized that "you didn't have to make films like Hollywood." Three years later, in 1981, Yang accepted an invitation from a friend to come to Taiwan and assist him on a film. There he discovered that Taiwanese actress-turned-Hong-Kong-star Sylvia Chang, herself an aspiring director, had pushed the leading Tai-wanese television station TTV to launch a series, *Eleven Women,* intended to give opportunities to new directors. On a whim, Yang sub-mitted his name to the producers and to his surprise, was asked to direct an episode.

Yang began spending time with other young movie types, inviting them to his house for cocktails and lively, occasionally heated discus-sion. The most regular visitors out of the ten or so who frequented these impromptu salons were a pair who would later become Yang's closest friends in the industry: Wu Nien-chen, a screenwriter then working as script supervisor for the Central Motion Picture Corporation, and an aspiring director named Hou Hsiao-hsien.

Born in Guangdong, Hou, like Yang, was raised in Taiwan; unlike

The grand master Hou Hsiao-hsien's *City of Sadness*. *Courtesy of Taiwan Film Archive.*

Yang, he stayed in Taiwan for school, and was forced to serve two years of compulsory military service, where he served in the film unit. Upon his discharge in 1969, he decided to make the movies his career, enrolling in film school at the National Taiwan College of the Arts, and beginning to work as an assistant scriptwriter and director's assistant soon after graduation.

In 1982, Wu Nien-chen and a colleague named Hsiao Ye (later the scripter for Yang's *The Terrorizers*) managed to convince Ming Chi, then the president of CMPC, to authorize a project that would give some of their closest friends exposure. The project, an anthology film called *In Our Time*, featured segments directed by Yang, Ko I-cheng, Tao De-cheng, and Chang Yi; it has been generally referred to as the origin point for the New Taiwanese Cinema.

Yang's piece, titled "Desires," was particularly acclaimed by critics; he was immediately offered the opportunity to make a feature film, which became 1983's *That Day on the Beach*, an epic, two-hour-and-forty-minute exploration of a woman's empowerment after the disappearence of her no-account husband. (Not coincidentally, it starred the actress whose lobbying had provided Yang with his first start in the business: Sylvia Chang.)

Though critically admired, the film was not a commercial success; nevertheless, firm in his belief in Yang's talents, Hou Hsiao-hsien offered to mortgage his house to underwrite Yang's second film, *Taipei Story* (1985), in which Hou would play the lead. The film, which details the deterioration of a yuppie couple's relationship, lasted in theaters just four days. Yang was crushed; Hou lost everything, just as his own career was on the rise.

In 1983, Hou had produced a commercially successful film called *Growing Up*, directed by seventies standout Chen Kun-hou, and directed a segment of another hit, *The Sandwich Man*—a three-part omnibus based on stories written by Huang Chun-ming, notable for being one of the first films to defy the KMT's edict against using the Taiwanese dialect in cinema. That year, Hou also made his feature debut, *The Boys from Fengkuei*, following it up the year after with the well-received *A Summer at Grandpa's* (1984). But Hou's 1985 financial disaster may have prompted the self-reflection that led to the film some see as his first great classic: the autobiographical *A Time to Live, a Time to Die* (1985), which won him the Critics Award at that year's Berlin International Film Festival—the first of the New Taiwanese Cinema's major international awards. A year later, in 1986, both Hou and Yang would release landmark films—Hou making the elliptical, nostalgic *Dust in the Wind*, written by Wu Nien-chen and loosely based on the scripter's childhood, and Yang making a work that fit his dark, post–*Taipei Story* mood: the brilliant and surreal urban nightmare *The Terrorizers*.

*Dust* and *Terrorizers* were released just as critical steps were being taken toward greater openness in Taiwanese society. President Chiang Ching-kuo, the son of Generalissimo Chiang Kai-shek, had begun a program of governmental reform by allowing the creation of Taiwan's first opposition party, the Democratic Progressives (DPP). The following year, he lifted the martial law that had ruled the country for forty years, allowing Taiwanese to contact and visit Mainland relatives for the first time since the KMT retreat in 1949. With his death in 1988 came one final reform: the inauguration of Taiwan's first native-born (*ben sheng ren*) president, Lee Teng-hui.

These changes in the political climate gave rise to a film that marked the end of the New Taiwanese Cinema's first creative wave: Hou Hsiao-hsien's 1989 *A City of Sadness*, the first film to examine the KMT's bloody "Er Er Ba" massacre of native Taiwanese. Gripping, impassioned, and often painful to watch, the film was the first to make a significant stir among Western audiences, after it was awarded the Golden Lion, the top prize at the prestigious Venice International Film Festival.

Nineteen eighty-nine would be a milestone year for the globalization of Greater China's other cinematic regions as well—marking the release of two films that would serve as Chinese cinema's first prominent representatives in Western theaters since the heyday of kung fu cinema: John Woo's thrill-charged ballistic ballet *The Killer*, and Zhang Yimou's mesmerizing rural shocker *Ju Dou* (1989).

## THE GUNSLINGER

Bodies fly through the air, defying common sense and physics as they spin through a murderous hail of bullets; jaded cops bond with noble criminals, before they go out together in a blaze of glory; duels end in standoffs, with multiple guns pointed at multiple targets, each shooter waiting for the wrong move to be made. No filmmaker has done more to shape the vocabulary of the modern action movie than John Woo, perhaps the greatest genre auteur of his generation (some would say the greatest ever).

John Woo, before the gun:
*Heroes Shed No Tears.*
*Courtesy of Celestial Pictures.*
*All rights reserved.*

Born in 1946, Woo moved with his family from Mainland China to Hong Kong at the end of the fifties, fleeing the Communist Revolution. His childhood was marked by poverty and social isolation. Enrolled in a Methodist-run school where he had few close friends, he eventually found solace in the movies—falling in love with Hollywood films and the Cantonese cinema, and then, in his later student years, embracing the French New Wave. Woo briefly considered becoming a minister; fortunately for film fans, he decided to follow his heart rather than his soul, and became a production assistant at Cathay Studios instead.

As Cathay's fortunes degenerated, Woo jumped over to the industry-leading Shaw Brothers studio, to apprentice under top martial arts director Chang Cheh. But in an industry and era where "young upstarts" were often in their forties, Woo was unwilling to pursue a slow, grinding path to film-making. At the tender age of twenty-six, he left Shaws to launch his own independent production company, making his directing debut with the martial arts actioner *The Young Dragons* (1973). Woo's final cut proved so savagely over-the-top that censors banned it for excessive violence.

Somehow, Raymond Chow—overlord of the equally upstart Golden Harvest, which had risen out of the ruins of Cathay—managed to get a look at the film and decided that Woo had talent worth polishing. Chow purchased and released *The Young Dragons* (albeit in a heavily edited version), while simultaneously dangling a three-year contract in front of the budding auteur. A grateful Woo accepted.

Woo's early Golden Harvest films were martial arts pictures like *Hand of Death* (1975), which gave a young Jackie Chan his first featured role, and *Last Hurrah for Chivalry* (1978), an old-school *wuxia* epic that previewed some of the themes and techniques that would eventually become Woo's trademarks. They also were unmitigated commercial disasters. Soon, Woo once again found himself looking for work.

Opportunity knocked in the form of a newly launched maverick studio, Cinema City, which offered him a job . . . if he agreed to turn his talents toward making comedies. With no other obvious prospects, Woo took the job.

Founded by the creative trinity of Karl Maka, Dean Shek, and Raymond Wong, Cinema City conspired to give Asian audiences a new kind of movie—one with Hollywood-style production values, but a distinctly Hong Kong sensibility. Their forte was comedies, and they achieved their pinnacle of success with the *Aces Go Places* series (1982–89), several installments of which set new Hong Kong box-office records.

The secret to Cinema City's success was their ultrapractical, "laugh factory" mindset. Each of their pictures followed a basic formula that combined stunts, slapstick, bankable stars, and celebrity cameos. Meanwhile, rather than depending on the uncertain inspiration of individuals, most of their films were made by committee. Cinema City set up a brain trust, headed by its founders, but later enlarged to include the likes of Tsui Hark and Eric Tsang, to oversee film development. Among the duties of this panel was the enforcement of a "joke quotient"—a yuks-per-minute measurement based on the number of reels in a film (with each reel being approximately ten minutes long).

The studio's first film, *Laughing Time* (1981), leveraged the strengths of the founders. Popular comedian Dean Shek starred, giving a Chaplinesque "Little Tramp" turn, and bald-headed comic foil Karl Maka played Shek's on-screen sidekick. The third member of the triumvirate, Raymond Wong, wrote the script, while newly hired employee Woo was put at the helm. Woo proved shockingly good at directing slapstick, and the film was a hit. What followed was a string of cheesy but successful farces, starring the likes of Ricky Hui and Josephine Siao. Short on plot and character, long on buffoonery and exaggerated spit-takes, Woo's commercial coups in the comic genre were a mystery even to him; he certainly had no interest in pursuing a career as the King of Comedy, and began to desperately seek a way to get back to making films with meaning, which to him meant movies about manhood, brotherhood, sacrifice, and self-respect.

The solution came in the form of impresario Tsui Hark, who'd gone from edgy New Wave auteur to master of the mainstream; Tsui had parlayed his work with Cinema City into an opportunity to launch his own production company, Film Workshop. According to Tsui, the mission behind Film Workshop was to "push the envelope" of the Hong Kong motion picture, incorporating high-end special effects, sophisticated cinematic techniques, and rich, complex screenwriting; seeing in Woo a kindred visionary, he invited him to take the opportunity to make the film he'd always wanted to make.

That film turned out to be *A Better Tomorrow* (1986), an emotionally charged melodrama that married Woo's personal obsession with honor and brotherhood to his uniquely kinetic sense of film action. A remake of an old Lung Kong classic, *Story of a Discharged Prisoner* (1967), it starred old-school Shaw Brothers hero Ti Lung, emergent superstar Chow Yun Fat, and pop idol Leslie Cheung.

The film struck a chord with audiences throughout Asia. Woo became the industry's most sought-after director; Ti Lung's acting career was revived, while Cheung's was launched into the stratosphere. And Chow, up to then best known for his TV work, found himself transformed into a cult icon, with legions of young men sporting the distinctive shades, toothpick, and duster outfit of his Triad-assassin antihero Mark Gor.

Chow was born in 1955 on tiny Lamma Island off the coast of Hong Kong. His family's poverty led him to quit school at seventeen to work a series of odd jobs: messenger, bellboy, door-to-door salesman, and cab driver. At the suggestion of a friend, he'd auditioned for and entered TVB's training academy; upon graduation, he had signed the standard TVB management contract—which tied him to the studio for fourteen years—and begun a long and successful television career. He became known through-

Chow Yun Fat in *Love in a Fallen City. Courtesy of Celestial Pictures. All rights reserved.*

out Asia as the star of the soap opera *Hotel* (1976), and then as a crime lord in *The Bund* (1977), before shifting to film with his poignant performance as a Vietnamese refugee in Ann Hui's *The Story of Woo Viet* (1981) and his bravura role in Po Chih Leong's *Hong Kong 1941* (1982), for which he won Best Actor at Taiwan's Golden Horse Awards.

But Chow's collaboration with Woo propelled him to superstar status—and it was just beginning. Chow's ability to project both heartfelt passion and effortless cool made him the perfect avatar for Woo's heroic ideal. After making two sequels to *A Better Tomorrow* (the second of which was directed by Tsui Hark, after he and Woo experienced sharp creative differences), Chow and Woo went into production on the film that would define Hong Kong action for the world: *The Killer*. Featuring for the first time Woo's full arsenal of tropes and clichés—leaping two-gun attacks, tense Mexican standoffs, flocks of startled doves—on the American arthouse circuit it played to jam-packed crowds, who'd never seen anything like it in their lives.

Over the course of the next decade, they'd see much, much more of the same.

## MAKING THE FIFTH

Meanwhile, right alongside Woo's bullet-riddled mayhem played a quieter, yet equally wrenching masterpiece—*Ju Dou*, the first film by a Mainland Chinese filmmaker to ever achieve broad United States release. It gave Western audiences a tantalizing glimpse of the state of Mainland cinema after the Cultural Revolution, a cinema in the process of reinventing itself virtually from scratch.

The leaders of this renaissance were a group of filmmakers called the "Fifth Generation"—a name they received after critics determined that they were the fifth generation of directors since the dawn of Chinese film. (The First Generation was held to be the early Shanghai pioneers; the Second, the "golden age" filmmakers of the thirties and forties; the Third, the "revolutionary film workers" of the fifties who were put in the service of early socialist realism; and the Fourth was the "interrupted" generation of directors who were trained in the early sixties, but prevented from making films by the onset of the Cultural Revolution.)

## SUPERCOPS: THE GOOD, THE BAD, AND THE BRUTAL

功夫

In a territory where nitro-burning action is a trademark, it should come as no surprise that Hong Kong loves its cops. The territory has produced an astronomical number of police procedurals over the past few decades (almost, but not quite, as many as the number of Triad films; after all, it's not the cops who've been financing the industry). What follows is a handy guide to a few of the filmmakers and stars who have made significant contributions to the genre.

- **Danny Lee:** A former Shaw Brothers contract player, Lee established himself as the crème de la crème of Copland by appearing in or producing over sixty police-related thrillers, many of which were made by his own Magnum Films company. Precinct houses across Hong Kong loved the publicity—with many officers even taking to calling him "Sir" when they spotted him in public. (Lee probably never got a parking ticket in his life.) Whether he's playing a patrolman, a house detective, or a cycle jockey, Danny Lee is Hong Kong's quintessential supercop.

- **Michael Wong:** Wong has played a cop in more than twenty-two films to date, practically carving a niche out of portraying officers of the SDU (Special Detail Unit; the equivalent of SWAT teams in Hong Kong), beginning with his debut in Dennis Yu's *City Hero* (1985). While he's not the world's most talented actor, it doesn't take a Barrymore to play a hardcore street commando.

- **Cynthia Yang:** If Danny Lee is the proverbial Adam of supercops, then Cynthia Yang (often billed as "Cynthia Khan") would be his Eve. She was groomed by D&B Films as the "next Michelle Yeoh," and a look at one of her fifteen or so police thrillers proves why. Beautiful, balletic, and ballistic, she can swing a kick with as much panache as she can fire a pistol.

*—Darryl Pestilence*

The Fifth Generation was composed of the 153 students who made up the first class of the reopened Beijing Film Academy, who graduated in 1982 having been exposed to a much broader range of international cinema than any earlier set of alumni. They shared common experiences of teenage years spent in turmoil, as members of the Red Guards or as exiled "sent-down" youth; this would serve as the context for their later work, which government censors would uniformly attack as subversive, degenerate, or both.

Meanwhile, because they were graduating into an era with a surplus of filmmakers—many of the veteran directors who'd lost positions during the Revolution were streaming back into the cities and retaking their jobs—these freshly minted graduates were sent to remote studio outposts in Guangxi and Xi'an, which had the unintentional effect of setting them free to express themselves with minimal Party oversight.

The first Fifth Generation film is generally held to be Zhang Junzhao's war story *One and Eight* (1984); however, the first to receive international attention was *Yellow Earth*, directed that same year by Chen Kaige. The film, a deceptively simple tale about a young man sent to the countryside to record rural folk songs, is a technical masterpiece—gorgeously shot, with a beautiful, complementary score; when screened for international audiences at the 1985 Hong Kong Film Festival, *Earth* generated an immediate buzz, focusing world attention on the film industry of the Mainland for the first time since the golden era of Shanghai. It also established Chen as something of a troublemaker, for coyly presenting what could be interpreted as controversial political allusions; this epithet would be applied to most of the Fifth Generation's leading lights.

Chen was born in Beijing in 1952, the son of a notable Fourth Generation filmmaker, Chen Huai'ai. Swept up in the frenzy of Mao's Cultural Revolution as a teen, he joined the Red Guards, and publicly accused his father of being a Kuomintang spy. For most of the next decade, Chen worked on behalf of the masses, as laborer on a rubber plantation, soldier, and factory hand.

As the Cultural Revolution staggered to a close, a disillusioned Chen decided to follow in the footsteps of the father he'd denounced. He found a job at Bejing's central film laboratory and gradually insinuated himself into the circles of top directors and cinematographers, winning admission to study at the prestigious Beijing Film Academy in 1978. (According to Chen, he actually failed his entrance exam, because the instructors disliked his "know-it-all attitude," which they ascribed to his being the son of a famous director; luckily, the academy decided to increase the size of that year's class and he got in under the wire.)[18]

Graduating in 1982, he was given the opportunity to work with the Beijing Film Studio, but chose to go to distant Guangxi Studios instead, in order to collaborate with two of his classmates—Zhang Junzhao and Zhang Yimou.

The latter Zhang was born in 1950 in the northern Chinese city of Xi'an. Because his father had been an officer in the Kuomintang, Zhang's family was treated with the contempt reserved for those of "black" backgrounds—socially ostracized, and largely excluded from economic or political advancement. Zhang himself was barred from becoming a member of the Youth League, a key prerequisite to joining the Communist party. The arrival of the Cultural Revolution seemed to offer a chance for a teenage Zhang—then sixteen—to distance himself from his paternal legacy. Quitting school, he headed for the countryside like so many of his peers, first working on a collective farm, and then in a textile factory—an experience from which he reportedly drew the inspiration for *Ju Dou*.

As the Revolution began to draw to a close in 1974, Zhang found himself in Shanghai, out of work and still without much by way of prospects. Always possessed of a strong visual imagination, he bought a second-hand still camera (reportedly with money earned by selling blood) and was able to make a living as a freelance newspaper photographer.

In 1978, he took the admissions exam for the Beijing Film Academy. Although he passed, the academy initially refused to admit him because of his age—at twenty-seven, he was considerably older than most of his fellow students. He brought his case before the Ministry of Culture and won his appeal. He spent his four years working toward a degree in cinematography, and upon graduation, was assigned to Guangxi Studios.

When Zhang, Zhang, and Chen arrived there, they were told that due to a shortage of teaching personnel, they would have to fend for themselves. They formed a "Youth Film Team" and petitioned the Ministry of Culture for permission to work on their own projects. From their independent efforts sprang *One and Eight* and *Yellow Earth*, both of which Zhang Yimou shot as cinematographer.

Zhang's work drew the attention of Wu Tianming, who had been placed in charge of Xi'an Studios, based in Zhang's old hometown. Eager to see what the cinematographer would do if given the chance to make his own films, Wu lured Zhang home with promises of a chance to direct. Obtaining approval from the new Ministry of Radio, Television, and Film to apply the proceeds from Xi'an's more commercial films toward "discretionary works," Wu was able to provide Zhang with the funds to make a film based on a story by novelist Mo Yan, starring Jiang Wen, China's best-known actor, and an unknown student actress.

The film was *Red Sorghum* (1987), and the actress was twenty-two-year-old Gong Li. *Sorghum* shocked China's cinematic establishment by winning the Golden Bear, the top prize at the Berlin Film Festival. It also launched a personal and professional partnership between Zhang and Li that would last for the next seven years.

A rattled MRTF refused to fund Zhang's next project; instead, the capital for *Ju Dou* came from Tokuma, a Japanese production company. It was his first to be nominated for an Academy Award in the United States It was also his first to be banned by the Chinese government. Despite multiple attempts made by Zhang to placate censors, including shifting the setting of the film to the remote twenties, the Ministry of Radio, Television, and Film simply decided that that the movie projected a negative image of China to the rest of the world. Zhang, like Chen, was now stigmatized as a "problem director," and for the remainder of the decade, his works would regularly be delayed from release or banned outright.

Still, the trials of Chen and Zhang were nothing compared to those of the third Fifth Generation filmmaker to win international acclaim. Like Chen Kaige, Tian Zhuangzhuang descended from cinematic blood. His father, Tian Fang, had been a leading actor in the early thirties who took on a new role in post-1949 China as the director of the Beijing Film Studio. Tian's mother, Yu Lan, was an award-winning actress who'd won acclaim for roles in classics like *The Lin Family Shop* (1959) and *Revolu-*

*tionary Family* (1961), and who'd gone on to serve as administrator of the Beijing Children's Film Studio after her retirement from the screen.

Despite, or because of, their celebrated background, Tian's parents suffered harsh persecution during the Cultural Revolution. Tian himself was "sent down" to the countryside. After a stint in the army, he joined his parents' industry as a cinematographer in the late seventies; after attending Beijing Film Academy and graduating, with his Fifth Generation peers, in 1982, he was restricted primarily to television and children's film, including the well-regarded *Red Elephant* (1982).

In 1985, he was finally given the opportunity to direct a feature film, after submitting a script set among the tribesmen of Inner Mongolia. Upon reaching the steppes, he decided to throw away his script and instead make the bold stylistic experiment *On the Hunting Ground*. The film, which examined the exacting traditions and customs of Inner Mongolian hunters, was shot in a documentary manner and in the indigenous dialect. It was a critical success internationally, but a financial flop at home.

Luckily for Tian, Xi'an Studio's iconoclastic, forward-thinking administrator, Wu Tianming, saw past the film's box office receipts and gave him the opportunity to make *The Horse Thief* (1986), a similarly avant garde film that focused this time on Tibetan rites, rituals, and hardships. Once again, chirping cricket noises could be heard at empty local cinemas. Tian also began to draw the ire of Chinese critics, who accused him of elitism. Although an embittered Tian responded to their attacks with equally harsh rejoinders, his subsequent projects—*Drum Singers* and *Rock 'n' Roll Kids* (1987), and *Li Lianying: The Imperial Eunuch* (1991)— were significantly more populist in tone.

Then, in 1993, he made *The Blue Kite,* a film in which he overtly criticized modern Chinese policies. The tale of a mother who marries three times to provide for her son, only to have all three husbands die in a manner relating to one of China's great contemporary political upheavals (the Hundred Flowers movement, the Great Leap Forward, and the Cultural Revolution), the film is episodic and somewhat emotionally distant, but intellectually resonant. The subject matter of the film—along with the fact that Tian exhibited it outside China without permission—resulted in Tian being banned from further filmmaking, a ban that would not be lifted until 1996.

The government's reaction is indication enough that the work of the Fifth Generation filmmakers, who also included Wu Ziniu (*Nanjing 1937*), Huang Jianxin (*The Black Cannon Incident; Dislocation; Samsara*), and Hu Mei (*Army Nurse*), the only prominent woman director associated with the group, was exciting and provocative, though it was well disguised with allegory and, in the eyes of some, superfluous exoticism.

More unvarnished provocation would come in the decade to follow, emanating from the wildly creative, aggressively insolent cameras of the group of renegades dubbed the Sixth Generation.

*—Jeff Yang, with Art Black (Hong Kong New Wave, TVB, Tian Zhuangzhuang), Curtis Tsui (Ann Hui, Stanley Kwan, Edward Yang, Hou Hsiao-hsien), Caroline Vié-Toussaint (John Woo, Chow Yun Fat), Matt Levie (Chen Kaige, Zhang Yimou)*

# 5

# The Best of Times, the Worst of Times: The Nineties

To me, a director is like a chef. I make the dishes that the audience wants to eat. Most directors love their movies, but I never fall in love with mine. When they are editing, it's like they are making love to the film. They hate to finish it. But I don't. I always edit my movies very fast. I try to give the audience what they want. That's the way I've done it for the last 20 years.

—Wong Jing, Hong Kong's king of commercial cinema[19]

As the nineties began, the Hong Kong movie industry had hit all-time highs in production, profitability, and popularity. They were beloved at home: in 1992, the top twelve movies on the local box office charts were all Hong Kong productions, with the highest-ranking imported film, *Basic Instinct*, crawling in at number thirteen. And increasingly, following the breakthrough of John Woo's *The Killer* (1989), they were finding a market abroad as well.

It seemed as if Hong Kong filmmakers had somehow chanced upon some kind of magic recipe for commodity motion pictures—one that blended Eastern verve and ingenuity with Western presentation. Suddenly, Hong Kong cinema's unpolished grit and lack of advanced special effects seemed like a conscious choice; a matter of stylistic preference rather than a logical consequence of minimalist budgets. Manufacturers have a term for low-priced, high-volume products that are consumed rapidly and continually, things like toothpaste, cakes of soap, and toilet paper. They call them FMCG, or fast-moving consumer goods. In essence, Hong Kong had created a recipe for FMCC—fast-moving consumer cinema.

The individual most responsible for concocting this formula was a man who emerged out of the late seventies New Wave to become one of the most reliable box office breadwinners of the eighties, and then the standard bearer for the first half of the nineties—the era when Hong Kong cinema hit its apex. During each of these periods, the films he directed or produced (most filmmakers he worked with suggested that he didn't see a great difference in the two roles) have inevitably ranked among the most original and successful of their era. Whether it's conceiving new trends, introducing new technology, or exploring new stylistic techniques, the impresario known as Tsui Hark—that's *Mr.* Tsui to you—has generally beaten a path for the rest of the industry to follow.

Of course, Tsui's success has not come without a price. His collaborators acknowledge, even proclaim to all within earshot, the difficulties of working with him, offering complaints ranging from "he interfered" (director Peter Wang, regarding the Tsui-produced *The Laserman,* 1990),

The second installment in Tsui Hark's unfinished "City Trilogy," *Shanghai Blues. Courtesy of Film Workshop Co. Ltd. All rights reserved. Special thanks to Janet Ma and Nansun Shi.*

to "he took things over completely" (director David Chung, on the Tsui-produced *I Love Maria*, aka *Roboforce*, 1988), to "he wrested away control of the sequel to my greatest masterpiece, and when I left to make the movie I wanted to make, rushed his version out just to make sure that mine was a flop" (director John Woo, on 1989's *A Better Tomorrow III*, which Tsui directed at a breakneck pace in order to beat Woo's 1990 *Bullet in the Head* to theaters).

Born January 2, 1951, in French Cochin China (now Vietnam), Tsui emigrated with his family to Hong Kong in 1966, ahead of the escalating war. Tsui left a few years later for the United States, where he studied cinema at the University of Texas, before moving to New York and working as a reporter and cameraman for a local Chinese-language television network. In 1977, Tsui returned to Hong Kong, where he, like many of his generation of overseas-educated filmmakers, found work in television. His first three movies—the existential martial arts mystery *The Butterfly Murders* (1979), the gross-out kung fu cannibal satire *We're Going to Eat You* (1980), and the politically charged *Dangerous Encounter—1st Kind* (1980)—polarized and alienated as many people as they impressed.

But it was the sweeping period fantasy of Hark's fourth film, *Zu: Warriors from the Magic Mountain*—a film he considered unfinished when he was compelled by Golden Harvest to release it in 1983—that established him as a filmmaker of revolutionary ideas and technique. It also motivated him to create his own production company, Film Workshop, allowing him to work at his own pace and in total command of his own creativity. (An indication of the degree to which Tsui needs to be in control: In 2001, he released a complete remake of *Zu*, entitled *The Legend of Zu*, just to show how the film should have ended up in the first place.)

Tsui's declaration of independence resulted in a string of startling successes. As a director, he made *Shanghai Blues* (1984) and *Peking Opera Blues* (1986), two segments of an as-yet-unfinished "city trilogy," as well as the goofy but brilliant comedy *Working Class* (1985), in which he also starred.

Meanwhile, as producer, Tsui enabled John Woo's groundbreaking *A Better Tomorrow* (1986), Ching Siu Tung's exhilarating action-horror-romance *A Chinese Ghost Story* (1987), and *Swordsman* (1990), the film that was supposed to serve as a triumphant comeback for classic *wuxia* director King Hu. All of these films were box office successes that launched multiple sequels. Each of them also generated whispers regarding Tsui's overbearing presence on the set—suggesting that, as a producer, he saw the director's role as essentially "doing the dirty work necessary to get the Tsui Hark Vision up on screen."

Tsui's meddlesome ways eventually led Woo to abandon ship after *A Better Tomorrow II*, prompting Tsui to take the reins for the third installment. King Hu walked out, or was kicked out, before completing *Swordsman*, leading Tsui to try to plug the hole with directors like Ann Hui and Raymond Lee, before throwing up his hands and finishing the film himself, hand in hand with action director Ching Siu Tung. (Ching seems to be the only major figure in Hong Kong cinema whom Tsui has been able to work with on a consistent and long-term basis, either because of Ching's congenial personality, or because of his apparent willingness to not eclipse Tsui in any way.)

But of all of the masterpieces that Tsui can justifiably be credited with bringing into existence, the one with which he is most associated is the *Once Upon a Time in China* series (six installments, 1991 through 1997), a set of films that singlehandedly revived the period kung fu genre, reenergized the Hong Kong film industry, and launched Mainland wushu master Jet Li's career into superstardom throughout Asia, and eventually, the world.

Born in Hebei, China, on April 26, 1963, Li was selected at the age of eight for training in wushu, the authentic, if formalized, warrior art that consolidates all of the many regional forms of kung fu, including mastery of the eighteen "traditional weapons." By age nine, he had won the Award for Excellence at the first national wushu competition to be held in China since the Cultural Revolution. At twelve, he was already the Chinese Men's All-Around National Wushu Champion, and a national superstar. His decision to become an actor simply added to his already enormous fame. After making a superlative debut with *Shaolin Temple* (1982) and its two sequels, *Kids from Shaolin* (1984) and *Martial Arts of Shaolin* (1986), Li was emboldened to take the directorial helm himself, with the awkwardly titled *Born to Defense* (1988). A leaden flop at the box office, it put Li's film career into a tailspin, until he met Tsui Hark. In Tsui's hands, Jet blossomed as an actor in the role he seemed born to resurrect: that of the legendary traditional healer and martial arts master Wong Fei Hung.

# THE SHAOLIN TEMPLE

功夫

Jet Li's wushu breakthrough, *Shaolin Temple*. *Courtesy of Fortissimo Films. All rights reserved.*

Even those who've never seen a kung fu film have probably heard of mystic Shaolin, home of the fighting monks; few, however, know of the reality behind the legends, in part because much of that reality was lost forever in the temple's three bouts with destruction. It's believed that Emperor Wen Di of the Northern Wei built the Temple in A.D. 495, as a base for an Indian Buddhist monk named Ba Tuo. The temple was named "Shaolin," for the Shaoshi Mountain above it and the forest ("*lin*") around it. The temple's destiny was changed forever in A.D. 527, when another Indian monk named Bodhidarma arrived, preaching the meditative form of Buddhism known as Ch'an, or Zen. Zen meditation required sitting for long periods of time; legend has it that Bodhidarma developed a set of exercises to help the monks physically handle the stress. Over the generations, the Shaolin blended these exercises with other disciplines, such as traditional boxing, to create the martial art known as wushu. Because of his impact on the temple, after his death in A.D. 535, Bodhidarma was revered as the "founder" of Shaolin.

The temple was never supposed to take part in worldly struggles, but history acknowledges that it did—and as a result, was attacked and burned to the ground three times. After the first of these fires, which occurred in 1674, surviving monks went south to Fukien, where they founded the Southern Temple. Among those who fled were the "Five Elders of Shaolin": Fung Doe Duk (ancestor of the White Tiger style); Bak Mei (ancestor of the White Eyebrow style); Mew Hin (ancestor of Choy Li Fut); Gee Sim (ancestor of the Hung Family style, or Hung Gar, and eventual abbot of the Southern Shaolin Temple); and a nun named Ng Mui, revered as the originator of Wing Chun. Under Abbot Gee Sim, the Southern Temple developed the legendary "35 Chambers," and opened up its training to "lay initiates." Since these non-monks were seeking to overthrow the Manchu, it was just a matter of time before the Southern Temple was attacked as well. The day of reckoning occurred in 1768, when a monk named Ma Fuyi betrayed his brothers, allowing Manchu troops to launch a surprise attack. The survivors, young rebels like Fong Sai Yuk and Hung Hei Kwoon, developer of contemporary Hung Gar, formed secret societies that spread Shaolin techniques and the anti-Manchu resistance throughout China.

In early 1900, the Qing emperor allowed the original temple to be rebuilt, only to have it burned down again in 1928 by the warlord Shi Yu San. But in 1983, after the release of Jet Li's wildly popular *Shaolin Temple,* the government began renovations to the ruins, unveiling it in 1989 as a monument to self-improvement, the fight against tyranny, and most of all, the incredible power of the human spirit.

*—Linn Haynes*

*Once Upon a Time in China* (1991) was a blockbuster success—with Li, as Wong, firmly reclaiming the mantle as one of the top action leads of the Chinese screen. While two sequels, released in 1992 and 1993, were equally successful, the familiar specter of artistic differences had reared its ugly head; a rift developed between Li and Tsui that led to Li leaving the series, to be replaced by fellow wushu champion Zhao Wen-zhou. Both Li and the series suffered—the former because he subsequently agreed to reprise his role as Master Wong in Wong Jing's lame ripoff, *Last Hero in China* (1993), the latter because Zhao, for all of his martial arts skill, was simply not up to replacing the original.

When Li and Tsui put aside their differences and reunited for a sixth *Once Upon a Time in China* film, crisis emerged from a new quarter. Tsui hired Sammo Hung to direct the film that subsequently became *Once Upon a Time in China and America* (1997); Hung's "opera brother" Jackie Chan—the other famous martial artist to portray Master Wong—was appalled to discover that the film's plot was identical to his own idea for an "Eastern Western," which he'd told Hung in confidence some years before. (Chan, himself a noted control buff, later made his version of the story in Hollywood as 2000's *Shanghai Noon*.)[20]

After *Once Upon a Time in China*, Tsui branched out in a series of scattershot yet fascinating directorial explorations (*The Lovers*, 1994; *Love in the Time of Twilight*, 1995; *The Blade*, 1996; *Tristar*, 1996). And then, like many of his peers, Tsui looked out beyond the boundaries of the Hong Kong market, to the glittering gates of Hollywood.

In 1993, Woo had become the first of a series of directors to follow that dream, moving to the United States to make the Jean-Claude Van Damme starrer *Hard Target*. He brought with him a mystique that few American action filmmakers could match—a reputation as the God of Guns, spread by such high-profile fans as Quentin Tarantino; reportedly, when a studio executive asked Tarantino if Woo could direct action scenes, he snapped back, "Sure—and Michelangelo can paint ceilings!"[21]

By the late nineties, Tsui, like many other A-list action directors, from Ringo Lam (*City on Fire*) to Corey Yuen Kwai (*High Risk*) had also taken the trans-Pacific leap. Curiously, while many Hong Kong–to–Hollywood transplants have been hired to helm projects for Van Damme, Tsui is the only one to have used the human green card twice. His first Van Damme vehicle, *Double Team* (1997), had the disadvantage of costarring former NBA star Dennis Rodman. His second, *Knock-Off* (1998), had the even greater disadvantage of perhaps the stupidest plot ever conceived for an action film: it features Jean-Claude Van Damme as a high-kicking gar-mento who must thwart a nefarious plot to destroy the world (or at least the world's buttocks) with exploding designer jeans.

There were many reasons for this frenzy of puddle-jumping by Hong Kong talent, but two loomed particularly large in the imagination.

The first was simple: As piranhas are drawn to a swimming cow, the burgeoning success of the motion picture industry in Hong Kong attracted all manner of unappealing characters. More and more, the average "independent producer" wasn't a hardscrabble hustler, looking to scrape together the spare change for a low-budget genre film. He was, instead, a man with a gun, big "friends," and the kind of negotiating leverage that comes of being willing to commit acts of senseless violence.

## DIRTY DEEDS DONE DIRT CHEAP

The insinuation of unsavory characters at all levels of the film industry also presaged a sharp shift in both the quality and tone of Hong Kong cinema; movies became gorier, more violent—and far more sexually explicit. Softcore pornography had long been an accepted part of the industry's output, which never had the kind of sharp delineation between "porn" and "legit" seen in the United States; *fengyue,* or "romance," films with names like *Sexy Playgirls* (1973) were a staple of major-studio production slates in the seventies and eighties.

Ironically, however, it was the introduction of the movie classification system in November 1988 that really opened the floodgates to adults-only entertainment. The new ratings system divided films into Category I (for general audiences) and Category II (still unrestricted, but deemed "Not Suitable for Children"). The division between mainstream and adult fare grew suddenly sharper; then, in the mid-nineties, when the system was modified to divide II into IIA and IIB (the latter indicating "Not Suitable for Young Persons and Children"), and to add Category III ("Persons 18 or Above Only"), the line became starker still.

The Cat III rating was theoretically conceived to allow for the domestic distribution of contentious releases like Martin Scorsese's *The Last Temptation of Christ,* and the early years of ratings saw Category III being handed out to everything from the relatively tame true-crimer *Sentenced to Hang* (1989) to the notorious wartime-atrocity exhibition *Man Behind the Sun* (1987). Over time, however, pornography began to dominate the rolls of Category III films, beginning with softcore sex comedies, and becoming increasingly extreme from there. To fans of the sleazier side of Hong Kong cinema, the result was a sort of golden age of smut, showcasing a new breed of gorgeous actresses in movies that feature overt sexual situations, generous amounts of nudity, and the occasional twist of bondage, S&M, or rape.

Unlike so-called adult films in the West, Cat III films are essentially mainstream; although they are still seen as a cinematic ghetto, they lack the stigma that damns its performers as "porn stars," as opposed to real stars. Category III films screen in many of the same theaters as standard action films, dramas, and comedies, and sometimes rake in higher box office takes. And otherwise reputable actors—at least some of them—occasionally descend into the world of Cat III and re-emerge, largely unscathed.

Former Miss Asia runner-up and ATV actress Veronica Yip was perhaps the first, moving away from genre offerings like 1992's *Retribution Sight Unseen* (opposite psycho Anthony Wong) and *Gigolo and Whore II* (with Simon Yam) to give an acclaimed performance in Stanley Kwan's *Red Rose, White Rose* (1994).

Loletta Lee's story is essentially a "there and back again" of Cat III erotica. Originally known as a fresh-faced teen star who went straight from high school to roles in wholesome offerings like the *Happy Ghost* series—even getting a Best Actress nomination for 1987's *Final Victory*—Lee shed her inhibitions and her clothes in revealing roles in films like *Crazy Love* and *Girls Unbutton* (both 1993). Thinking better of her new notoriety, Lee changed her name to Rachel, and won a Golden Horse as Best Actress for her performance in Ann Hui's drama *Ordinary Heroes*.

But Category III's most notable success might well be Taiwanese ingenue Shu Qi, who went from porn princess to "It Girl" of Hong Kong cinema, seemingly overnight. Born Lin Li-huei in Taiwan on April 16, 1976, to what she describes as a "traditional" family, she was a fiercely independent child with an implacable hatred for the tedious routine of school. As a teen, Lin frequently ran away from home, once for as long as six months. Her original ambition was to be a model, but—despite her striking beauty—was told she was too short to walk the runway.

Unbowed, the ambitious eighteen-year-old chose another path to stardom. Changing her name to Shu Qi on the advice of her agent, she began posing nude for picture books and magazines. So it was that producer Manfred Wong saw one of Shu Qi's magazine spreads and wooed her to Hong Kong to appear in Wong Jing's latest Category III flick, *Sex and Zen II* (1996). Fortunately for her, the film turned out to be an outrageous exploitation classic, with Shu Qi stealing the (freak) show as an innocent new bride turned hermaphroditic demon whore-beast. Shortly thereafter, legit auteur Derek Yee cast her opposite Leslie Cheung in his critically lauded *sendup* of Category III filmmaking, *Viva Erotica* (1996). It proved to be the breakthough role Shu Qi needed, earning her both the Best Supporting Actress and Best Newcomer awards at the 1996 Hong Kong Film Awards.

Since then, with her Category III days firmly behind her, she has appeared in more than forty films and played opposite the biggest stars of Hong Kong, including Jackie Chan (1999's *Gorgeous*), Leon Lai (1998's *City of Glass*), and Ekin Cheng (*Young and Dangerous 5*, 1998); she was reportedly even Ang Lee's first choice for the role that eventually went to Zhang Ziyi in the staggeringly successful *Crouching Tiger, Hidden Dragon* (2000).

Others besides Shu have used Cat III stardom to propel themselves into mainstream recognition, including Chingmy Yau, who graduated from unremarkable roles in forgettable genre films to stardom after her unforgettable performance in Clarence Fok's Cat III classic, 1992's *Naked Killer*. An acknowledged marquee draw thereafter, she alternated performances in Cat III exploitationers like the ostensible *Naked Killer* sequel *Raped by an Angel* with more prestigious roles alongside the likes of Jet Li, Jackie Chan, and Chow Yun Fat, before effectively retiring from the screen following her dramatic performance in Stanley Kwan's *Hold You Tight* (1998). Carrie Ng was another actress with a long career, giving overlooked performances in dozens of films of all genres. But after appearances in *Sex and Zen* and *Naked Killer*, she struck a blow for Cat III sisterhood when she took home the Golden Horse as Best Actress for her role in Clarence Fok's true-crime epic *Remains of a Woman*—a rare *quality* Cat III film.

# CATEGORY III EROTICA

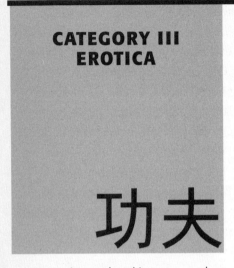

功夫

Consumers interested in more than just bare flesh will find that the most entertaining and offbeat Hong Kong sex films are almost invariably the ones that feature period history and Chinese mythology. Michael Mak Dong Kit's hugely successful 1991 feature *Sex and Zen* (the most lavish of several films based on the seventeenth-century Chinese sex novel *Yu Pui Tsuen)* is the most notable example of this genre; its box-office success led to a wave of period erotica in the early nineties. (The prolific Wong Jing produced its two sequels, as well as the far more lurid, S&M-laced 1994 films *A Chinese Torture Chamber Story* and *Sex and the Emperor,* and the comparatively classy 1995 opus *Lover of the Last Empress.)*

Besides bare-breasted flocks of second-tier Miss Hong Kong contestants, many of these films have one thing in common: the bald and glowering presence of Hong Kong's most traveled Cat III actor, Elvis Tsui. In fact, anyone planning on exploring this genre to any degree should be prepared to see Tsui's trademark grimace and insatiable sexual appetite in movie after movie after movie. Notching more appearances in this genre than possibly all of his female costars put together, Tsui is the unrivaled king of Hong Kong erotic cinema. (In *Viva Erotica,* King Elvis is wonderful in a role where he essentially plays himself: a family man making a living in a less-than-respectable business.)

Although Category III films have floundered since their heyday in the early 1990s, when over half of the films produced in Hong Kong bore their triangular logo, new actresses continue to appear, sometimes seemingly ripping off their clothes and vanishing, sometimes establishing tentative careers. As to the future of the Cat III industry, it may well fall victim to its own success; now that the envelope has been pushed up against the boundary of hardcore, the potential for government crackdown has become more real, while the more pervy of Cat III's consumers are rapidly migrating to harder fare, available via the Internet or illicit foreign import.

*—John Charles*

But not every star of Category III cinema has as pleasant a story to tell as the lovely and lucky Shu Qi. As rougher elements moved in behind the cameras, industry folk whispered rumors of female celebrities subjected to extortion, kidnapping, or worse, in the course of "convincing" them to work on the skinny side of the business. Anyone who knows the story of Bugsy Siegel knows that Hollywood, too, has had its share of rats in the woodwork.

In Hong Kong in the early nineties, the rats were gnawing away in broad daylight.

## MOB RULE

Triads, as members of Hong Kong's mob underworld are called, have been an element in the Chinese motion picture industry since the heyday of old Shanghai (influential thirties producer Zhang Shankun was publicly known to have gangland connections); indeed, given that the roots of the Triads were in the rebel "secret societies" that infiltrated Beijing opera companies during the anti-Qing resistance, it's likely that organized crime and Chinese cinema grew up together as siblings, with Triads turning into gangsters just as opera players were turning into screen stars. "If you want to make a film in Hong Kong, you're going to be dealing with Triads," one acclaimed filmmaker has been quoted as saying. "The trick is to deal with the *good* Triads."

But as the nineties dawned, things were rapidly getting out of control. On May 4, 1992, Canto-pop diva and star actress Anita Mui (*Rouge; Rumble in the Bronx*) was accosted at a karaoke bar by a man named Wong Long Wai, who was affiliated with the bloody 14K Triads. She dismissed his overtures, and in the ensuing altercation was slapped in the face. Shortly therafter, Wong ended up dead—allegedly at the hands of a Triad fan of Mui's named Andely Chan, the "Tiger of Wanchai." Upon hearing the news, Mui fled for a quick round-the-world trip. A year later, Andely Chan was gunned down by a trio of helmeted assassins.[22]

Mui's experience was far from unique. Earlier that year, an armed quintet of brutes had attempted to heist the negatives for a Lunar New Year movie starring Leslie Cheung; later that year, action star Jet Li's manager, Jim Choi (who reputedly was an Amsterdam-based heroin smuggler before turning film producer), was shot dead by two men in the hallway of his pro-duction offices. (His company was then in preproduction on a Triad flick called *Secret Signs* [1993]. To pad its running time, a *documentary* on Tri-ads, specifically of the Amsterdam-based heroin-smuggling variety, was shot and tacked on to the front of it for its theatrical release. It remains a highly suspect, and deeply eerie, tribute to its deceased producer.)

Although some three hundred motion picture professionals subse-quently took to the streets in protest (calling themselves "Show Business Against Violence"), the peaceful march seemed to have little effect. The following year, pop idol Andy Lau's personal assistant was hospitalized after a bomb went off in her flat, and schlock-king Wong Jing needed extensive dental work after being beaten by three unknown men.[23]

The film industry, which had spent much of the past decade valorizing gangsters onscreen, was not as keen on them in real life—at least the crude, thuggish ones who were causing street-level mayhem. Rumors had it that numerous individuals in loftier positions, from top producers to eminent directors to studio executives like Charles Heung, the powerful head of Win's Entertainment, were past or present Triad members; in the case of Heung, given that his father founded Hong Kong's biggest Triad society, Sun Yee On, the speculation makes sense, although he and his brother Jimmy have always denied any connection to the "family business."

## REAL-LIFE TRIADS

功夫

Given the generous involvement of the mob behind the scenes, it's understand-able that gangsters have been some of Hong Kong cinema's most popular pro-tagonists. But when the Hong Kong movie industry took a downturn after 1995, producers filled screens with a unique brand of "reality show": low-cost, culturally conservative biopics of real-life thugs. Here's a rogue's gallery of who's who in Criminal Cinema.

- **Wan Kuok Koi:** Better known as Broken Tooth Koi, this violent Macanese Triad leader was played by Simon Yam in *Casino* (1998), just one of Yam's countless mobster performances (at least eighteen to date); the film was financed with HK$14 million of Wan's own cash. Wan had been at the center of a bloody Macanese gang war that left more than twenty dead, before being sent away for fifteen years. On the eve of the movie's release, he gave *Time* magazine's Asia edition a series of self-aggrandizing interviews, which later became key evidence in his trial. To his credit, Wan did invent a guaranteed antipiracy device, regularly sending men wielding lead pipes to visit shops selling pirated *Casino* VCDs.

- **Cheung Tze Keung:** Immortalized by Simon Yam in *Operation Billionaire* (1998), Cheung specialized in kidnapping the sons of Hong Kong's elite. He was arrested in Mainland China for his Hong Kong crimes; *Operation Billionaire* opened on the first day of his trial. The flick offers a winning portrayal of Cheung as a mischievous rogue. Mainland authorities were not amused, and after reading his ninety-minute verdict (about the running time of the film), they took Cheung outside and had him shot.

- **Yip Kai Foon:** An old prison buddy of Cheung Tze Keung. If there was anything Yip liked more than rounding up his ex–Red Army pals and knocking over a Hong Kong jewelry store, it was using his AK-47 to mow down cops as he subsequently made his escape through crowded midday streets. Simon Yam (again) plays Yip in *King of Robbery* (1996). The real Yip ended his career in a wheelchair in Stanley Prison serving three consecutive life sentences for a botched Yip/Cheung kidnap plot.

- Just in case you were starting to think that *every* Triad in a movie was played by Simon Yam—you're right. That's when they're not playing themselves. The ranks of Triads-turned-actor include **Frankie Ng, Chan Wai Man** (who's played a Triad in more than 100 movies to date), and **Nam Yin,** Ringo Lam's brother and a successful writer/producer in his own right, who drew on his real-life prison stories in scripting Lam's 1987 hit *Prison on Fire*.

—Grady Hendrix

Fruit shoots—the director at work.
*Courtesy of Golden Network. Special thanks to Lammy Li.*

But, as some stars noted, at least the Triads were a known quantity; they were, in many ways, infinitely preferable to the dark unknown that would descend upon Hong Kong in 1997—when Hong Kong was scheduled to be handed over to (or "reunified with") the Mainland.

## COUNTING DOWN

Nineteen ninety-seven was the other overriding concern of Hong Kong's show business community, who feared that the ex-colony's media and entertainment industries would face Party censorship—or worse, outright persecution—once the reunification took place. The abuses of the Cultural Revolution were just two decades past, and Tiananmen, a mere handful of years; nor did the Chinese government's treatment of premier filmmakers like Zhang Yimou inspire trust among concerned Hong Kong residents.

As a result, many stars established secondary homes in Australia, Canada, and the States. Others emigrated altogether, unwilling to risk their careers or lives against an uncertain future. For those who stayed behind, 1997 became an overarching theme in most, if not all, creative pursuits. It came out in off-the-cuff comic quips, in passing pop references, and in the bleak, time-obsessed visions of auteurs like Wong Kar Wai; to some, it was a source of inspiration, to others, merely an expiration date.

The final word on 1997 may have sprung from the imagination of Fruit Chan, one of the earliest and foremost directors in Hong Kong's late-nineties Indie Wave. With his "Handover trilogy," which began with 1997's *Made in Hong Kong* and concluded with *The Longest Summer* (1998) and *Little Cheung* (2000), he unpacked lingering 1997 dread and malaise from the island's collective baggage and sorted out the issues that remained—scarce (and dangerous) housing, juvenile delinquency, unemployment, disaffected public servants, and rampant class inequity.

Born in Guangzhou, in 1959, Chan spent the first decade of his life in the island's notorious public housing projects. It is in these poor and violent legacies of British colonial administration that Chan chose to set his works, beginning with *Made in Hong Kong*. Coproduced by actor/popstar Andy Lau, the movie was made with a five-man crew for a modest HK$600,000, using some forty thousand feet of leftover film stock. Despite, or perhaps because of, its guerrilla production standards, the film had a raw, gut-wrenching tone and visual impact that was like nothing the island's audiences had ever seen. It won 1997's Hong Kong Film Award for Best Picture, and brought fame and acclaim to Chan, until then a virtual unknown, and to Sam Lee, a former electrician whom Chan had plucked out of obscurity to serve as the film's lead.

The magnitude of Chan's accomplishment shocked Hong Kong critics. *Made in Hong Kong* was undoubtedly original, emotionally resonant, and, most of all, politically timely. Though Chan has rejected characterization of his works as "art movies," *Made in Hong Kong* was undoubtedly an "important" film; along with the other two installments in the "Handover trilogy," the film aptly captures for posterity a slice of the personal and emotional reactions to the island's reunification with the Mainland.

Hair today; gone tomorrow. A still from Fruit Chan's *Durian Durian*. *Courtesy of Golden Network. Special thanks to Lammy Li.*

## POWER TO THE SIXTH

Throughout the early nineties, the Mainland government professed surprise at the Hong Kong artistic community's consternation over the imminent arrival of 1997, pointing to the Joint Declaration's provision of fifty years of rule under the existing system as protection for Hong Kong's media and entertainment industries. Who knew what would happen in half a century? After all, China had changed dramatically in just a couple of decades. And though Party leaders would never point to them as an example, the indie malcontents of the Sixth Generation were a prime example of just how much.

In 1970, to invoke taboo issues like drug addiction, homosexuality, or democratic egalitarianism in a film would have led to instant imprisonment and censure, if not worse. Filmmakers were coerced to obey rigid socialist construction guidelines, such as the rule of "Three Prominences," which said that films should stress positive characters, highlight only their heroic characteristics, and feature their most obviously positive and heroic figures as protagonists.[24]

"Independent cinema" did not exist during the Cultural Revolution, because such cinema was, by definition, counterrevolutionary. In the late seventies and eighties, it did not exist because lack of capital and the studio system made it impractical.

But in 1990, a young recent graduate of the Beijing Film Academy named Zhang Yuan, using funds provided by friends and family, managed to assemble the film stock and equipment necessary to make a movie called *Mama*. The black and white picture, shot in gritty neodocumentary style, is about a young mother's struggle to rear her autistic child in an unsympathetic society. After completing the film, Zhang was able to sell it to Xi'an Studios—still the most progressive of China's studios—and pay back his "investors," while generating the funds necessary to make another indie picture.

Though the film itself did not challenge the system, the way it was created did. Soon, other filmmakers, many of them disenchanted and disenfranchised fellow graduates of Beijing Film Academy, began making "outside" movies, including Wang Xiaoshuai (1993's *The Days*), He Jian-

Zhang Yuan, the first to jump the rail.
*Courtesy of Locarno Film Festival.*

jun (1995's *Postman*), Ning Ying (1995's *On the Beat*), and Jia Zhangke (1997's *Xiao Wu*).

The films—minimalist in style, plot, and dialogue, and usually made with nonactors, who often played characters based on their real-life identities—were a studied reaction not just to Chinese government and social policy, but also to their cinematic forebears, particularly the directors of the Fifth Generation. Though the Sixth Generation had even less cohesion as a "movement" than that earlier cohort, rarely choosing to work together or even associate, they were united in condemning what they viewed as the Fifth Generation's exotic pandering in pursuit of Western acclaim—with the exception of Tian Zhuangzhuang, in whose films they perceived a like-minded disregard for authority and audience.

Like Tian, the Sixth Generation has experienced profound government censure, ranging from the withholding of their films from distribution—none of the Sixth Generation works have ever been released in China—to blacklisting and loss of privileges, including bans on traveling outside the country, a punishment imposed by the government on Zhang Yuan, the first and still the most prolific of the group (his other films include the 1993 rock-underworld film *Beijing Bastards* and 1997's gay tango *East Palace, West Palace*).

Though their films have yet to be seen by their intended audience, the existence of the Sixth Generation filmmakers is proof enough that there are cracks in the monolith, and that something—a crop of hardy weeds and illicit wildflowers—is germinating within.

## NEON GODS, PEACH BLOSSOMS, AND WEDDING BANQUETS

Meanwhile, the film industry of Taiwan was experiencing the exact opposite problem—a gradual *loss* of its filmmakers' independence, as the motion picture industry became increasingly dependent on government subsidy for survival. Despite the arthouse chic and film festival acclaim of the New Taiwanese Cinema's stalwarts, their commercial successes in the eighties were few and far between. As a result, despite Taiwan's persistent economic growth, private investors shied away from backing film production, seeing it as a risky business beset by impossible competition from Hollywood in the West and Hong Kong in the East. By the nineties, the number of films being produced by the entire Taiwanese movie industry was down to the low double digits.

Fearing the industry's total collapse, the Government Information Office quickly established a system of public grants, given to production companies based on the merits of their projects. The initial sum offered was NT$30 million (about $900,000), doled out in three lumps of NT$10 million; the amount set aside increased each year, as well as the number of grants awarded. By 1996, five of the eighteen films produced in Taiwan received these grants; by 1997, the ratio was fifteen out of twenty-nine. The list of directors whose work they supported reads like a virtual roll call of contemporary Taiwanese film.[25]

These grants were originally meant merely to provide "supplemental" production funds. Gradually, however, they turned into a life support system for some producers, and an ugly profit opportunity for unscrupulous ones, who made a living out of winning NT$10 million grants and making NT$7 million films. Meanwhile, production executives began to condemn the grants, even as they accepted them, calling them a force that had transformed Taiwan's motion picture industry into a factory for boring art films that played to empty houses.

In 1996, the GIO attempted to address these concerns by decreeing that the grants would henceforth be divided equally between five "art" awards and five "commerce" awards, each consisting of NT$10 million. The commerce awards would go to films that were assessed by the judging panel to have particularly strong box office viability. Unfortunately, these pictures—like Kevin Chu Yen-ping's *The Sexy Story* (1997), which grossed less than NT$600,000—turned out to be no more successful than their art award counterparts.

Chu—one of Taiwan's few remaining bankable filmmakers—subsequently declared that *The Sexy Story* was, for him, an "experimental" work, and should not have been seen as a commercial picture. "For my real commercial films, I don't need the grants, wouldn't apply for them, and wouldn't win them if I did apply," he said. The following year, the GIO eliminated the two-tier system and went back to a single category of grants.[26]

Tsai Ming-liang's *Vive l'Amour.*

*Courtesy of Fortissimo Films. All rights reserved. Special thanks to Marnix van Wijk.*

However, the question remained whether the grants were getting the Taiwanese film industry back on its feet, or merely propping up a sagging corpse. The answer may lie with a group of filmmakers who have been called Taiwan's "Second New Wave"—a handful of directors who have begun to emerge from arthouse obscurity into the international spotlight, and whose films, in many cases, have had commercial success back home. All of them benefited from GIO subsidy programs, and some still continue to do so.

Perhaps the most distinctive (yet least commercial) of the Second Wave directors is Tsai Ming-liang, an ethnic Chinese born in Kuching, Malaysia, in 1957 who moved to Taiwan at the age of twenty, and graduated with a joint degree in drama and film from the Chinese Cultural University in1982. After completing a directorial apprenticeship, during which he also wrote experimental plays and film and television scripts, he made his first feature, *Rebels of the Neon God,* in 1992. This award-winning film of teenage angst in the urban wasteland of Taipei established his pivotal place among Taiwan's young, emerging filmmakers. Tsai's trademark touches included an unusual mix of vérité and painstaking pictorialism in his cinematography; a brooding aura of alienation and unfulfilled desire; and minimal dialogue, allowing situations suffused with absurdist humor and horror to speak for themselves. In *Vive l'Amour* (1994), a young man lies masturbating beneath the bed where a man he's in love with is having sex with a woman; in *The River* (1997), an encounter in a dark sauna leads to an accidental incestuous experience between father and son; in *The Hole* (1998), a woman must balance a bucket on her head to go to the bathroom.

Another prominent Second Wave figure is Stan Lai, whose primary career is as a leading playwright and stage director, and the head of the Performance Workshop Theater Company, which he founded in 1984. His film debut was an adaptation of his own acclaimed play *Peach Blossom Land* (1991); the story's central conceit is that a mistake has caused two wildly different dramas to be booked into the same rehearsal space: *Peach Blossom Land,* a period fairy tale, and *Secret Love,* a contemporary story about a couple, separated in Shanghai during the war, who rediscover each other in Taiwan. The format allows for humorous backstage farce (props are constantly being rearranged in a war for space) and pungent social allegory; with Brigitte Lin Ching-hsia in the lead, the movie became a considerable box office hit. His only other film to date is *Red Lotus Society* (1994), a quasi-mystical exploration of the decline of traditional values in the modern metropolis.

Two other Second Wave filmmakers have achieved critical attention and, perhaps more important, commercial success: Chen Kuo-fu, a former film critic and stage director who made his feature-film debut with *School Girls* (1989) and whose second film, *Treasure Island* (1993), was produced by Hou Hsiao-hsien, won sudden acclaim for 1998's *The Personals,* starring Taiwan's most popular ingenue, Rene Liu, as a woman whose hobby of interviewing "applicants" who have responded to her personals ad gets out of hand. In a vérité touch, some of the suitors are played by real-life respondents to a personals ad Chen placed himself. Meanwhile, Lin Cheng-sheng began his career as a baker in a bread factory, before enrolling in a film work-shop in 1986. He received a GIO grant to make his debut feature, *A Drifting Life* (1996), following that up with such critical favorites as *Murmur of Youth* (1997), *Sweet Degeneration* (1997), *March of Happiness* (1999), and most recently, *Betelnut Beauty* (2001).

But the standout director of the government-subsidized Second Wave is also the exception that suggests how rare it is for a filmmaker to translate publicly supported work into consistent commercial success. Born and raised in Taiwan, Ang Lee moved to the United States in 1978 to earn a Bachelor of Fine Arts in theater at the University of Illinois. From there, he went on to New York University film school, where he earned his masters in film production. His body of student work—including his forty-five-minute-long thesis feature, *Fine Line*—drew the interest of Good Machine producers Ted Hope and James Schamus. The latter became his regular collaborator, producing all of Lee's films from his debut *Pushing Hands* (1995) through his global breakthrough *Crouching Tiger, Hidden Dragon* (2001).

Lee's acclaimed early work—what he has referred to as his *"Father Knows Best* Trilogy"—was developed under the auspices of a GIO screenwriting pro-gram. Focusing on generational tension and the tug of war between modern and traditional values, the three films—*Pushing Hands, The Wedding Ban-quet* (1993), and *Eat Drink Man Woman* (1994)—each feature veteran Tai-wanese actor Sihung Lung in the linchpin role of an aging patriarch, a rock of solemn pride awash in the dynamic eddies of his children's Westernized ways. All three films were successful, with *The Wedding Banquet* astronomi-cally so. But Lee truly hit his stride when he was picked to direct 1995's *Sense and Sensibility*, whose British dialect and turn-of-the-century setting made him the unlikeliest of choices (barring, perhaps, his surname-sharing fellow NYU alumnus Spike). From there, Lee unveiled surprise after surprise, with every project forcing him to test the limits of his creative flexibility.

Now one of the world's premier directors, Lee has used his formidable clout to change perceptions of Taiwanese film and Chinese-language film in general. Yet a case can be made that he is a product of the system who no longer works in the system, leaving the viability of Taiwanese cinema in doubt.

Ultimately, the same quandary faced by judges of the GIO's grant-making panel—"art" or "commerce"?—is one that afflicts each of Greater China's film industries, to greater and lesser degrees. For Hong Kong, the fading center of commercial cinema in the region, that quandary may be a matter of life or death.

## GOOD, BAD, AND UGLY

As the nineties waned, so too did the Hong Kong motion picture industry. According to the Hong Kong Trade Development Council, for the first time in 1997, foreign films, mostly from the United States, had a higher share of Hong Kong box office receipts than domestic movies, by a count of $84 million to $70 million. The following year, the ratio swung to $70 million for foreign films and $54 million for domestic. In 1999, domestic films generated just $45 million in total box office revenues, compared to $68 million generated by imports—with no floor in sight. The number of films being produced dwindled in tandem with falling revenues, hitting a modern-day low of just eighty-four films in 1998.[27]

The reasons given for the sudden decline were manifold: Some pundits blamed out-of-control competition during the fat years of the early nineties, which drove up costs and drove down profitability, others, the collapse of secondary markets in Southeast Asia, which slashed margins (and thus production budgets) for producers dependent on "presales" to places like Thailand and Vietnam. Still others pointed to the loss of big stars to Hollywood in the years preceding 1997; the nosediving stock market, bitten by the "Asian flu"; and runaway video piracy from cheap black-market VCDs, which often were available on street kiosks simultaneously with theatrical releases. All of these were valid, and each played a role in Hong Kong cinema's fall, but the most basic reason why audiences were staying away in droves was simple: The movies just weren't very good.

Of course, "good" can be a subjective term. A hormone-charged teenager will have one definition of a good movie, a connoisseur of world cinema will have another, and never the twain shall meet. But to film industry professionals—emphasis on the "industry"—good should also have an *absolute* meaning. By these standards, a good movie would be technically adept, properly presented, and engineered to appeal to its target market.

## PIRACY

功夫

On March 17, 1999, a brigade of show-biz luminaries, led by Jackie Chan, Tsui Hark, and Tony Leung Chiu Wai, took to the streets of Hong Kong to protest the scourge of the entertainment industry: video piracy. Illegally copied VCDs—extremely cheap to manufacture, easy to transport, and better in quality than commercial videotapes—had become epidemic throughout greater China and Southeast Asia; bootlegged films often appeared in seedy VCD stalls long before they even hit theaters. The Hong Kong government was doing little to thwart this blatant piracy, even after United States Customs authorities, responding in part to widespread bootlegging of *Titanic,* placed China and Hong Kong on its list of trade law violators in 1997.

Normally law-abiding citizens saw little harm in buying bootlegs; like MP3 trading and software copying, it seemed like a "victimless" crime. But over 90 percent of the titles being pirated were domestic films, made by studios whose razor-thin margins made them vulnerable to the slightest box office dips. As theatrical revenues shrank, production values plummeted; 1999 bore witness to some of the most abysmal films Hong Kong had ever produced.

Today, after the deployment of an antipiracy task force—a direct result of the highly publicized protest—Hong Kong officials contend that piracy's plague has been nearly eradicated, and effectively driven into the shadows.

But while piracy of easily accessible commercial product might be indefensible, the bootlegging of otherwise unavailable films is a different matter entirely. Since Western distributors long ignored popular Asian cinema, many film fans abroad discovered the Hong Kong New Wave only through bootleg videos garnered on underground trading circuits. The experience of watching such "forbidden" films through the blurry, nth-generation haze of ill-gotten dupes imparted a kind of democracy to fans enslaved by the whims of commercial distributors and major film festivals. Fans pointed to the fact that artists weren't losing any money, because there wasn't anywhere they could buy these films in the West. Today, of course, Chinese cinema enjoys an unprecedented popularity, and once-rare films are easily available at mainstream video stores. But could this current explosion of interest have been commercially viable without a longstanding fan movement fueled primarily by piracy? The sad truth is, conventional attitudes still prevent the broad distribution of many Chinese films. Even in the age of *Crouching Tiger, Hidden Dragon,* Mainland and Taiwanese films are generally labeled arthouse fare, while most Hong Kong films distributed theatrically in the West are poorly dubbed, grossly reedited martial arts films, suggesting that retrograde seventies stereotypes of the industry have not been completely overcome—and as a result, that the defiant, empowering, oddly liberating act of piracy may not yet be entirely obsolete.

*—Andrew Grossman*

By the late nineties, Hong Kong movies were falling short on all three counts. They often looked like shoddy, low-budget grindhouse flicks, even when they weren't. They were misleadingly marketed—big-name performers were touted as leads, even when their appearance amounted to little more than a cameo; unrelated and inferior movies were packaged in ways that confused those seeking established hits. Worst of all, the vast majority of films were being made with little consideration for their audiences. Producers had no idea what the typical Hong Kong moviegoer wanted, and generally didn't care. Instead, they put their faith in the three C's of nineties Hong Kong cinema: naked chicks, bloody choppers, and Stephen Chiau.

By the mid-nineties, Chiau, the most popular comedian in the history of Chinese cinema, had parlayed his enviable talents—a machine-gun mouth, an elastic face on a rubber-band body, and the kind of comic je ne sais quoi that causes even people who don't speak his language to chortle at his antics—into near-domination of the Hong Kong box office.

## DISTURBING HORROR

功夫

A scene from the shocker *Human Lanterns.*
*Courtesy of Celestial Pictures. All rights reserved.*

The introduction of the adults-only Category III rating in the late 1980s certainly raised the bar as to the degree of gore and violence local filmmakers could deliver, but the stomach-churning tradition of Hong Kong horror extends back a decade earlier. While the major taboos were only occasionally being challenged in Western horror films of that time, Hong Kong studios gleefully stretched the envelope of taste from the very beginning, depicting a gruesome array of cannibals, dark magicians, undead creatures, and maniacal killers. Shaw Brothers, in particular, produced such seminal skin-crawlers as *Killer Snakes* (1974) and *Black Magic I* and *II* (1975, 1976) (the sequel would be retitled *Revenge of the Zombies* for its English-dubbed release in America), as well as *Human Lanterns* (1982), *Seeding of a Ghost* (1983), and *The Boxer's Omen* (1983) a few years later.

However, the territory's nastiest cinematic nightmares didn't emerge until the "True Crime" trend of the early nineties. This notorious subgenre kicked off in 1989 with the relatively tame *Sentenced to Hang,* notable as the first film to ever receive the Cat III tag. It soon grew much darker with the release of *Dr. Lamb*

(1992), a tawdry thriller based on the revolting extracurricular activities of cab driver/serial killer Lam Guo Wen (memorably portrayed by Simon Yam Tat Wah). It was a box office success, and producer Danny Lee Sau Yin followed it up with the even more infamous cannibal killer tale *The Untold Story* (1993). Anthony Wong Chau Sang's startling lead performance in the film netted him Best Actor at the Hong Kong Film Awards; the combined success of these two pictures resulted in a relentless wave of imitations, many of which were headlined by Yam or Wong.

The recent trend in local horror has been toward lightweight ghost stories seemingly pitched to high-school students out on their first dates. However, as anyone who follows Hong Kong moviemaking knows all too well, it only takes one hit to launch a tidal wave of imitations, meaning that the SAR's darkest tales of the unimaginable may still be yet to come.

*—John Charles*

---

Born in Hong Kong in 1962, the only boy of four children, he applied to join TVB's acting school after graduating from high school but was rejected as neither attractive nor talented enough to have real promise. A friend pulled a few strings, and Chiau was grudgingly accepted. But upon finishing the training program, he was given the less-than-stellar job of hosting a children's program called *430 Space Shuttle*—basically a holding slot used by TVB to house performers for whom they had no immediate use. (Ironically, however, the gig has evolved into a harbinger of future stardom. Among others who were originally assigned to host the program are Tony Leung Chiu Wai, Ekin Cheng, and Athena Chu.)

After making his big-screen debut in Parkman Wong's *Final Justice* (1987), for which he won Best Supporting Actor at the Taiwan Golden Horse Awards, Chiau was given opportunity to display his dramatic chops in films like John Woo's *Just Heroes* (1987) and *Dragon Fight* (1988), starring Jet Li. Oddly, however, Chiau's comic talents were largely ignored, until his supporting turn in Wong Wah Kei's 1988 dueling-barber comedy *Faithfully Yours* drew the attention of a director with one of the most offbeat comic sensibilities in the business, Jeff Lau, who, in collaboration with action-comedy master Corey Yuen, had decided to make a parody of Chow Yun Fat's 1989 blockbuster *God of Gamblers*. To

Good Chiau, bad Chiau? A scene from *Love on Delivery. Courtesy of Celestial Pictures. *

make the shtick stick, they needed a performer with the ability to project an unusual combination of ersatz suaveness and sarcastic stupidity. Going out on a limb, Lau and Yuen cast *All for the Winner* (1990) with Chiau in the lead, as a country bumpkin with extrasensory gambling powers. The film was an instant success, ending up as that rarest of comic beasts, a lampoon that grossed more than the film it mocked.

As a result, Chiau was hired to reprise the role in two official sequels to the original *God of Gamblers,* hybridizing the satire with its target. The weird idea worked, and Chiau's career soared like a 430 Space Shuttle into the stratosphere of Hong Kong stardom.

It was the beginning of a half-decade in which nearly everything Chiau touched turned to gold. He mocked old-school kung fu (*Fist of Fury,* 1991), the education system (*Fight Back to School,* 1991), the legal system (1992's *Justice, My Foot!* and 1994's *Hail the Judge*), Japanese and American trademarked characters (1994's *Love on Delivery*), Jin Yong's *wuxia* epics (1992's *Royal Tramp I* and *II* and *King of Beggars*), James Bond (*From Beijing with Love,* 1994), and even the gods themselves (1993's *The Mad Monk;* 1993–94's *A Chinese Odyssey 1* and *2*). In the process, he created a genre of humor referred to as *"mo lei tau,"* an indescribable blend of verbal pyrotechnics, physical shenanigans, and indefinable comic oomph that at its best was both ridiculous and sublime, and at its worst was painfully unwatchable.

But even bad Chiau made money—which, in turn, made producers increasingly lazy.

## MASTER WONG VS. MASTER WONG

As the nineties progressed, a certain running theme began making its appearance in comedies like the Anita Yuen vehicle *Whatever You Want* (1994), porn-industry satire *Viva Erotica* (1996), and the nostalgic farce *Those Were the Days* (1998). The theme in question: "Wong vs. Wong," in a battle for the soul of Hong Kong movies.

One Wong was Wong Jing, the portly lord of anything-goes exploitation; the other was Wong Kar Wai, sunglasses-wearing king of opaque but stylish arthouse favorites. The Wongs are diametric opposites, yet they both successfully make "good movies" in the show business sense of the term: technically superior, terrifically marketed, and precisely targeted films that happen to be aimed at fundamentally different audiences— markets that could be divided, for simplicity's sake, into "hormone-charged teenagers" and "connoisseurs of world cinema."

The Two Mr. Wongs: Jing (L) and Kar Wai (R). *Courtesy of Hong Kong Film Critics Association.*

Wong Jing is the most commercially successful film director in modern Hong Kong history. His cinematic canon is a chaotic maelstrom of slapstick, toilet humor, and exploitation, largely unencumbered by artistic merit and firmly tethered to the lowest common denominator. The son of sixties director Wong Tin Lam (*The Wild, Wild Rose*), Wong graduated from college with a degree in Chinese literature (which he readily refers to as "useless") before launching his film career as a screenwriter for Shaw Brothers in the early eighties.

Twenty years later, with seventy-five films under his belt and his name listed as producer or writer on over a hundred more, he claims to come up with a film's subject matter first, its poster second, and the script third. The formula seems to work. His movies—aptly described by local critics as "a taste of sugar and a taste of crap"—please crowds, in an era when ticket-buying crowds Hong Kong are few and far between.

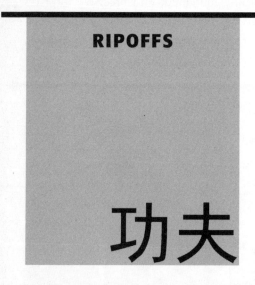

# RIPOFFS

When was the last time you checked out a Chinese James Bond? Or Jack and Rose of *Titanic*, played by middle-aged Asians? As a horny teenager, you may have seen *Porky's* or *Meatballs*, but what about . . . *Porky's Meatballs* (1987)? Call 'em what you will—homages, parodies, reinterpretations, or just plain old ripoffs—Hong Kong cinema is a dominated by the principle that the next best thing to using other people's money is to filch other people's ideas.

Since the success of *Crouching Tiger, Hidden Dragon* (2000), a confusing rash of movies has tried to cash in, including *Roaring Dragon, Bluffing Tiger* and *Flying Dragon, Leaping Tiger*, among others. Joseph Lai, *Roaring Dragon*'s producer, has stressed that his movie is set in China circa 1946 and features guns, while *"Crouching Tiger* had only swords and sticks."

Sometimes, however, the swipes are more pronounced. Even if it's just for laughs, Herman Yau's *Fascination Amour* (1999), an Andy Lau romantic comedy set on a big boat, often plays as a grating series of "best of" moments from the already grating *Titanic*. 1994's *Mermaid Got Married* is Ron Howard's *Splash* (1984) gone Asian, Kirk Wong's terrific *Gunmen* (1988) is Brian De Palma's *The Untouchables* (1987), but with even harder-hitting violence, and Sammo Hung's *Eastern Condors* (1987) is obviously indebted to *The Dirty Dozen* (1967).

On top of poster ripoffs, title ripoffs, and straight-out concept ripoffs, Hong Kong is also rife with a kind of ripoff that would cause most American viewers to firebomb theaters: The *nonsequel* sequel. Take *Return to a Better Tomorrow* (1994), a gangster stinker that has neither Chow Yun Fat nor John Woo's stamp of approval, or *Raped by an Angel,* which bills itself as *Naked Killer 2* but has no connection to the original other than perky, seminude Chingmy Yau.

It must be said that the artistic burglary is far from a one-way street. Hollywood has been just as sticky-fingered with Hong Kong stories and ideas. By now, everyone but Quentin Tarantino has accepted the debt owed by *Reservoir Dogs* to Ringo Lam's *City on Fire* (1987). And John Woo's trademark double-gun action and slow-mo lateral dives can be seen everywhere from *The Crow* (1994), to *Desperado* (1995), to Bruce Willis's *Last Man Standing* (1996), even if Woo himself inhaled his flair for mayhem from Sam Peckinpah to begin with. Last but not least, Jackie Chan fan Sylvester Stallone pulled the entire bus-stopping stunt from Chan's 1985 *Police Story* (1985) and fitted it into his *Tango & Cash* (1989) . . . not that Chan should complain, given that he adopted *Raiders of the Lost Ark* for his 1986 *Armour of God,* and readily acknowledges his debt to silent-era Hollywood stars like Buster Keaton and Harold Lloyd.

In the end, though, the bottom line isn't just the bottom line, it's entertainment. Given that even Shakespeare pinched all of his plots from the ancients, as long as we leave theaters with smiles on our faces, who are we to complain?

*—Curtis Tsui*

And then there's Wong Kar Wai. Dubbed by critics as the leader of the "Next Wave" of Hong Kong cinema, Wong has become a cottage industry of arthouse cool, generating inventive, improvisational creations that read like urgent dispatches from lonely souls trapped five seconds in the future: swordsmen marooned in an endless desert, yuppies caught in a blooming urban sprawl, hustlers stranded in Buenos Aires, not-quite-lovers in a tango of forlorn, forbidden desire.

Wong began as a screenwriter, writing for nearly every Hong Kong director of note, before he got the chance to direct *As Tears Go By* (1988). Starring pop stars Andy Lau and Jacky Cheung in a scenario reminiscent of Scorsese's *Mean Streets,* the film demonstrated Wong's ability to extract gripping performances from his actors, as well as his flair for the perfect pop moment—in one scene, a Cantonese version of Berlin's "Take My Breath Away" swells up on the soundtrack as the screen flares to white, and two lovers kiss in a phone booth. The film became an instant classic.

Given unusual leeway by his overwhelming commercial and critical success, Wong invoked for the first time a production process that would become his trademark: booking a bevy of top stars, retreating to some out-of-the-way locale, and screwing up nineteen other productions by holding everyone hostage as he genially throws everything against the camera to see what sticks. The sophomore effort that resulted, *Days of Being Wild* (1990), starred virtually every young, popular face in the industry. Though audiences expected fireworks, what they got instead was a leisurely but intense meditation on the passage of time. Though viewers were stunned and disappointed, critics were entranced by the film's sterling performances (including some from actors not known for their thespian skills) and its heady vapor of wasted youth, embracing the film as a masterpiece.

But they hadn't seen anything yet. Next up was Wong's bravest act of all: the abduction of every star in the Hong Kong cosmos, trapping them in the remote Chinese desert while he shot what may be the biggest puzzle of a movie ever made—1994's *Ashes of Time.* It may mean everything; it may mean nothing. Furthermore, you may not be able to see any of Sammo Hung's award-winning action choreography through Chris Doyle's exquisitely obscurantist camerawork. Still, there's something, some tantalizing enigma, in *Ashes* that keeps people watching. With each repeated viewing, something new emerges—revising the degree or even the polarity of one's reaction toward the film.

After *Ashes*—which ate up sixteen months in an industry where month-long production schedules are not uncommon—Wong sought a break from remote locations and enormous casts. In the process, he offhandedly tossed off a classic: 1994's compact and brilliant *Chungking Express*, which says in ninety minutes everything there is to be said about city living in Hong Kong. The film remains his most accessible work to date, and turned gaminesque popstar Faye Wong and blonde-bewigged Brigitte Lin Ching-hsia (in her final screen appearance) into icons of the American arthouse. (The film, which has sequences taking place on the long network of escalators that connects downtown Hong Kong to the residential towers of the Mid-Levels, also has the unique distinction of having prompted its own city ordinance: Tourists taking the journey will note regularly spaced signs barring the shooting of movies on the system.)

After *Chungking* came its semisequel, *Fallen Angels* (1995)—a straight shot of Wong Kar Wai right to the jugular, with a last frame that bids a final fleeting goodbye to pre-1997 Hong Kong, and all that it entails. With that, Wong was finally ready to go back on the road.

This time, however, Wong had the benefit of international renown. Critics were waiting patiently for Wong Kar Wai's next move, and would likely have given him a standing ovation if he'd announced he was directing a TV commercial. What he gave them instead was *Happy Together* (1997). As with *Ashes*, the six-week shoot stretched into infinity, ultimately lasting over a year, and stranding stars Tony Leung Chiu Wai and Leslie Cheung in Argentina along with Wong and his band of merry movie men. However, the film won Wong a Best Director nod at Cannes and paved the way for Wong's return to his *Days of Being Wild* roots, eschewing edgy urban modernity for the achingly slow heartbreak tango of 2000's *In the Mood for Love*, between Maggie Cheung and Tony Leung Chiu Wai, in which art direction is transfigured into a kind of religious ecstasy.

As famous as the movies he's made are the volumes of footage he's left on the cutting-room floor. Each of Wong's films after his first has essentially been assembled during the editing process, with the actors, the cinematographers, and even Wong himself having no idea what the finished product will look like, or even be about. *Ashes of Time* left thousands of fabled feet of film on the cutting-room floor. *Days of Being Wild*'s cryptic coda is all that remains of an entire third segment of the film, which focused on Tony Leung Chiu Wai's late-entry character and was shot in the legendary, now-demolished Walled City of Kowloon. *Happy Together* had an hour shaved from its running time, totally eliminating Shirley Kwan's character. And of course, there are the never-seen sex scenes from *In the Mood for Love* (the Criterion DVD actually includes long swatches from Wong's edits, including a hilarious scene in which Cheung and Leung intently line-dance in a hotel room).

One would think that the arrant whimsy of Wong's reshoots and reboots, his refusal to adhere to shooting schedules, and his adamantly improvisational approach to moviemaking would cause performers to flee him like the plague; far from it. Actors seek him out because of his artistic credibility and studied mystique, and discuss their Wong Kar Wai shoots as if they were some kind of exhilarating New Age experience—like fire walking or

Art or Commerce? Two faces of romance: Wong Jing's *Prince Charming* and Wong Kar Wai's *In the Mood for Love. Courtesy of Celestial Pictures (L) and Kino International (R). All rights reserved. Special thanks to Marnix van Wijk.*

deep colonic cleansing. "You need to make yourself very flexible with Kar Wai. You have to turn yourself inside out," said Tony Leung Chiu Wai. "I've worked with people on his movies and they are very frightened, very nervous at first, and they come up and ask me what the heck is going on. And I always tell them, with Kar Wai, you don't ask, you just *feel.*"[28]

Imagine now two gates, each leading to a different movie future, and each guarded by one of the two Hong Kong Wongs. Wong Jing's door— the Gate of Commerce—might open onto a room full of uniform, shrink-wrapped, candy-coated lozenges of entertainment, each containing a full day's supply of sex, violence, and bathroom humor. Wong Kar Wai's door—the Gate of Art—might open into a gaping void, or a pastoral paradise, or a hellish inferno . . . a different world each time, not always to your liking, and never according to your choice. If the decision truly were solely between one Wong or the other, Hong Kong cinema might well be doomed. But what if a third way existed?

The otherwise mediocre *Whatever You Want* introduced a character named "Wong Jing Wai," a caricature-director portrayed as embodying both Wong Jing's abrupt crudeness and Wong Kar Wai's airy pretentiousness. If instead of the very worst of each filmmaker, Wong Jing Wai exemplified the best . . . what love-child of Art and Commerce might result? Would he or it be able to create films suffused with personal vision, but still bound by the mandate of pleasing the masses? After appropriate blending and distillation, could two Wongs make a right?

Attempts to marry artistic merit and entertainment value had been made in the past, notably with the United Filmmakers Organization, a creative collective founded in the early nineties by the likes of Peter Chan (1996's *Comrades, Almost a Love Story*), Claudie Chung (executive producer, 1986's *Peking Opera Blues*), and Eric Tsang (1982's *Aces Go Places*). Their ambition was to make high-quality films that were also commercially viable, and for a period of time they were successful, but as 1997 approached, their conscious focus on the urban romantic-comedy genre limited their ability to engage anxious audiences. At the end of the decade, when their many-headed structure grew politically complicated, they disbanded, transferring their brand and intellectual property to Golden Harvest.

There's an edge to the best Hong Kong films; sometimes it's rusty and black, sometimes sleek and glittering, sometimes warped and cracked. But that edge, that danger, is there. The finest films of both Wongs display their edges keenly; though UFO's films were sophisticated and entertaining, they were also soft and harmless. It would be another production company, founded just as UFO was fading out, that would display the means of preparing a proper Hong Kong combination of art and commerce—with an edge as sharp as heartbreak, and as cool as winter wind.

*—Jeff Yang, with Ric Meyers (Tsui Hark, Stephen Chiau),*
*Yvonne Teh (Fruit Chan), Gary Morris (Tsai Ming-liang),*
*Matt Levie (Ang Lee), Peter Nepstad (Hsu Qi),*
*Art Black (Category III Girls),*
*Grady Hendrix (Wong Jing, Wong Kar Wai)*

# Epilogue:
# 2000 and Beyond

If we cannot rejuvenate the [Hong Kong film] industry, give it support, and make it more exciting, then perhaps investors will have no interest in putting more money into it. Why does an investor want to put money into the Hong Kong film industry? To make a profit. At Milkyway Image, we aim for a balance between the kind of movies we like and the kind of movies audiences like. That is our goal. A few years ago, we only did the movies we liked. That would make the industry dead.

—*Milkyway Image's Johnnie To*[29]

The dark little production company known as Milkyway Image slipped onto the scene in 1996, just as the Hong Kong film bubble burst and the Asian economic crisis dragged the colony to the edge of destruction, and immediately began creating films that offered searing, discordant visions of crime and punishment—dark, doomed, hyperstylized thrillers that propped up the industry's self-respect at its artistic nadir.

But though their films were critical triumphs, they were commercial failures—until the final movie in Milkyway's "first phase," the cat-and-mouse technothriller *Running Out of Time* (1999). Kinetic and buoyant, but full of Milkyway's signature twists and kinks, the film marked a creative turning point for the duo at the company's helm—veteran director/producer Johnnie To and his writing partner Wai Ka Fai. Despite this surprise success, for the next two years, To and Wai put Milkyway on hold, with To joining Charles Heung's China Star Enterprises/100 Years of Film as COO and Wai returning to his home base, television.

But in the backs of their minds, thoughts of that last success lingered. Finally, To and Wai decided to give Milkyway another chance, after agreeing to adhere to a rigid new production strategy. Every genre-exploding "personal movie" they made would now be paired with an "audience movie"—a film whose commercial returns could underwrite the costs of their acts of creative expression. So, Milkyway's second phase began, with frothy crowd-pleasers like *Needing You* (2000), *Help!!!* (2000), *Love on a Diet* (2001), and *Wu Yen* (2001) alternating with off-kilter mind-bombs like Derek Chiu's *Comeuppance* (2000), Lawrence Ah Mon's *Spacked Out* (2001), and To and Wai's *Fulltime Killer* (2001).

Some of their personal films, like *Fulltime Killer*, have turned out to be unexpected commercial successes; more important, however, every single one of Milkyway's "audience movies" to date has been a hit—and in many cases, seemed like lonely domestic islands amid the Hollywood-dominated sea of the box office charts.

Critics have suggested that the string of winners can't last; that eventually, the streak will end, and the Milkyway boys will fall into the same malaise being experienced by other industry lights—with even studio giant Golden Harvest being forced to sell key assets and shutter its storied backlot in recent years. In response, To and Wai have suggested that if only the rest of the Hong Kong movie industry were to follow their lead, the industry's survival would no longer be in question. Rather, Hong Kong cinema's best days could still be ahead.

And To and Wai have a point. Hong Kong, and Taiwan, and the Mainland, three film-producing regions that have all seen days of glory and days of shame, contain within their borders a staggering array of talent. China—newly admitted to the World Trade Organization—represents the largest potential media market in the world; Taiwan, after years spent in an economic haze, finally seems ready once more to unleash its huge and pent-up supplies of capital. The worst predictions of years gone by—that 1997 would bring with it a harsh crackdown on Hong Kong freedoms, or that Taiwan's shifting internal politics would provoke the Mainland to exert its military might—now seem unlikely, and already, the region's most forward-thinking artists have begun to align themselves to take advantage of the opportunities.

Precedent certainly exists, as blueprinted by the majestic Hsu Feng, a diva whose contributions onscreen and off have marked her as one of the most influential individuals of all three of China's film industries. Born in Taipei in 1950, Hsu was just sixteen years old when she signed a six-year contract with Taiwan's Union Film Company, making her film debut with a small role in King Hu's *Dragon Gate Inn* (1967). With her star turn in Hu's *A Touch of Zen* (1971), Hsu established the persona that she would inhabit throughout her cinematic career—as a queen of the silver screen with a gaze so chilly it could freeze Hell itself; a warrior woman who intimidated opponents not with thunderbolt kicks or lightning blows, but with the most expressive set of eyes this side of the Great Wall.

In 1980, after an illustrious performing career, and shortly after winning her second Golden Horse Best Actress nod for *The Pioneers*, Hsu married a wealthy real-estate mogul and retired from acting. Four years later, she founded the Tomson Film Company, announcing her intention to produce films that balanced artistic aspirations and commercial entertainment, while embracing the talent of all three of Greater China's industries—from Hong Kong's Ann Hui (1988's *Starry Is the Night*) and Yim Ho (1990's Mainland-filmed *Red Dust*), to Taiwan's Yeh Hung-wei (1991's *Five Girls and a Rope*), and the Mainland's Chen Kaige (1993's *Farewell My Concubine* and 1996's *Temptress Moon*).

With luck and continued détente, Hsu's example could eventually prove to be the norm. "Before the Handover, it was impossible for Hong Kong directors to release our movies in China," says Dennis Chan of the Hong Kong Directors' Guild. "It was possible to arrange coproductions, but we would still have no right to release the movie until we passed their censors. But after [the Handover], it was quite a big surprise to all of us: Coproduction opened up, it's become easier to get script approval . . . we're moving toward a better atmosphere."[30]

Meanwhile, entrepreneurs have hardly been standing on the sidelines; Media Asia, which owns the distribution rights to the largest library of films in China, including Golden Harvest's entire backlist, debuted with a strong lineup of productions in the late nineties, and weathered the defection of its managing director Thomas Chung to affirm their status as one of the biggest players on the Greater Chinese cinema map. (Chung has launched his own holding company, Han Entertainment, in partnership with actress Michelle Yeoh.) China Star Entertainment, run by Charles Heung (who parted ways with his brother Jimmy in the late nineties, leaving Win's Entertainment in his hands), is another important trans-China player, while newer guns have recently made big splashes, such as Albert Yeung's Emperor Movie Group, a spinoff of the massive Emperor food conglomerate, and Celestial Pictures, funded by Malaysian capital and run by former Sony executive William Pfeiffer. Celestial announced that it had struck a deal with Shaw Brothers to license and release the studio's seven-hundred-plus backlist of classic films, fulfilling the dreams and wishes of Hong Kong cinema fans everywhere.

As the cinematic industries of China throw off their slumber and show signs of life, American audiences should remember that they've had only the merest taste of the banquet that is to come. Save room for dessert.

—*Jeff Yang, with Grady Hendrix (Milkyway Image)*
*and Art Black (Hsu Feng)*

# Capsule Reviews

## THE DAWN OF CHINESE FILM: 1896–1949

***Along the Sungari River*** (1947; Mainland, Dr) D: Jin Shan C: Zhang Ruifang, Wang Renlu, Zhou Diao, Pu Ke

A patriotic love story set against the backdrop of the 1931 Japanese occupation of Manchuria. Reviewers called it "film as poetry"; "potent" moviemaking, and one of the "high points of international film history."

***Big Road*** (1934; Mainland, Dr) D: Sun Yu C: Jin Yan, Zhang Junli, Han Lan'gen, Li Lili, Chen Yanyan

This enormously successful silent epic about a ragtag group of young idealists building a highway for the war effort spawned one of China's first "soundtrack hits," when the patriotic theme song sung by the movie's youthful characters, "Dalu Ge" ("Song of the Big Road"), attained blockbuster popularity. Reviewers called it "passionate, expansive, and exciting"; though "obviously a recruiting poster," the film "transcends" thanks to its "remarkable realism" and the "stand-out personalities" of its cast.

***Burning of Red Lotus Temple, The*** (1928; Mainland, Ac, Dr, Pd) D: Zhang Sichuan C: Zheng Xiaoqiu, Xia Peizhen, Gao Lihen

Adapted from a well-known "wandering-swordsman" novel, *Red Lotus Temple* was the most famous early action epic, and essentially the ancestor of the entire genre known as *wuxia pian*. Reviewers called the film "seminal" and "profoundly influential"; its popularity was so huge that its director set another Chinese tradition, by making eighteen sequels.

***Cheng the Fruit Seller*** (1922; Mainland, Cm) D: Zhang Shichuan C: Zheng Zhegu, Yu Ying, Zheng Zhengqiu

A madcap farce featuring a crafty but amorous fruit vendor, who's intent on wooing the beautiful daughter of the village doctor. Reviewers called this, the earliest surviving Chinese film, a work of "surprisingly clever slapstick."

***Children of Troubled Times*** (1935; Mainland, Dr) D: Xu Xinzhi C: Wang Renmei, Yuan Muzhi, Tan Ying, Gu Menghe, Lu Luming

After the invasion of Manchuria, many students and intellectuals volunteered to serve against the Japanese. This story follows two university graduates who flee their home in the north of China and travel cross-country to Shanghai, where they join the forces of the resistance. Reviewers note that the theme to this "stirring patriotic ode"—"Volunteers Marching On," written by Nie Er, the greatest composer of early Chinese cinema—was eventually chosen as China's national anthem.

***Crows and Sparrows*** (1949; Mainland, Dr) D: Zheng Junli C: Chen Baichen, Shen Fu, Wang Lingu, Xu Tao, Zhao Dan

Set during the fading days of the Kuomintang regime, this classic social commentary film plays out China's civil war in miniature, as a group of poor workers struggle against the wealthy and corrupt owner of their boarding house. Reviewers called it a "tremendously well-acted and -directed melodrama" with a "passionate, but not doctrinaire political conscience."

**Difficult Couple, The** (1913; Mainland, Dr) D: Zhang Shichuan, Zheng Zhengqiu C: Unknown

A short feature documenting the efforts of a matchmaker to negotiate a marriage, this seminal work was the first feature work to be made in China. "Primarily notable for its pioneering status," say reviewers. In a carryover from Beijing Opera tradition, all roles in the film (both male and female) were played by men.

**Eight Thousand Li of Cloud and Moon** (1947; Mainland, Dr) D: Shi Dongshan C: Bai Yang, Gao Zheng, Tao Jin

This film follows the exploits of an opera company as they entertain soldiers on the front and even, when pressed, take part in battle themselves. After the war, the players return home to Shanghai, where they struggle to keep the troupe alive in a difficult period of rebuilding and revival. Reviewers called it "masterful," with "appealing, richly drawn characters."

**Goddess** (1934; Mainland, Dr) D: Wu Yonggang C: Ruan Lingyu, Zhang Zhizhi, Li Keng

A beautiful young woman, driven to prostitution to support her family, suffers from daily abuse at the hands of cops and the local headman. But when her son begins experiencing the same problems at school, she is driven into madness, lashing out around her in a futile attempt to protect herself and her child. Reviewers praised Ruan's "moving performance," and the film's "deep and universal impact."

**Myriad of Lights** (1948; Mainland, Dr) D: Shen Fu C: Lan Ma, Shang-guan Yunzhu, Wu Yin, Shen Yang, Gao Zhen

At the end of the 1940s, Shanghai—a shadow of its glamorous former self—is home to thousands of returning refugees, who enter an economy already stretched to the limit by efforts to rebuild. Hu Zhiqing, an employee at a trading company, lives in a tiny apartment with his pregnant wife Youlan and young daughter, barely able to make ends meet. Things only get worse when Hu's mother, brother, and sister-in-law arrive from the countryside and unexpectedly decide to move in. Reviewers called it "a tangled, but beautiful" tale of "familial warfare and sacrifice."

**New Woman** (1934; Mainland, Dr) D: Cai Chusheng C: Ruan Lingyu, Zheng Junli, Yin Xu, Wang Naidong

A gripping melodrama inspired by the suicide of actress Ai Xing, who took her life after a scandal ruined her reputation. Complimenting Ruan's "vivid display of her charms," reviewers called it "bleak" and "emotionally overwhelming," particularly given that Ruan, beset by some of the same troubles as the title character, took her own life shortly after making this film.

**New Year's Coin, A** (1937; Mainland, Dr) D: Zhang Shichuan C: Gong Qiuxia, Hu Rongrong, Li Minghui, Gong Jianong

The titular coin is a gift from a grandfather, Mr. He, to his granddaughter Rongrong for Lunar New Year—when *hong bao,* or red envelopes containing money, are tradtiionally given by elders to children. Rongrong subsequently buys firecrackers with the coin, and it passes from hand to hand through Shanghai society. Reviewers said it provides a "fascinating tour" of Shanghai society, though from a "self-consciously leftist" point of view.

**Orphan on the Streets, An** (1949; Mainland, Dr) D: Zhao Ming C: Wang Longji, Guan Hongda, Wang Gongxu

This film was based on one of China's most popular cartoons, which followed the adventures of a young street urchin named San Mao ("Three Hairs"). Here San Mao decides to "sell" himself to a wealthy family, hoping for a better life, before realizing that riches do not equal happiness. Reviewers called this a "brilliant" work of social realism, but criticized the story's "inevitable coda," celebrating the victory of communism. In its original (and nonpolitical) guise as a children's comic by Zhang Leping, the character of San Mao had a popularity akin to Mickey Mouse in the West. He was so beloved, in fact, that Hong Kong actor/director/action star "Sammo" Hung Kam Bo adopted the Cantonese version of the name as his professional identity.

**Orphan Rescues Grandfather** (1923; Mainland, Dr) D: Zhang Shichuan C: Wang Hanlun, Wang Xianzai, Zheng Xiaoqiu, Zheng Zhegu

A melodrama about a wealthy man named Yang who is faced with naming a new heir after the untimely death of his son, Daosheng. Greedy nephew Daopei asks

Yang to adopt him, and Yang agrees, unaware that Daosheng's wife Weiru is pregnant with his grandson. Reviewers called it a "simple but effective" film, and noted that its popularity saved its studio from bankruptcy.

***Sing-Song Girl Red Peony*** (1930; Mainland, Dr) D: Zhang Shichuan C: Hu Die, Wang Xianzai, Xia Peizhen, Gong Jianong

A melodrama with the distinction of being one of China's first sound films, this film concerns an actress named Red Peony, whose beauty and vocal talents have brought her fortune and throngs of male admirers, but who is tied to a brutal, abusive wastrel of a husband. Reviewers called it a "pioneering achievement" that "holds up remarkably well."

***Spring in a Small Town*** (1948; Mainland, Dr) D: Fei Mu C: Wei Wei, Shi Yu, Li Wei, Zhang Hongmei

A beautiful woman, bound in a marriage to a dying man she does not love, finds her fidelity challenged when her husband's best friend returns to their village. Reviewers laud the "striking" cinematography and the many "subtle, delicate moments" that director Fei Mu finds between the characters, calling it "one of the finest films of the period."

***Spring River Flows East*** (1947; Mainland, Dr) D: Cai Chusheng, Zheng Junli C: Bai Yang, Shu Xiuwen, Wu Yin, Shangguan Yunzhu, Tao Jin

This epic two-part melodrama tells the story of Zhang Zhongliang, a patriotic young man who leaves his wife and son to volunteer for the war effort against the Japanese. Despite his initial idealism, as the battle winds down, he becomes drawn into the decadent world of the postwar rich, turning his back on his family and betraying his lofty aims. Reviewers called this, the most influential film of the postwar period, a "grand masterpiece"; "China's *Gone with the Wind*."

***Street Angel*** (1937; Mainland, Dr) D: Yuan Muzhi C: Zhao Dan, Zhou Xuan, Wei Heling

The war in China's northeast drives two young girls, Xiao Yun and Xiao Hong, to flee their homes and seek refuge in Shanghai. Unfortunately, the big city has its own dangers, and the girls are coerced into working at a brothel—one as a prostitute, the other as a dancer. Reviewers praised it as a "true classic" that provides a "rich and vivid portrait" of the urban underclass in thirties China.

### *Unchanged Heart in Life and Death* (1936; Mainland, Dr) D: Ying Yunwei C: Yuan Muzhi, Chen Boer, Li Qing, Liu Liying

In this political thriller, an imprisoned revolutionary makes a stunning jailbreak; during the hunt for the fugitive, an uncanny physical resemblance leads the authorities to arrest an innocent man. The multitalented Yuan Muzhi essayed both of the film's leading roles—the abused innocent and the passionate revolutionary. Reviewers called *Heart* an "effective exploration" of the "oppressive paranoia of life during wartime."

### *Zhuangzi Tests His Wife* (1913; Hong Kong, Dr) D: Li Minwei, Li Beihai C: Li Beihai, Li Minwei, Yan Shanshan

This is an adaptation of a folk tale about the ancient sage Zhuangzi. Married to a young and pretty wife, the master decides to test her loyalty and fidelity. He fakes his own death, then disguises himself as a wandering prince in an attempt to seduce her. More of a stage production put to celluloid than a full-fledged work of cinema, *Zhuangzi* is nonetheless notable as one of the first features to be produced in China, as well as the very first film with a female cast member. Codirector Li Minwei played Zhuangzi's wife, while Minwei's real-life wife Yan Shanshan took the supporting role of a maid. The cast of this family affair was rounded out by Minwei's brother Beihai as the philosopher himself; Beihai had also starred in the film generally considered to be Hong Kong's first—a short feature called *Stealing the Roast Duck* (1909).

# SWORDSMEN AND REVOLUTIONARIES: THE FIFTIES AND SIXTIES

***Chinese Boxer, The*** (1969; Hong Kong, Ac, Dr, Pd) D: Jimmy Wang Yu C: Jimmy Wang Yu, Lo Lieh, Chen Sing, Yuen Woo Ping, Fang Mien

Jimmy Wang Yu plays Lei Ming, who has vowed to take revenge on the Japanese martial artists who killed his master. Knowing that the skill of his enemies is too great for any ordinary technique, Lei heads for the mountains of Korea to learn the secrets of the "Iron Palm." This picture launched the modern kung fu era, and the elements of most later works are all here: A student seeking to avenge his teacher, a mystical kung fu style that can only be learned through rigorous and unusual training, and a climactic face-off between the hero and his enemies, who are startled (and then defeated) by his unorthodox new skills. Reviewers called it an "interesting point of reference" for the golden age of martial arts cinema, "still watchable and entertaining today."

***Cinderella and Her Little Angels*** (1959; Hong Kong, Cm) D: Tung Wang C: Linda Lin Dai, Peter Chen, So Fung, Wang Lai

This whimsical musical comedy is a showcase for the beautiful Linda Lin Dai. Lin Fu (Chen) is a quiet and kindhearted tailor who lives a simple and rather boring life. The only sparkle in his existence is Dan Yee (Lin), a lovely girl from a nearby orphanage. Lin is completely taken with her, but too timid to ever let her know; instead, he lavishes affection on a clothes mannequin that looks exactly like her. Needless to say, everything's resolved in time for a happy (and romantic) ending. Reviewers lauded the movie's spectacular "fashion parades" and Lin Dai's "exciting presence"—marking her as "every bit the superstar" she would become.

***Come Drink with Me*** (1966; Mainland, Ac, Dr, Pd) D: King Hu C: Cheng Pei Pei, Yueh Hua, Chen Hung-lieh, Yeung Chi-hing, Simon Yuen

An imperial officer and his guards are overwhelmed by bandits, and the official is held for ransom as a bargaining chip for the release of the bandit chieftain, currently being held in the local prison. Rather than freeing the prisoner, the officer's father—the magistrate of the province—sends his daughter, Golden Swallow, to deal with the situation through diplomacy or swordplay, at her discretion. When the thieves attempt to ambush Swallow at a roadside inn, her choice becomes obvious: swordplay, of course.

Reviewers called it "a work that all Chinese film fans must see—one of the movies that started it all," and praised the epic's "intoxicating" "romantic sweep."

### Dragon Gate Inn (1967; Mainland, Ac, Dr, Pd) D: King Hu C: Polly Shang, Jun Shi, Ying Bo, Jian Tsao, Han Xue

Chief Eunuch Cao executes Defense Minister Yu, a Ming loyalist, and declares his family outlaw; as Yu's children are escorted to the border, Cao orders them assassinated before they even reach exile. His agents converge with operatives loyal to Yu at Dragon Gate Inn, a small hostel near the border, setting the scene for a majestic clash of wills and blades. Polly Shang plays a mysterious swordswoman seeking to save the two youths; the small role of Yu's daughter is played by Hsu Feng, who would star in many of Hu's subsequent films. Reviewers noted that it was one of Hu's few box office smashes, featuring "thrilling action" and "outstanding direction and choreography"; an "important" and "entertaining" film, with a lead actress in Shang who "steals the show."

### Golden Swallow (1968; Hong Kong, Ac, Pd) D: Chang Cheh C: Jimmy Wang, Cheng Pei Pei, Lo Lieh, Chu Sam Yin, Wu Ma

In this sequel to King Hu's classic *Come Drink with Me,* Chang Cheh introduces a pair of suitors for the incredible warrior woman Golden Swallow, played here again by Cheng Pei Pei. One of them is Silver Roc (Wang), a driven master bladesman out to avenge his murdered family by killing all of the members of the evil Golden Dragon Gang. The other is fellow swordsman Han Tao (Lo), who has long wished to test his skills against his respected rival. "Not nearly as good as either *One-Armed Swordsman* or *Come Drink with Me,*" says one reviewer. Absurdly, while "Silver Roc is a human death machine" who "kills what appears to be everyone in the entire universe," the "much more interesting" Golden Swallow "gets the short end of the stick here."

### Lin Family Shop, The (1959; Mainland, Dr) D: Shui Hua C: Xie Tian, Lin Bin, Yu Lan, Chen Shou

Adapted from a famous short story by contemporary author Mao Dun, this film follows the trials of a shopkeeper named Lin, whose business is being squeezed from a number of directions: increasing Japanese aggression, the corrupt ways of

KMT officials, and an excessive load of debt held by banks, creditors, and vendors. Reviewers praised its "momentum of quiet nightmare."

***Lin Zexu*** (1959; Mainland, Dr) D: Zheng Junli, Qiu Fan C: Zhao Dan, Han Fei, Gao Bo, Qin Yi, Wen Xiying

A biopic on the Qing Dynasty official of the same name, whose open confrontation with Western opium importers led directly to the Opium War, and indirectly, to the ceding of Hong Kong to the British. This film was produced as part of the tenth anniversary of the founding of the People's Republic of China, but was subsequently criticized by Maoist critics, who referred to it as a "poisonous weed" that "slandered" China and its people. Reviewers called it perhaps the "most ambitious" film to be created in the first decade after communism.

***Love Eterne, The*** (1963; Hong Kong, Dr, Pd) D: Li Hanxiang C: Betty Le, Ivy Ling, King Hu

This "triumphant" adaptation of the opera classic *Liang Shanbo and Zhu Yingtai* (aka the "Butterfly Lovers") is notable for having been an enormous hit throughout the Chinese-speaking world—despite going up against a rival project that starred then-superstars Li Lihua and Lucilla Yu Ming. In Taiwan, audiences queued up for blocks to see it, and watched and rewatched it time and again (some as many as five hundred times!). "Two hours of solid entertainment," say reviewers, who compare the popular reaction to the film to "*Star Wars* mania."

***Mambo Girl*** (1957; Hong Kong, Dr, Cm) D: Evan Yang C: Grace Chang Ge Lan, Peter Chen Hou, Kitty Ting, Liu Enjia, Tong Yeuk Jing

This portrait of a free spirit, whose ecstatic journey through a life punctuated with song and dance numbers is interrupted when she discovers she was adopted, established Grace Chang Ge Lan as the top chanteuse of her era, and Peter Chen Hou—playing the straight-arrow guy indoctrinated into the world of rhythm by "mambo girl"—as the period's most popular romantic comedy lead. Reviewers called it a "vibrant hipster fantasy," confirming Chang as "a phenomenal singer and dancer"; one reviewer called Grace Chang the female "Fred Astaire of Mandarin musicals," and Peter Chen "the genre's Ginger Rogers."

***New Year's Sacrifice*** (1956; Mainland, Dr) D: Sang Hu C: Bai Yang, Wei Heling, Li Jingpo

Based on a short story by Lu Xun, one of China's most prominent contemporary writers, this film takes place shortly after the fall of the Qing Dynasty, in rural Zhejiang Province. It follows the trials, tribulations, and descent into poverty and self-destruction of a young girl named Xianglin. Driven insane by her repeated misfortunes and left to wander the streets, she dies of exposure on New Year's Eve. Reviewers praise this "successful adaptation" that has become a "popular classic"; "it doesn't get any more melodramatic than this."

***One-Armed Swordsman, The*** (1967; Hong Kong, Ac, Pd) D: Chang Cheh C: Jimmy Wang, Pan Yinzi, Guk Fung, Wong Chung Shun, Tin Fung

A swordmaster raises his dead servant's son as his own; the boy, Fong Kong, turns out to have tremendous natural skills, and soon rivals his adoptive father as a bladesman. Unfortunately, Fong's success triggers the envy of other pupils, including the master's daughter, who leads a treacherous attack against him. Fong survives, but loses his sword arm in the process. He is nursed back to health by a peasant girl, and creates a new, potent one-handed style. Reviewers called it "groundbreaking in its extreme violence and brutality," but "highly recommended"; "Chang allows the tension to build until you're at the edge of your seat."

***Our Sister Hedy*** (1957; Hong Kong, Dr, Cm) D: Tao Qin C: Julie Yeh Feng, Jeanette Lin Tsui, Muk Hung, So Fung

In contrast to most films revolving around siblings, the stars of this family comedy are the two middle girls out of four: hot-blooded second sister Helen (played by Julie Yeh Feng) and earnest third sister Hedy (Jeanette Lin Tsui). Helen, a flirt and a charmer, consistently draws boys into her orbit, exasperating the other girls, and Hedy most of all. The film's storyline throws out a heady (no pun intended) array of developments in its two-hour run—with plot twists involving an auto accident, an elopement, a sister-on-sister catfight, three big song-and-dance extravaganzas, and an endless stream of dress-up parties. Reviewers call it "one of the brightest Mandarin comedies of the fifties ." The film turned Lin Tsui, who plays Hedy, into a star; the cast and director reunited for a sequel in 1959, *Wedding Bells for Hedy.* Three decades later, Lin Tsui appeared as the mother in a remake, *Four Loves* (1989).

**Oyster Girl** (1964; Taiwan, Dr) D: Li Jia, Lee Hsing C: Wang Mochou, Wu Jiaqi, Gao Xinzhi

A "wholesome" melodrama about a young woman named Ah Lan, who supports her alcoholic father and younger brother by gathering oysters on the shore. A rivalry develops between honest fisherman Jinshui and rascal Huo for her attentions, although Lan's heart belongs to the former. Love (and good) defeat lust (and evil) in the end. Reviewers called it a "pleasant" melodrama that remains one of the classics of sixties Taiwanese cinema.

**Stage Sisters** (1965; Mainland, Dr) D: Xie Jin C: Xie Fang, Li Wei, Cao Yindi, Shangguan Yunzhu

In this forties-era period melodrama, a traveling theater company finds a stowaway hidden amidst its baggage—Chunhua, a young girl attempting to run away from an arranged marriage. Yuehong, the daughter of the troupe's leader, befriends the girl and begs for her to be allowed to stay. The two follow starkly different paths through life. Reviewers called this, one of the last films to be produced before the Cultural Revolution temporarily ended film production, a work of "cleverly staged agitprop" whose "revolutionary thrust was intensified in mid-shoot" by its wary director as time went on and the political climate shifted. Still, it's a "real delight," with "terrific performances" and a "fluid and elegant" directorial style.

**Sun, Moon, and Star** (1961; Hong Kong, Dr) D: Evan Yang C: Lucilla Yu Ming, Grace Chang Ge Lan, Julie Yeh Feng, Zhang Yang, Ouyang Shafei

This two-part epic melodrama follows the story of a young man named Xu Jianbai and the three remarkable women in his life—all of whom he loves, and none of whom he is ultimately able to win. Reviewers called it a "richly drawn" masterpiece, starring three of the biggest Hong Kong actresses of the day—Lucilla Yu Ming, Grace Chang Ge Lan, and Julie Yeh Feng.

**Teddy Girls, The** (1969; Hong Kong, Dr) D: Patrick Lung C: Josephine Siao, Nancy Sit, Lydia Shum, Kenneth Tsang, Seung Gwun Yuk

Though, like most works of its period and genre, it is difficult to find in the United States, this film is an interesting and uncommonly dark example of the teen movies that took Hong Kong cinema by storm in the late sixties. Josephine Siao, the era's top girl star, plays the troubled adolescent lead, who is arrested for fighting at a club, and sentenced to a year in a home for female delinquents. Although Siao originally welcomes the opportunity to get away from home, she soon finds that reform school is no picnic, and escapes along with some of her fellow "teddy girl" friends. The fugitive lasses, seeking justice for past injuries, soon find themselves in a spiral of crime that includes robbery, beatings, and ultimately, murder. Reviewers call it a "strikingly composed" film with "top-notch performances by young stars Josephine Siao and Nancy Sit," although the "social message ultimately becomes overwhelming."

### White-Haired Girl, The (1950; Mainland, Dr) D: Wang Bin, Shui Hua C: Tian Hua, Chen Qiang, Li Baiwan, Hu Peng

Dachun, a young peasant, is in love with Xi'er, the beautiful daughter of his neighbor Yang. While Yang approves of the match, he has racked up large debts to landlord Huang Shiren. Threatening Yang with arrest, Huang coerces him into selling Xi'er into his service as a maid. Unable to face what he has done, Yang commits suicide; Huang proceeds to rape Xi'er and drive Dachun off his property. With the help of a sympathetic fellow servant, Xi'er escapes into the hills, where she takes up residence in a secluded cave and steals temple offerings to survive. Worshipers, noting the disappearance of their sacrifices, begin to tell tales of a mysterious mountain deity—particularly when they catch fleeting glimpses of Xi'er, whose hair has turned snow white. After years of separation and turmoil, the star-crossed lovers are reunited at last. Reviewers called it an "arresting" romantic drama with an "unusual mythic backdrop," given its era.

### Wild, Wild Rose, The (1960; Hong Kong, Dr) D: Wong Tin Lam C: Grace Chang Ge Lan, Zhang Yang, Wang Lai, So Fung, Tin Ching

In this loose, noiresque adaptation of Bizet's Carmen, Grace Chang Ge Lan plays a femme fatale with a surprisingly kind heart. Zhang Yang, one of the era's top male stars, plays the teacher-turned-alcoholic-turned-pianist who is hired to accompany Chang's Wanchai nightclub act, but who soon accompanies her to bed. Miscommunication, jealousy, and murderous rage ensue, as things spin toward an easily foreseen tragic ending. The film's signature song, a ditty called "Ja Jambo," became an enormous hit. Reviewers say that "Chang gives the best performance of her illustrious career," while "Zhang is surprisingly effective in the 'Don Jose' role." "There's magic to this musical!"

# MARTIAL ARTS AND MELODRAMA: THE SEVENTIES

*Arch, The* (1970; Hong Kong, Dr) D: Tang Shuxuan C: Lisa Lu, Roy Chiao, Zhou Xuan

This film, directed by the era's foremost woman filmmaker, explores the archaic and oppressive mores of feudal China. By tradition, a woman was bound to her husband even beyond the grave; for a widow to fall in love again was frowned upon, and for her to marry again was out of the question. A "properly chaste" woman was celebrated by the construction of a memorial arch in her honor, which could just as well be a grave marker. Lisa Lu plays the widow, Madame Tung, and Roy Chiao, the cavalry officer that she loves—or would love, if it were possible. In a wrenching turn of events, when Lu hesitates to follow her heart, Chiao marries her daughter instead. "A remarkable precursor of the Hong Kong New Wave," say reviewers. "Evocative and haunting."

*Butterfly Murders, The* (1979; Hong Kong, Ac, Pd) D: Tsui Hark C: Lau Siu Ming, Michelle Mai, Eddy Ko, Hsia Guang Li, Wong Shee Tong

This strange and atmospheric period detective story, about a hero tasked with investigating a series of deaths committed by clouds of blood-sucking butterflies, confirmed Tsui's status as one of the foremost figures of the Hong Kong New Wave. Fong, an author and investigator of unusual phenomena, is summoned to the ancestral mansion of an aristocratic clan. He brings with him Green Shadow, his acrobatic female assistant, and together they conceive of a plan to protect the family from further insect attacks: draping the entire edifice with netting. Unfortunately, the fluttering menaces find alternative ways into the castle, slaying the patriarch of the family—and things only go downhill from there. Reviewers called Tsui's directorial debut "offbeat and highly satisfying"; "a preview of his now-familiar themes and style."

*China Behind* (1974; Hong Kong, Dr) D: Tang Shuxuan C: Shao Xiaoling, Feng Baoxian, Zeng Jilu, Pan Rongmin

The second of female director Tang Shuxuan's tremendously significant works (the other being the 1970 feminist drama *The Arch*). This film tells the story of a group of young scholars who flee the Cultural Revolution for Hong Kong, leaving "China behind"; they first must travel cross-country, and then swim across the straits to arrive in the sanctuary of the island. The film was understandably banned by the Communist party, which declared that it would "damage relations with other territories." Reviewers stressed that the film is hardly a propaganda piece, displaying nuanced ambivalence about both communism and capitalism. "A work that grows in strength each time you see it," say reviewers. "Inspired and powerful."

**Chinatown Kid** (1977; Hong Kong, Ac) D: Chang Cheh C: Alexander Fu Sheng, Sun Chien, Johnny Wang, Phillip Kwok, Lo Mang

This was the film that established the boyish Alexander Fu Sheng as a legitimate martial arts superstar, until his career was cut short by his untimely and accidental death. Here Fu plays a youth named Tan Tung, who shows up on his grandfather's doorstep in Hong Kong after fleeing the turmoil on the Mainland. Despite his grandfather's poverty-stricken circumstances, he welcomes Tan, and Tan swears to someday become rich enough to repay his grandfather's kindness. The two set up an unlicensed business selling orange juice on the street, but are forced to stay on their toes by police harassment. Then a swaggering gangster named Cho Hao observes Tan cheerfully crushing oranges in his palms; stunned by the boy's strength, he offers Tan a job—without telling him his true profession. The first order he gives his new hire is to go retrieve his "kidnapped cousin," actually a runaway prostitute (played by Kara Hui Ying). Tan finds her, but upon learning the truth from her takes her home to her father instead. This understandably enrages Cho, who sets up Tan to be arrested on false drug charges. Tan escapes, and with the help of the prostitute's father makes his way to San Francisco Chinatown, where he starts his life anew. But Tan soon finds that Cho's reach extends across the ocean as well. "One of the best martial arts movies ever made," says one reviewer. "Clever touches, like the use of a digital watch to symbolize the brave new world of America, make this actioner effective"; "Fu Sheng is the heart of this film, and he shines."

**Chinese Connection, The** (1973; Hong Kong, Ac, Pd) D: Lo Wei C: Bruce Lee, Wei Ping, Riki Ao, Robert Hashimoto

This follow-up to Lee's blockbuster debut, *The Big Boss,* manipulated residual anti-Japanese hostility to rouse Chinese audiences, and ultimately proved to be an even bigger hit than its predecessor. Lee plays Chen, the top-ranked student at a

Shanghai martial arts school, who comes back from a trip to find his classmates mourning their *sifu*—allegedly dead from a case of pneumonia. Lee soon uncovers the truth: His master was murdered by associates of a rival Japanese karate school. The rest of the film is classic kung fu vengeance. Reviewers call it "possibly Lee's most balanced and accomplished film," and note that the scene where Lee shatters the park sign that says "NO DOGS OR CHINAMEN" with a single kick "still gets Chinese audiences cheering."

**Contract, The** (1978; Hong Kong, Cm) D: Michael Hui C: Michael Hui, Sam Hui, Ricky Hui, Yeung Wei

In this showbiz satire, Michael Hui plays an actor consigned to the television equivalent of hell: a gig as host for a ludicrous game show where contestants bet the lives of their loved ones in exchange for the chance to win big prizes. When he unexpectedly gets his big break with a generous offer at another network, he's ecstatic . . . until he realizes that his contract with his channel, MTV (!), represents an iron-clad eight - year commitment. Desperate to get out, he calls on his brother Ricky, a brilliant but goofy inventor, to help him steal his contract out of the MTV safe. Reviewers called it "perhaps the best of the Hui Brothers laugh-fests," particularly praising the "dead-on parody of Hong Kong TV behind the scenes." "Highly recommended!"

**Dirty Ho** (1979; Hong Kong, Ac, Pd) D: Lau Kar Leung C: Gordon Lau Kar Fai, Yung Wang Yu, Lo Lieh, Kara Hui, Johnny Wang

Gordon Lau Kar Fai plays Wang, an apparent layabout who's actually an incognito prince, hiding out from the thugs of his murderous brother, the "Fourth Prince." Running into a con man named Ho in a tavern—while both are flirting with the same girls—he initiates a rivalry that ends with Wang tricking Ho into becoming his apprentice. (This happens during a hilarious "fight by proxy" scene in which Wang defeats an angry Ho using his servant, played by Kara Hui, as a prop.) Over time, Ho grows to respect Wang as he learns the prince's powerful martial arts; when Wang is badly injured by hitmen sent out by his brother, Ho builds him a special wheelchair to transport him to the Fourth Prince's palace to seek revenge. Reviewers called it "one of the great classics," with "kinetic camera work" and "incredible choreography"; "thoroughly entertaining!"

**Drunken Master** (1978; Hong Kong, Ac, Cm, Pd) D: Yuen Woo Ping C: Jackie Chan, Simon Yuen, Hwang Jang Lee, Dean Shek, Yuen Shun Yee

After the breakthrough success of 1977's *Snake in Eagle's Shadow,* Jackie Chan needed to push the envelope further to prove that he was more than just a flash in the pan. The result was *Drunken Master,* a film that took the risky step of depicting Chinese culture hero Wong Fei Hung before he became a hero. Chan plays Wong as a lazy, shiftless, and irresponsible youth who so enrages his father that he gets kicked out of the house and sent to study with an eccentric, drunken beggar named So (memorably played by Yuen Clan patriarch Simon Yuen). So's "lessons" are a series of brutal training exercises that push Wong to the limits of his stamina and sanity, but the hard work pays off; when Wong's father is targeted by a brutal hitman hired by a greedy rival, Chan and his new "Eight Drunken Fairies" style kung fu are able to save the day. "Classic kung fu, classic Jackie Chan," say reviewers. "Still enjoyable today."

**Enter the Dragon** (1973; Hong Kong, Ac) D: Robert Clouse C: Bruce Lee, John Saxon, Jim Kelly, Shek Kin, Ahna Capri

The film that launched a thousand video games, this is the last film that Bruce Lee completed before meeting his untimely end. Lee plays a martial artist recruited by the British government to infiltrate the operation of a mob boss named Han (veteran actor Shek Kin, in a thoroughly menacing performance); since Han's men killed Lee's sister (played by Angela Mao Ying in an all-too-brief appearance), and since Lee's *sifu* instructed him to terminate Han for being a renegade against the Shaolin Way, Lee has plenty of motivation to comply. The only way to get onto Han's island is to participate in his win-or-die ultimate fighting tournament, so Lee accepts an invitation to enter. Reviewers note that there are "too many iconic scenes to mention," and call it "a cinematic landmark," although one mentions that "the dazzling fight scenes and Lee's charisma help you to forgive the racial stereotypes, gratuitous nudity, and blatant rip-off plot."

**Fate of Lee Khan, The** (1973; Taiwan, Ac, Dr, Pd) D: King Hu C: Li Lihua, Angela Mao Ying, Hsu Feng, Pai Ying, Helen Ma

King Hu took more than three years to complete this epic, set during the Mongol rule of China. A group of Chinese rebels hope to obtain a secret map that is being transferred into the hands of Mongol prince Lee Khan; discovering that the exchange will take place at a remote inn, they conspire with the innkeeper (Li Lihua) to place four killer operatives on her staff as waitresses (one of whom is played by the lovely and acrobatic Angela Mao Ying). Reviewers rave about the "masterfully textured plot," with "layers of drama and tension, laid on in delicate single sheets"; the movie "grabs your interest and never lets go."

### Five Deadly Venoms (1978; Hong Kong, Ac, Pd) D: Chang Cheh C: Phillip Kwok, Chiang Sheng, Lo Mang, Sun Chien, Lu Feng

The head of the Poison Clan is on his deathbed, and only one disciple is left to attend him. Before he expires, the chief tells his student to seek out the five original disciples of the clan, each of whom has mastered a different "animal style" kung fu technique: Snake, Centipede, Scorpion, Lizard, and Toad. His mission will be to assess whether any of them have turned to the "dark side" of kung fu, and if so, to eliminate them. Reviewers called it "one of the great classics," but noted that "although it has some real innovation in its fight scenes, its promise is ultimately not fulfilled." This film was most significant for having introduced the Five Venoms, what Chang Cheh called his "second team" of stars: Philip Kwok Choy, the acrobatic, sardonic antihero; Chiang Sheng, his lively gymnastic ally; Lo Mang, the large-muscled, kind-hearted, but often thick-headed sidekick; Lu Feng, the sullen, duplicitous back-stabber; and Sun Chien, an accomplished master of kicking techniques who could play villain and hero with equal ease. They would go on to star as a unit in fourteen films, and in many more as pairs, trios, or quartets.

### Five Fingers of Death (1971; Hong Kong, Ac, Pd) D: Cheng Chang Ho C: Lo Lieh, Meng Fei, Chiao Hsiung, Kung Hsun Nun, Wang Ping

Although Bruce Lee is usually credited with the global breakthrough of kung fu cinema, it was actually this film that broke open the floodgates. Originally titled *King Boxer*, it was licensed by Warner Brothers, dubbed, and renamed to appeal to more bloody-minded fans; released shortly after Lee's death, it broke all box office records for a foreign film, and made it possible for a tidal wave of kung fu exports to follow. Lo Lieh plays Chao, a brilliant martial arts student who is engaged to Ying Ying, the daughter of his *sifu* Shen Wu. When Master Wu hears of an upcoming martial arts tournament, he decides to send Chao as his school's representative. Chao bids Ying Ying goodbye and makes his way to Shen's school, not knowing that a rival teacher, Meng, is set upon having his own sons win the tourney. To stack the deck, Meng is sending thugs out to break or kill the competition. When Master Wu is killed by Meng's hired killers, Chao demands to learn a style powerful enough to defeat Meng and his men—the invincible "Iron Fist" technique. Reviewers called the film "highly recommended for those who like this sort of thing"; the "amount of violence and bloodshed in this movie is staggering."

### Flying Guillotine, The (1974; Hong Kong, Ac, Pd) D: Ho Meng Hua C: Chen Kuan-tai, Ku Feng, Wei Hung, Liu Wu Chi, Ai Ti

In this very strange cult classic. Chen Kuan-tai plays a soldier who has been initiated into a crack fighting force, trained in the use of a secret "invincible weapon," the flying guillotine. Basically a razor-edged hatbox on a chain, it's used by being flung over the head of an enemy and then yanked sharply back. If done properly, both the guillotine and the head return to sender. Chen, the best practitioner in the unit, goes AWOL when he realizes that his emperor is an insane tyrant. Fleeing into hiding, he begins to develop a weapon that can defeat the invincible weapon—a steel umbrella-skeleton sporting sharpened ribs. "Not really a kung fu film at all, but what it lacks in kung fu it makes up for with an endless parade of gory decapitations," says one reviewer.

### Game of Death (1978; Hong Kong, Ac) D: Bruce Lee, Robert Clouse C: Bruce Lee, Kim Tai Yong, Gig Young, Dean Jagger, Hugh O'Brian

This film might have been Bruce Lee's masterpiece, if he'd ever had the opportunity to complete it. Sadly, he died after having shot only the film's final eleven minutes of fight sequences, including a memorable battle with his real-life pupil, NBA star Kareem Abdul-Jabbar. Golden Harvest unconscionably decided to hire Robert Clouse to complete the film using a Korean martial artist as Lee's double. To get around the fact that Kim looked nothing like Lee, they put him in sunglasses for most of the movie and used other dubious techniques to hide the obvious, like pasting a paper cutout of Lee's face on a mirror. Reviewers called it "easily Lee's worst film, if you can even call it *his* film"; "truly unwatchable."

**Games Gamblers Play** (1974; Hong Kong, Cm) D: Michael Hui C: Michael Hui, Sam Hui, Ricky Hui, Dean Shek, Roy Chiao

This seminal seventies farce, the debut of the "Hui Brothers" as a cinematic team, was a blockbuster success when it was released in 1974, hitting number one in the box office and essentially inventing the Canto-comedy genre. Deadpan Michael plays a gambler and swindler who meets a naïve wannabe (his brother Sam) in jail. With nothing but time on their hands, the two make plans to partner up after their eventual release. Sam's refrain is "How can we fail?" Stupid question. Reviewers called it a "milestone" that "still holds up"; one reviewer appreciates the fact that "the duo never learns their lesson."

**Infra-Man** (1976; Hong Kong, Ac) D: Hua Shan C: Danny Lee, Wang Hsieh, Terry Liu, Lin Wen Wei, Yuan Man Tzu

This film was an attempt to emulate the successful live-action superhero shows of seventies Japan—notably, costumed crimefighter films like *Ultraman* and *Kamen Rider*. The film stars Danny Lee as a motorcycle-riding hero called into action to defend Earth from the menacing Princess Dragon Mom and her underground army of rubber creatures. It's almost impossible to describe; readers interested in the so-called "plot" will have to actually unearth a copy of this rare cult classic. Reviewers called it "colorful, action-packed, and fun," if you can overlook its "absence of basic cinematic logic," its "penny-ante special effects," and its "moronic conceit that space alien invaders would attack using kung fu, instead of, say, missiles or death rays."

**Raining in the Mountain** (1979; Taiwan, Ac, Dr) D: King Hu C: Hsu Feng, Sun Yue, Wu Ming-tsai, Tung Lam, Paul Chun

Unlike *Legend of the Mountain*, Hu's other Buddhist-themed epic, filmed almost simultaneously with this one, *Raining* is driven by action. Esquire Wen (Sun), Gold Lock (Wu), and White Fox (Hsu) are bandits who have partnered to steal a precious Buddhist sutra from a cliffside temple, only to find themselves caught amidst a political struggle among three of the temple's monks. Reviewers call this "Hu's most satisfying film," with "delirious camerawork" and an "awesome level of intensity."

**Run Lover Run** (1975; Taiwan, Dr) D: Richard Chen C: Brigitte Lin, Alan Tang, Liu Shan-chian, Hsia Ling-ling

A frothy romantic comedy starring Brigitte Lin as Li-ping, a twenty-one-year-old tomboy whose mother is desperate to marry her off, this picture showcases a very young-looking Brigitte engaged in a variety of sporting activities, from track and field to basketball—a novel sight for those used to seeing her in period Hong Kong fantasies. (In one scene, as Li-ping's mother is attempt to market her daughter as the most gentle and feminine of girls, she returns home covered in mud clutching a huge dead bird.) Alan Tang plays I-fan, a friend of the family coming back from getting his graduate degree in the United States, which makes him Li-ping's ideal match as far as her mother is concerned. But getting Li-ping to agree may not be so easy. Reviewers called it "light-hearted and winning"; "Brigitte and Alan show great chemistry." "You'd never guess, but Asia the Invincible has a great jump shot!"

**Secret, The** (1979; Hong Kong, Dr) D: Ann Hui C: Sylvia Chang, Gigi Chu, Norman` Chiu, Lee Hoi Suk, Alex Man

Director Hui's debut film, this thriller features women in virtually all of its behind the scenes roles, from composer Violet Lam, to writer Joyce Chan, to director Hui and producer Audrey Li. Atmospheric cinematography lends a chilling touch to this story based on a real-life murder case, with Norman Chiu playing a seemingly harmless man who just might be hiding a psychopathic streak. Reviewers praised Sylvia Chang's performance as Lin Ming, as well as the "rich palette of psychological details" Hui uses in painting this tale.

**Snake in the Eagle's Shadow** (1978; Hong Kong, Ac, Pd) D: Yuen Woo Ping C: Jackie Chan, Simon Yuen, Hwang Jang Lee, Dean Shek, Peter Chan

This was Jackie Chan's first big hit, and for good reason; it's here that Chan first infused martial arts with his inimitable blend of acrobatics and slapstick, building a foundation for the classic *Drunken Master* (1978). Chan plays Chien Fu, an abused janitor at a local kung fu academy, who does his best to save a weird old man (Simon Yuen) from harassment at the hands of the students of another school. (The old man actually saves himself, using Chien Fu as a puppet!) As a reward for his kindness, the beggar teaches Chien Fu the secrets of Snake Fist, not knowing that a rival master, Eagle Claw stylist Chien I Kun (Hwang), is seeking to assassinate all initiates of the Snake Fist style. Realizing that Snake Fist alone is not powerful enough to defeat the Eagle Claw, Chien Fu notices a cat defending itself against a snake's attack. Reviewers called this "fun-filled enterprise" a "clear indication of Chan's talent," although "honestly, 'Cat Claw' is more ridiculous than it is intimidating."

**36th Chamber of Shaolin, The** (1978; Hong Kong, Ac, Pd) D: Lau Kar Leung C: Gordon Lau Kar Fai, Lo Lieh, Yung Wang Yu, Norman Tsui, Lee Hoi Sang

Gordon Lau Kar Fai plays Liu Yu Te, a young man who finds sanctuary in the Shaolin Temple after his family is murdered by marauding Manchu troops. As the novice "San Te," he painstakingly proceeds through the temple's "35 Chambers," each of which offers lessons in a different martial skill. Upon completing many inventively grueling training exercises, he is transformed into a fighter powerful enough to avenge his family. After obtaining his revenge, he returns to the temple to form a "36th Chamber" of Shaolin, where nonmonks can be schooled in how to defend themselves against oppressors. Reviewers called it a "true classic," with "brilliantly sadistic training sequences." Followed by the entertaining *Return to the 36th Chamber of Shaolin* (1980), which featured Gordon Lau in a sharp-eyed spoof of this film.

**Touch of Zen, A** (1971; Taiwan, Ac, Dr, Pd) D: King Hu C: Shih Jun, Hsu Feng, Pai Ying, Roy Chiao

Perhaps the *wuxia* master's greatest work, this was the first to receive limited art-house distribution in Europe and the United States; it was originally close to four hours in length, but practicality (and Hu's studio, Union Film Company) forced him to trim it to about three hours. Loosely based on a famous short story by ghost-tale author Pu Songling, this film was shown at Cannes to awards and great acclaim. A scholar named Ku, who is living in a supposedly haunted fortress with his mother, sees a mysterious figure in the woods; this is followed by Ku's encounter with a beautiful but enigmatic girl named Yang, who turns out to be a fugitive from a government coup, and a powerful swordswoman in her own right.

The other figure, meanwhile, is revealed to be a bounty hunter hired to take her and her band of rebels down. Reviewers called this film "on par with Kurosawa at his best," with an "unforgettable" battle in a bamboo glen that would influence all *wuxia* films to follow. "One of the landmark films not just of Hong Kong or China, but of all of cinematic history."

### *Way of the Dragon* (1972; Hong Kong, Ac) D: Bruce Lee C: Bruce Lee, Nora Miao, Wong Chung Shun, Bob Wall, Chuck Norris

Bruce Lee's wife and daughter have called this their favorite of the Dragon's films, since it's the only one to truly have Lee's creative fingerprints all over it from beginning to end. In the film, shot on location in Italy, Lee plays Tang Lung, a boy who goes to Rome to help out a relative's restaurant, which is being threatened by local gangsters. Lung's interference sets off a cascade of vengeance, but there's no question that the Dragon will eventually save his own. Reviewers call this "Lee's most personal work," and a "masterful pastiche of humor, revenge clichés, and incredible kung fu." This was released in the United States after Lee's death under the title *Return of the Dragon.*

# NEW WAVE DREAMS AND BALLISTIC KISSES: THE EIGHTIES

*Aces Go Places* (1982; Hong Kong, Ac, Cm) D: Eric Tsang C: Sam Hui, Karl Maka, Sylvia Chang, Dean Shek, Chen Sing

The first in a highly successful series of caper films, this Cinema City classic features pretty Sam Hui as a superthief and bald Karl Maka as the Chinese-American detective who's spent his career trying to hunt him down. After a series of highly entertaining cat-and-mouse escapades, the two team up to fight a pair of deadlier rogues. Reviewers praised Maka's "gift for physical comedy" and noted, among other pluses, the film's "incredibly catchy theme" music and "hilarious" hat-tips to Hollywood, including a "great *Godfather* in-joke." Followed by four sequels featuring Hui and Maka (the so-called "Best Partners") and one ill-advised attempt to revive the series, *Aces Go Places '97*, starring Alan Tam and Tony Leung Chiu Wai.

*All the Wrong Clues (For the Right Solution)* (1981; Hong Kong, Cm) D: Tsui Hark C: George Lam, Teddy Robin Kwan, Karl Maka, Kelly Yiu, Eric Tsang

An early work by Hong Kong New Wave impresario Tsui Hark, this Cinema City comedy, set in the thirties, features pop singer George Lam as a penny-ante private investigator who provided the evidence required to bust a big-time gangster, "Ah Capone," played by bald comic Karl Maka. When Capone is released from prison, his first order of business is to rub out his nemesis. Lam enlists the support of a bumbling top-cop played by Teddy Robin in an attempt to survive Capone's deadly quest for vengeance. Some reviewers called it "delightful," while others dismissed it as having "more energy than laughs." Still, "watch out for the classic final shootout!"

*All the Wrong Spies* (1983; Hong Kong, Ac, Cm) D: Teddy Robin Kwan C: George Lam, Teddy Robin Kwan, Brigitte Lin, Paul Chun, Tsui Hark

This unrelated sequel to Tsui Hark's popular original, set in 1939, finds George Lam's stumblebum "Agent Yoyo" and director Teddy Robin's goofy cop drawn into a mysterious conspiracy involving the plans for the atomic bomb. A Jewish physicist has stolen the plans from the Nazis, but is slain before he can deliver them to Allied authorities at a drop zone in Hong Kong. Brigitte Lin, in one of her first Hong Kong roles, plays a flamboyant (and drop-dead gorgeous) femme fatale in black;

Tsui Hark hiimself plays a debonair enemy spy who goes by the name "Hiroshima." Reviewers called it "pleasantly enjoyable," with numerous parodies of both classic Hollywood and Hong Kong films—if "not particularly original." They also note that the final joke in the film is in "shockingly bad taste."

### *Angel* (1987; Hong Kong, Ac) D: Raymond Leung, Tony Leung C: Moon Lee, Elaine Lui, Hideki Saijo, Yukari Oshima, Alex Fong

Although some point to its 1977 predecessor *Deadly Angels* as the first official entry in the "girls with guns" genre, it was the surprise box office success of this actioner that made pistol-packing femmes ubiquitous—inspiring two official sequels and about a hundred similarly themed films. When DEA officers destroy a crop of opium poppies in an assault on a Golden Triangle drug ring, the traffickers decide to get revenge in blood. Fellow agent Alex Fong turns to the only group that can stop them: the Angels, a trio of sexy merecenaries. Fong hires them to take out the drug runners and their new leader Madame Yeung (Oshima, who, like Lee and Lui, would become a regular in this genre). Despite its status as the "godmother of the genre," reviewers call it "disappointing" in retrospect, with fewer action sequences than later entries in the category.

### *Armour of God* (1986; Hong Kong, Ac, Cm) D: Jackie Chan C: Jackie Chan, Alan Tam, Rosamund Kwan, Lola Forner, Bozidar Smiljanic

In this flamboyant actioner—clearly inspired by *Raiders of the Lost Ark*—Chan plays Asian Hawk, a freelance hunter of antiquities who has retrieved a trio of rare artifacts that together make up most of a legendary "invincible" suit of armor: The discovery of the missing pieces draws the attention of a satanic cult, which kidnaps Hawk's ex-girlfriend Lorelei and demands the relics in exchange for her life. Hawk borrows the pieces from Bannon, the millionaire who commissioned him to find them, but is forced to take along Bannon's daughter as insurance against their return. In the meantime, Hawk's former best friend (and Lorelei's current fiancé) also demands to come along on the quest. "Okay if you don't ask questions," says one reviewer; "fast and furious," says another. During the filming of this movie, Chan nearly died hitting his head in a stunt that went awry; he still has a hole in his skull as a result.

*As Tears Go By* (1988; Hong Kong, Dr) D: Wong Kar Wai C: Andy Lau, Maggie Cheung, Jacky Cheung, Alex Man, Ronald Wong

Wong Kar Wai's debut film shows the traces of his immense talent, although its pacing, editing, and style are nothing like those of his later works. Wah is a street-level gangster who is constantly bailing his "Little Brother" Fly out of trouble. In part because of his urge to protect Fly, he has never been able to rise in the Triad ranks. When Wah's cousin Ngor comes to Hong Kong to receive medical attention, initial attraction blossoms into love, and Wah considers leaving the criminal life entirely. Until Fly requires his help one last time—precipitating a tragic series of consequences. Reviewers called it "uneven," but with "flashes of brilliance."

*Autumn's Tale, An* (1987; Hong Kong, Dr) D: Mabel Cheung C: Chow Yun Fat, Cherie Chung, Danny Chan, Gigi Wong, Wong Man

A classic romantic drama, pairing two of the era's biggest stars—Chow Yun Fat, in his finest "lovable slob" mode, and Cherie Chung, making the most of her glamorous-girl-next-door looks and irresistible air of naïveté. Filmed on a minuscule budget on location in New York City, for years after its release, Hong Kong tourists to Chinatown would look for "Figgy's apartment" in vain (it's supposed to be somewhere under the Manhattan Bridge, a region currently occupied by a shopping mall). Chow is Sam "Figurehead" Pang, an ex-sailor who's called upon to take care of a distant cousin, Jennifer, when she moves to the city in search of her wayward boyfriend. Although initially put off by Figgy's rough ways, she grows to appreciate his heart of gold. The two part ways after a misunderstanding, with Jennifer taking a position as a live-in nanny to a young girl named Anna. But it's a foregone conclusion that their paths will cross again. Reviewers called the movie "moving and subtle"; a "lighthearted and well-written charmer," with "perhaps the greatest final line ever."

*Better Tomorrow, A* (1986; Hong Kong, Ac) D: John Woo C: Chow Yun Fat, Leslie Cheung, Ti Lung, Waise Lee, Emily Chu

If action cinema were a professional sports team, this film would be referred to as "the franchise." Its blend of relentless machismo, heartfelt emotion, and pulse-racing gun-play essentially created the cinematic genre referred to by fans as "heroic bloodshed," while setting box office records in Asia and inspiring legions of Chow Yun Fat wannabes. Old-school Shaw star Ti Lung plays Ho, a noble gangster working for a counterfeiting syndicate alongside his best pal Mark Gor (Chow) and an ambitious newcomer named Shing (Lee). When the gang is busted, Ho takes the fall out of loyalty to his boss. During Ho's years in prison, his younger brother Kit—a police officer—finds himself blocked from promotion due to his connection to a convicted felon; when Ho is released, Kit rejects his conciliatory overtures. Meanwhile, Mark, crippled in the police raid, is now homeless, and eking out a pathetic existence, while Shing has become the syndicate's boss. Ho, who has discovered that Shing was responsible for betraying the gang to the police, enlists Mark in a mission to obtain revenge. Reviewers called it "unforgettable," a "career-making masterpiece for its creators and cast"; despite its "now-cliché elements" and its "heavy dosage of melodrama," it "ages like wine." Followed by two sequels—one starring Chow as Mark's "twin brother" Ken, the other a prequel showing Mark's early gunslinging days, directed by Tsui Hark.

### Black Cannon Incident (1985; Mainland, Dr) D: Huang Jianxin C: Liu Zifeng, Ming Gao, Gerhard Olschewski, Zhao Shuxin

This debut feature by maverick Fifth Generation filmmaker Huang Jianxin is a dark comedy about a mild-mannered engineer who finds himself under political investigation after he sends an innocent telegram referring to a "lost black cannon." Narrow-minded party officials don't believe that the engineer is referring to a Chinese chesspiece. The ensuing chaos causes the engineer's important project to go off schedule, and finally, to end in disaster. Reviewers compared the lead, Liu Zifeng, to a "Chinese Woody Allen," and called the film "incredibly inventive"; "filmmaking firing on all cylinders." Followed by a sequel, Dislocation (1986).

### Boat People (1982; Hong Kong, Dr) D: Ann Hui C: George Lam, Season Ma, Cora Miao, Andy Lau

In this "affecting" and "powerful" drama by Hong Kong New Waver Ann Hui, George Lam plays a Japanese photojournalist assigned to investigate the condition of Vietnam after the war. The communist government brings him on an official tour, showcasing a happy populace. Determined to uncover the real story, Lam connects with Cora Miao's jaded bar girl and a young man desperate to escape the country's dire poverty (a very young Andy Lau in his acting debut). Sympathy drives him to help a pair of young orphans, with tragic results. Reviewers called it a "powerful document of its time," and noted that its commercial and critical success made it an object of "intense political scrutiny," with many suggesting that Vietnam was merely an allegorical stand-in for the Mainland.

### Chinese Ghost Story, A (1987; Hong Kong, Dr, Hr, Pd) D: Ching Siu Tung C: Leslie Cheung, Joey Wang, Wu Ma, Lau Siu Ming, Sit Chi Lun

In this vision of forbidden love between the quick and the dead, Leslie Cheung plays an imperial tax agent whose kindheartedness makes him rather inept at his job. Strapped for cash, he decides to spend the night in an abandoned temple. The only living being for miles appears to be a bizarre adventurer (Wu). Then Cheung encounters the lovely Joey Wang, only to discover that she *isn't* a living being, but a ghost-maiden enslaved to a soul-eating tree demon. Determined to free her from the demon's clutches, Cheung enlists Wu's help in a quest that takes them to hell and beyond. Reviewers lauded its "moody, lusciously crafted" atmosphere, and notes that the leads are "perfectly cast," especially Wang, who "thankfully, doesn't really have to act." "A classic." Followed by two equally impressive sequels, the last of which features Tony Leung Chiu Wai; Joey Wang is the lovely thread that binds all three together. (Wang would go on to make numerous other appearances as a maiden of supernatural origin, including 1988's superior *Portrait of a Nymph* and 1989's *The Reincarnation of Golden Lotus*.)

### City of Sadness, A (1989; Taiwan, Dr) D: Hou Hsiao-hsien C: Tony Leung Chiu Wai, Shin Shu-fen, Li Tian-lu, Jack Kao, Ikuyo Nakamura

This film examines the KMT takeover of Taiwan from the viewpoint of the Taiwanese, who were freed of a half-century of Japanese colonization, only to be occupied once more by Nationalist forces retreating from the Mainland. On February 28, 1947, the KMT engaged in a massacre of natives, whose subsequent riots triggered the bloody and repressive onset of martial law. The events surrounding this climactic period in the island's history—memorialized by Taiwanese activists as *Er Er Ba*, "Two Two Eight"—are viewed through the eyes of members of the Lin clan, a Taiwanese family that struggles to adapt and survive in an increasingly oppressive environment. Reviewers called it an "elliptical and impressionistic portrait" by one of the most "profoundly original auteurs in contemporary cinema." *City of Sadness*, which won the Golden Lion at the 1989 Venice Film Festival, was the first Taiwanese film to be shot in synch sound.

**City on Fire** (1987; Hong Kong, Ac) D: Ringo Lam C: Chow Yun Fat, Danny Lee, Suhn Yueh, Roy Cheung, Kong Lau

This film—a portrait of male bonding and betrayal that served as the template for Quentin Tarantino's indie phenom *Reservoir Dogs*—features Chow Yun Fat as an undercover policeman assigned to infiltrate a Triad gang, who must choose between his duty and his friendship with a young thug played by Danny Lee. Reviewers called it "gritty and realistic," with a "wrenching climax."

**Club, The** (1981; Hong Kong, Ac) D: Kirk Wong C: Michael Chan, Norman Tsui, Kent Cheng, Phillip Ko

This grim thriller, starring acknowledged former gangster Michael Chan, effectively launched the era of the contemporary Triad movie. Chan plays Sai, a thug assigned to guard a hostess club owned by his boss and coveted by a number of rivals. After his boss is eliminated in a horrific mob execution, the war over the club becomes increasingly bloody. Viewers applauded lead actor Chan's "striking presence" and called it a "true classic" that "should be seen at least once," even if "its look and feel are painfully dated."

**Coast of Departure, The** (1987; Taiwan, Dr, Ac) D: Wan Jen C: You An-shung, Yuan Jie-ying, Wang Yu-wen, Hsu Le-mei

This bleak thriller by one of the lesser-known lights of the New Taiwanese Cinema tells the story of Ah-chen, a young man who has just been released from a prison sentence for accidental manslaughter. Attempting to set his life straight, he finds a job as a waiter, but soon becomes romantically involved with Hsiao-huei, a pretty but troubled prostitute. Ah-chen convinces her to quit her job and give up drugs, and the two move in together, enjoying momentary peace before one of Ah-chen's old prison friends shows up on their doorstep. Events soon spiral out of control. Reviewers called it a "mesmerizing achievement," "black with despair."

**Dangerous Encounter—1st Kind** (1980; Hong Kong, Ac) D: Tsui Hark C: Lin Ching Chi, Lo Lieh, Tse Bo Law, Lung Tin Sang, Au Siu Keung

This early actioner by Tsui is shot through with electric streaks of black humor and out-and-out nihilism. Lin Ching Chi plays a young woman with an unsettlingly sadistic personality (her character is introduced with a few sequences of all-too-real animal torture); when she happens to see a trio of teenagers commit a hit and run, she blackmails them into serving as her apprentices in an escalating orgy of mayhem. Reviewers found it "exciting and disturbing"—a "low-budget testicle-shrinker" that sends "blood flowing down the gutters."

### Dead And The Deadly, The (1983; Hong Kong, Hr) D: Wu Ma C: Sammo Hung, Cherie Chung, Wu Ma, Lam Ching Ying, Chung Fat

A stingy hustler named Ma (played by Wu Ma) comes up with a scheme to fake his demise so as to sell the heirloom antiques that would be buried with his corpse. He pulls two equally unscrupulous friends into the plot—but when they discover that Ma's wife would receive an inheritance dwarfing the amount Ma is paying, they decide to make his death permanent. The enraged ghost of Ma then haunts his goodhearted if cowardly friend Fatboy (director Hung) until the latter agrees to assist him in gaining revenge: Fatboy, a sorcerer in training, allows Ma's spirit to possess his body—but warns Ma that if he doesn't leave before dawn, Fatboy will die himself. Ma ignores the warning and Fatboy finds himself trapped without a body, leading his Taoist master (played here, as in dozens of other films, by Lam) and his girlfriend (Chung) to go to drastic lengths to save him before he's dragged into the underworld. Despite its rather "cornball, lowbrow humor," it's "campy fun" for those seeking a "competent B-movie." Along with Hung's *Encounter of the Spooky Kind* (1981) and Ann Hui's *The Spooky Bunch* (1980), this film launched the "comic horror" wave of the early eighties.

### Dragons Forever (1988; Hong Kong, Ac) D: Sammo Hung C: Jackie Chan, Sammo Hung, Yuen Biao, Yuen Wah, Deanie Yip

The last, and in some ways the most interesting collaboration between the "Three Brothers," Jackie Chan, Sammo Hung, and Yuen Biao; all three are cast in unusual and not all that sympathetic roles—Chan as a dodgy lawyer, Hung as a freelance weapons salesman, and Yuen as a freelance surveillance expert with a paranoid schizophrenic streak. Reviewers called it "occasionally silly" but "marvelously entertaining," and said it "sets a new standard for fight choreography."

**Dreadnaught** (1981; Hong Kong, Ac, Pd) D: Yuen Woo Ping C: Yuen Biao, Leung Kar Yan, Kwan Tak Hing, Yuen Shun Yee, Lily Li

This film represents the last time that veteran actor Kwan Tak Hing essayed the role of Chinese culture hero Wong Fei Hung, a character he played to great success in nearly a hundred movies during the early years of Hong Kong cinema. Yuen Biao plays Mousey, a mild-mannered young fellow who accidentally incurs the wrath of White Tiger (Yuen Shun Yee), a murderous martial artist who has hidden from the law by joining a traveling opera troupe. Fortunately for Mousey, his friend Leung Foon (Leung Kar Yan) is the apprentice of the great Wong Fei Hung. Reviewers called it "a novel standout," mostly due to seventy-year-old Kwan's "unexpected grace and agility" and some terrific fight sequences staged by director Yuen Woo Ping.

**Dust in the Wind** (1986; Taiwan, Dr) D: Hou Hsiao-hsien C: Xin Shufen, Wang Jingwen, Li Tian-lu

Ah-yuan and Ah-yun are childhood friends, a boy and girl who together move from the countryside to bustling Taipei to find work. Neither has enough money to complete their education, and their families rely on them for support. Slowly, their friendship begins to evolve toward romance, until Ah-yuan is drafted into the military. Before he leaves, Ah-yun gives him 1,096 envelopes, already stamped and addressed, telling him that he must write her a letter a day. But after he sends his last letter—telling Ah-yun that he's coming home—he finds out that Ah-yun has taken up with the man who has been delivering his letters to her. One reviewer called the final scene of the movie "the best I've ever seen in my entire life"; another praised it as "poignant and profound," but warned that the movie moves at "glacial" speed.

**Eight Diagram Pole Fighter, The** (1984; Hong Kong, Ac, Pd) D: Lau Kar Leung C: Gordon Lau, Kara Hui, Alexander Fu Sheng, Lily Li, Ku Ming, Lau Kar Fai

A bleak, brutal old-school epic that served as the cinematic epitaph of Shaw Brothers star Alexander Fu Sheng, killed in a tragic accident while this film was still in production. Fu Sheng and Lau Kar Fai play brothers of the Yang family, which has been betrayed in battle, with all of the other men in the family slain. After witnessing the massacre, Fu has lost his mind, and is no longer capable of even taking care of himself. Lau, meanwhile, has lost the ability to feel anything but a desire for revenge. He joins a Buddhist temple, but soon becomes a problem for the brothers there, who point out to Lau that the only reason they practice pole-fighting is to defend themselves against mountain wolves, and even then, rather than killing them, they "defang" them. Lau and Fu's mother sends Kara Hui, playing Lau and Fu's sister, to retrieve her prodigal son, but she is captured by the same killers who slew the family's men. When Lau hears the news, he heads out to rescue her. The bloody climax, which takes place on a literal pile of coffins, has Lau on the verge of being overwhelmed, until the brothers of the temple show up to assist him in "defanging the wolves." "Brilliant fights, with a stark, cruel violence rarely seen in Lau's work," say reviewers. "The darkness throughout this film may be related to Fu Sheng's unexpected death."

### God of Gamblers (1989; Hong Kong, Ac, Dr) D: Wong Jing C: Chow Yun Fat, Andy Lau, Joey Wang, Cheung Man, Charles Heung

In an iconic role that launched a legion of imitators, Chow plays Ko Chun, the world's greatest gambler, who regresses to a childlike state after being struck on the head by a rock. He is discovered by a down-and-out couple played by Lau and Wong, and his incredible abilities lead them into dreams of wealth and luxury. But unbeknownst to the amnesiac Ko, his former associate Yee has begun to take over his former boss's empire—even moving in on his mourning girlfriend. Reviewers called this a "classic tale" full of "surprising plot twists" and "terrific action, of both the gunslinging and gambling-showdown variety." Followed by a pair of hilariously entertaining sequels starring Stephen Chiau that combined his *All for the Winners* character with the *God of Gamblers* legend; both Chiau vehicles were moved "out of canon" when Chow Yun Fat came back for the mediocre "true sequel" *The God of Gamblers' Return* (1994), which was in turn followed by a prequel starring Leon Lai as Ko Chun, *God of Gamblers 3: The Early Stage* (1996).

### Hibiscus Town (1986; Mainland, Dr) D: Xie Jin C: Liu Xiaoqing, Xu Songzi, Jiang Wen, Zhang Guangbei, Zhu Shibin

Town beauty Hu Yuyin and her husband Guigui open a small but successful bean curd shop, which soon allows them to save enough for a new house. This, however, draws the jealous attention of a local bureaucrat named Li, who accuses them of being "rich peasants" as the Cultural Revolution begins to rise. The house is confiscated, Guigui is driven to kill himself, and Hu sentenced to a demeaning street-cleaning job. Her assigned partner is a man named Qin Shutian, whom others refer to as Madman Qin. Despite his nickname, he is actually a kind and supportive individual who helps Hu with her difficult menial labor. They fall in love, and Hu becomes pregnant; Hu's pregnancy is declared a criminal act by the town's party representative. Qin is sentenced to ten years in prison, and Hu almost dies when she has to give birth to her baby alone. After Qin is freed, he returns to Hibiscus Town and finds Hu and their child. They open a new bean curd shop together. Reviewers call it a "powerful reexamination of the suffering experienced during the Cultural Revolution."

### Homecoming (1984; Hong Kong, Dr) D: Yim Ho C: Josephine Koo, Siqin Gaowa, Zhou Yun, Zhang Jugao

Making her screen debut in this Hong Kong–Mainland coproduction, Koo plays Coral Zhang, a businesswoman who has traveled back to her home village to visit the grave of her recently deceased grandmother. There she meets childhood friend Pearl (Siquin), who has lived in the small town all her life, marrying and becoming headmistress at the local school. Coral envies Pearl's peace in her simple life, but soon realizes that Pearl has similar feelings about Coral's cosmopolitan existence. Reviewers called this "Yim's most successful work"; "a perceptive, beautifully scored drama."

### In Our Time (1982; Taiwan, Dr) D: Tao De-chen, Edward Yang C: Laan Sheng-wen, Anni Shi, Sylvia Chang, Li Liqun

This omnibus film, featuring short works by four directors, including Tao De-chen, Edward Yang, Ko I-cheng, and Chang Yi, was essentially the opening chapter in what would become the New Taiwanese Cinema. The first segment, directed by Tao, is entitled "Dinosaurs": Set in the sixties, it concerns an introverted boy named Mao who lives in his own fantasy world. The second segment, directed by Yang and entitled "Desires," follows a young girl named Feng as she develops a crush on a boarder at her family's house, but her puppy love is shattered when she finds out that her older sister and the tenant are already having an affair. The third segment, directed by Ko, is called "Leap Frog," and concerns a university student named Du who feels unanchored and adrift, until he finds his focus in competitive swimming. Finally, the fourth segment, directed by Chang, is called "Show Your I.D." A blackly humorous examination of the perils of losing your identity, it follows a young couple as they move into a new flat, and the wife begins a new job. Because the wife does not yet have her ID card, she finds herself unable to gain admittance to her workplace, while at home, her unemployed husband is mistaken for a burglar and beaten by their neighbors. Reviewers called it a "seminal work" that "clearly establishes the fresh vision of a new, humanist generation of Taiwanese filmmakers."

## *Ju Dou* (1989; Mainland, Dr) D: Zhang Yimou C: Gong Li, Li Baotian, Li Wei

Yang Jinshan, the cruel owner of a silk-dyeing factory, purchases a young and beautiful wife named Ju Dou (Gong Li), hoping that she can bear him an heir; however, because Yang is impotent, he turns to torturing her as a way of sublimating his frustration. Ju Dou's terrible screams evoke the pity of the third leg of the household triangle, Yang's nephew Tianqing, who begins to peep in on his uncle's abusive nocturnal activities, first out of sympathy, and then out of growing sexual excitement. Eventually, Ju Dou and Tianqing begin a furtive affair, which leads to Ju Dou becoming pregnant. At first, Yang is excited by the birth of his long-awaited heir, Tianbai, until he is confronted with the reality of Tianbai's parentage. Rage causes Yang to have a stroke and become a quadriplegic, allowing the lovers to cavort openly before him. However, this has a damaging psychic effect on Tianbai, who sees their passion as a betrayal of the man he thinks is his father, with tragic consequences. Reviewers called this "disturbing," "heartfelt," and "one of the decade's most provocative pieces of cinema."

## *Killer, The* (1989; Hong Kong, Ac) D: John Woo C: Chow Yun Fat, Danny Lee, Sally Yeh, Paul Chu, Kenneth Tsang

This classic cop-versus-noble-hitman actioner was Woo's first work to hit American arthouses, and effectively converted him from an obscure cult figure into an acclaimed "action auteur." Chow Yun Fat plays one of his many signature roles as Jeff, a mob assassin who is ready to retire from his life of bloodshed, but accidentally blinds a young cabaret singer named Jenny while completing his final hit. Struck by guilt, Jeff decides to take on one last assignment in order to pay for corneal transplant surgery that will restore Jenny's vision. But this last job may be one too many: Triad boss Johnny Weng (Shing) has secretly set Jeff up to be killed, to cut off any possible trail of evidence. Although Jeff is too good at what he does to die from such a simple trap, the incident leads him to suspect that the heat is on, and indeed, it is. Obsessed supercop Inspector Li (Lee) is on Jeff's trail, and soon manages to actually confront the assassin, face to face and gun to gun, in a comical scene at Jeff and Jenny's apartment (blind Jenny has no idea that the two are millimeters away from killing each other, and offers to make them tea!). As Li continues to stalk his prey, he becomes increasingly admiring of him, developing a bond of respect that is cemented when the two find themselves both targeted by Weng's killers. The climactic final battle, Li and Jeff against what seems to be the army of an entire third-world nation, is an impossible, incredible, indefinable slow-motion ballet of flying lead, splashing blood, and acrobatic leaps, tumbles, and falls, with "a wrenching emotional payload" that has "few equals in contemporary cinema"; "perhaps Woo's finest achievement, and by extension, one of the finest action films ever."

### King of the Children (1987; Mainland, Dr) D: Chen Kaige C: Xie Yuan, Yang Xuewen, Chen Shaohua, Zhang Caimei, Xu Gouqing

This film, set during the Cultural Revolution, follows Lao Gan, a young teacher (in rural idiom, "king of children"), to his first posting at a rural village; there he faithfully executes the lesson plans given to him by the central directorate, which consist of repetitive copying of political slogans. When Wang Fu, the school's brightest student, finally accuses him of not knowing how to teach, Lao Gan changes his style—taking his students out of the classroom and into the great outdoors. This naturalistic way of teaching soon sparks the ire of the authorities, and he is asked to resign—but in the process, has truly become the "king of the children." Reviewers called it "odd, ambitious, and beautifully shot"; "for all of its philosophy and allegory, ultimately a tedious exercise."

### Kuei-mei, a Woman (1985; Taiwan, Dr) D: Chang Yi C: Yang Hui-shan, Li Liqun

Kuei-mei, a refugee from the Mainland whose fiancé was killed during China's civil war, arrives in Taiwan at the invitation of a cousin, but soon realizes that she must find her own way in life. She accepts an arranged marriage to a restaurant worker who already has three children; soon after, she gives birth to twins of her own. But her match is far from a happy one, as her husband turns out to be a drunkard, a gambler, and an adulterer to boot. The story follows Kuei-mei's life until her death in her sixties from cancer, showing her strength and toughness in the face of repeated difficulties; reviewers called it "perhaps the most powerful portrait of the Taiwanese woman's experience." Dissenters suggest that this film merely "valorizes women's suffering."

### *Law With Two Phases* (1984; Hong Kong, Ac) D: Wong Siu Man C: Danny Lee, Eddie Chan, Parkman Wong, Tai Po

This gritty policier is the film that made Danny Lee a star. Here he plays a cop known only as B, who has been assigned to break in a new partner named Kit (Chan). Although their differences initially lead to tension—to B, the end always justifies the means, while Kit is a fresh-faced, by-the-book rookie—they eventually grow to become close friends. When a misjudgment by B leads Kit to be shot and killed, B descends into a spiral of doubt and emotional turmoil. Reviewers called it "efficient" and "consistently interesting."

### *Long Arm of the Law* (1984; Hong Kong, Ac) D: Johnny Mak C: Lam Wai, Huang Jian, Jiang Lung, Chen Jing, Shum Wai

This film of a heist gone wrong stars a cast almost entirely composed of first-time actors, lending a "remarkable sense of authenticity" to the proceedings. A group of former Red Guards plans a "Big Circle" caper, which involves slipping into Hong Kong, committing a lucrative robbery, then bolting back to the Mainland to escape prosecution. However, things begin to go wrong at the outset, when the gang shows up at the jewelry store they intend to knock over and discover that it is already being robbed. The gang escapes, killing a cop in the process, then comes up with the brilliant idea of waiting for the heat to die down and committing the crime anyway, figuring that no one will expect the place to get robbed twice. Reviewers called this critical and commercial hit "both enormously entertaining and artistically original"; "a true classic that culminates in one of the greatest showdowns in action cinema history." Followed by two unrelated sequels, of which only the last is worth hunting down.

### Miracle Fighters, The (1982; Hong Kong, Ac) D: Yuen Woo Ping C: Leung Kar Yan, Eddy Ko, Yuen Hsun Yee, Yuen Cheung Yan

This "Yuen Clan" outing is nominally set during the Ching Dynasty, with Kao, an upstanding Manchu general, finding himself marginalized in a court full of magicians and corrupt eunuchs. When he dares to marry a Han (Chinese) woman, the chief eunuch gives him two options: kill her immediately or be executed himself for treason. His choice is to attack the uppity eunuch with his sword, but his attack is halted by the appearance of Evil Sorcerer Bat, who unleashes a monster on Kao—the "Urn Man," who could be charitably described as a killer clown in a jar. The plot only degenerates from here, but by the time of the film reaches its climax, audiences will be treated to a fighting stick figure, a barber/beautician assassin in drag, flying drillbits, acrobatic cheerleader demons, killer midgets, and, of course, the triumphant return of Urn Man, most of which makes little sense but shows tremendous creativity. Reviewers called it "jaw-dropping," and "completely entertaining, if you suspend all disbelief, taste, and judgment."

### Mr. Vampire (1985; Hong Kong, Hr, Cm, Pd) D: Ricky Lau C: Ricky Hui, Chin Siu Ho, Lam Ching Ying, Moon Lee, Billy Lau

This genre-launching horror-farce features youngest Hui Brother Ricky as Man Choi, apprentice to a Taoist priest played, in a career-defining role, by Lam Ching Ying. The priest has been summoned to discover why a wealthy merchant clan has been experiencing two decades of misfortune, and quickly realizes that a malicious feng shui expert improperly buried the clan's deceased patriarch twenty years earlier; he has the corpse disinterred, and noticing that it has not decomposed, he prepares for the inevitable supernatural complications. That evening, the corpse rises as a *gyonsi,* or "hopping vampire," and proceeds to kill his own son, who also becomes a vampire. The priest fights off the latter, but the former manages to bite Man Choi, who finds himself infected with creeping *gyonsi*-ism. Meanwhile, the priest's other assistant (Chin) has his own supernatural problems: A beautiful girl-ghost (Lee) has fallen in love with him, and wants him to join her on the "other side." *Mr. Vampire* launched a genre that lasted into the early nineties, giving rise to such bizarre variations as kiddie *gyonsi,* chemically enhanced mutant *gyonsi,* and even *gyonsi* prostitutes. "You could die laughing," say reviewers, who call it a "silly classic" that "far outshines its many imitations."

***My Lucky Stars*** (1985; Hong Kong, Cm) D: Sammo Hung C: Sammo Hung, Sibelle Hu, Richard Ng, Eric Tsang, Charlie Chin

In this successful followup to the unexpected hit *Winners and Sinners* (1983), Chan and Yuen play undercover cops Muscles and Ricky, while Hung, Ng, Tsang, and Taiwanese hunk Charlie Chin play a motley crew of rascals who grew up in the same orphanage as Muscles. When Ricky is captured by a cop-turned–criminal kingpin and Muscles is forced to go fugitive, it's up to the "Lucky Stars" to save them both. Reviewers called this "fast-paced action comedy" "less than the sum of its parts," although the girl-on-girl fighting scene between Sibelle Hu and Michiko Nishiwaki is "not to be missed."

***My Young Auntie*** (1981; Hong Kong, Ac, Cm) D: Lau Kar Leung C: Lau Kar Leung, Kara Hui Ying Hung, Hsiao Hou, Johnny Wang, Gordon Lau

A young widow named Tai Nan (Hui) travels to Guangdong to meet with cousin-in-law Ching Chuen (director Lau), bearing the will that names him as her husband's heir. There she meets Ching's son Charlie (Hsiao), a modern boy infatuated with all things Western. Although the two are about the same age, Tai is deeply traditional and somewhat appalled at Charlie's impudent and jazzy attitude. Still, she allows him to take her out on the town to see how the "other half lives," and soon starts to appreciate the boy's joie de vivre. But then Yung Sheng, her late husband's cruel and greedy brother, hears how his hated sibling has snubbed him in favor of Ching; he immediately sends some of his men to break into Ching's house and steal the title documents to all of the extended family's property. Only Tai and Charlie, the two best martial artists of the family, can successfully get them back—and only if they work together. An "incredible showcase for the beauty and talent of Kara Hui Ying Hung," and a "refreshing, lighthearted masterpiece that will have you seeing Lau Kar Leung in a whole new light," say reviewers.

***Narrow Street*** (1981; Mainland, Dr) D: Yang Yanjin C: Guo Kaimin, Zhang Yu

This experimental film is told through an interwoven series of interviews and flashbacks, in which the picture's protagonist—a blind man named Xia—reminisces about Yu, a girl he'd met all too briefly during the Cultural Revolution. Ten years later, after looking for Yu everywhere, he is resigned to having lost her for good; he and the interviewer consider the poor girl's possible fates. Finally Xia takes his leave and departs; on the train, Xia hears a familiar voice—and realizes that it is the one he has been waiting to hear for an entire decade. Reviewers called it "a simple story told in the most complex of fashions," with "sometimes puzzling continuity." However, they also call it a "striking, both visually and conceptually."

### *Old Well* (1987; Mainland, Dr) D: Wu Tianming C: Zhang Yimou, Liang Yujin, Lu Liping

Zhang Yimou starred in and shot this tale of a mountain village called Old Well, whose source of water has gradually dried up, over the generations, putting the village at risk of dissolution. Sun Wangquan (Zhang) is one of the few educated boys in town, and as such is an important part of the community's search for a new supply of potable water. Although he has long had a mutual affinity for his former classmate Qiaoying, his family marries him off to a young widow with a sizable dowry instead. As he and Qiaoying lead a group to explore some local caves, they find themselves trapped underground, just as they've discovered the water everyone's been looking for. Believing themselves doomed, the two young people admit their feelings for each other, leading to an awkward situation when they're finally rescued. Reviewers called this film, winner of multiple awards at international festivals, a "celebration of the needs of the collective outweighing the desires of the individual," and praise Zhang's "underplayed, naturalistic performance."

### *On the Hunting Ground* (1985; Mainland, Dr) D: Tian Zhuangzhuang C: Autegen Bayaer, Laxi, Bayanertu

A "challenging" experimental film by the Fifth Generation's most controversial director. Tian made this exploration of the lives of Mongol tribesmen at the invitation of the Inner Mongolia Film Studio. Although the original script he was given was a focused, complex story of rivalry and jealousy, Tian essentially threw it away and made a film that has no real story, shot with documentary precision using real tribesmen as his actors. The movie focuses on Wangsen, a hunter accused of poaching game against the rigid code of hunting ethics laid down by Genghis Khan, who must thus accept a suitable punishment—to be beaten by his mother.

The herders and hunters he cast were delighted at his work, telling him it was a highly accurate portrait of their lives, but the local authorities were extremely upset—declaring that the film cast a bad light on Mongolians by portraying them as poor and backward. Perhaps more critically for Tian's immediate career, the film was dubbed cryptic and unwatchable, and effectively went unreleased. (Tian would later say that this film and its similar followup, *The Horse Thief,* were films made for the "next century," to which a film official then retorted that that was when Tian could pick up his paycheck.) Reviewers called this "a film that almost dares you to stop viewing," but "truly beautiful in its pastoral setting, and mesmerizing if given the chance."

### *One and Eight* (1984; Mainland, Dr) D: Zhang Junzhao C: Tao Zeru, Chen Doming, Lu Xiaoyan, Xie Yuan

This film and Chen Kaige's *Yellow Earth* (1986) essentially served as the beachhead for the movement later dubbed the Fifth Generation. Shot by classmate Zhang Yimou, *One and Eight* is a war movie about a cordon of nine condemned criminals—eight of whom are clearly guilty, and one of whom is a wrongly accused Communist official. As they're being escorted to their execution during the Sino-Japanese War, they and their guards are surrounded by enemy troops; the guards briefly consider killing them to get them out of the way, then decide to let them fight for their lives instead. The "one and eight" end up showing tremendous bravery, with the film's final frames dominated by the alleged traitor, the "one," bearing one of his wounded former captors on his shoulders. Reviewers lauded its "bravura visual style" and "theatrical touches," celebrating it as an "obvious cinematic breakthrough." They also noted that the film experienced real troubles with censors, who required over seventy cuts and delayed the picture's release for two years—something that would become a pattern for Fifth Generation works.

### *Osmanthus Alley* (1987; Taiwan, Dr) D: Chen Kun-hou C: Lu Hsiao-fen, Lin Hsiu-ling, Simon Yam, Emil Chow

According to a fortuneteller's reading, young Ti-hung (Lu) is destined for a tragic life. By the time she is twelve, she finds herself orphaned, and by the time she is sixteen, her younger brother has also died in a tragic drowning. Although a handsome young fisherman named Chiang-hai courts her, she is not willing to tie herself to a life of poverty, and she rebuffs him. Her great assets are her nimble fingers, with which she creates beautiful embroidery, and her tiny "lotus feet," cruelly bound since was a young girl. These make her a prize despite her sad history, and she marries into a wealthy family; unfortunately, her husband dies when she is just twenty-three, leaving her alone in a household where her status is uncertain. By the time she reaches her sunset years, she understands the true nature of her tragedy, which is that despite all of the turmoil she has overcome, she will die alone. Reviewers called this adaptation of a historical novel by Hsiao Li-hung a "stylized drama" that "traces the emergence of modern Taiwan through its protagonist"; a "tour-de-force" for lead actress Lu Hsiao-fen.

***Painted Faces*** (1988; Hong Kong, Dr) D: Alex Law C: Sammo Hung, Cheng Pei Pei, Lam Ching Ying, John Sham, Wu Ma

This film is a slightly fictionalized telling of the childhood history of some of Hong Kong cinema's greatest talents—notably, Sammo Hung, Yuen Biao, and Jackie Chan, who grew up together in the harsh environment of Yu Jim Yuen's Beijing Opera academy. Hung plays his own former master here, winning Best Actor at the Hong Kong Film Awards for his tough but sensitive turn (which, by all accounts, was an extremely forgiving depiction of Sifu Yu!); his students are played by a group of unknown child actors, selected for acrobatic skills and remarkable physical resemblance to their real-life counterparts "Big Nose," "Biao," and "Sam-mo." The movie follows this trio of young performers as they undergo their harsh training and engage in youthful hijinks, but the story is really about the waning days of Beijing Opera itself, which was being replaced as a popular medium by the motion picture. Reviewers called this film, one of the only coproductions between bitter rivals Shaw Brothers and Golden Harvest, a "deeply touching drama" that serves as a "remarkable debut" for director Law. "Every aspect of this production is phenomenal," which explains its avalanche of awards at film festivals throughout Asia.

***Papa, Can You Hear Me Sing?*** (1983; Taiwan, Dr) D: Yu Kan-ping C: Suhn Yueh, Liu Ruiqi, Jiang Hsia, Li Liqun

A retired soldier, struck mute by a wartime injury and now supporting himself as a junk collector, finds an infant girl abandoned on a trash heap. He brings her home and names her Mei, but his impulsive decision infuriates his wife, who leaves him. With the support of his friendly neighbors, the soldier brings Mei up on his own, entertaining her with music since he is unable to speak. Mei turns out to have a gift for singing, and is recruited out of high school to become a popular singer. While Mei is on tour, the old soldier languishes at home alone, listening to Mei's songs on the radio, until a neighbor hears Mei dedicating a tribute melody to her father and calls in, begging for her to return. Years later, the mute dies of old age, with Mei's lovely voice the last sound he hears. Viewers called it "sad but beautiful."

### *Peking Opera Blues* (1986; Hong Kong, Dr, Cm) D: Tsui Hark C: Brigitte Lin, Sally Yeh, Cherie Chung, Mark Cheng, Kenneth Tsang

In 1913, China is in turmoil, as warlords battle for control of Beijing, and revolutionaries huddle in darkened rooms to plot the overthrow of imperial rule. Against this setting, three of the greatest Hong Kong actresses of the mid-eighties play out an inventive comic tango of conspiracy, mistaken identity, and female bonding. Sheung Hung (Chung) is a singsong girl with material ambitions; Pat Neil (Yeh) is an opera veteran's daughter, who's dreamed all of her life of appearing on a stage restricted to men; and Tsao Wan (Lin) is the daughter of the local warlord, who is willing to betray her father for the sake of China. Snow would have to fall in summertime before each of their dreams come true. The three women cross paths, cross swords, and even cross-dress, as they seek to fulfill their individual objectives. Sheung gets her riches. Pat stars on stage. Tsao Wan betrays her father and saves her nation. And in the middle of the summer, it begins to snow. Reviewers called this film a "landmark that must be seen," a work of "vertiginous excitement"; "every performance is outstanding, and every aspect of the film, from story to soundtrack, remarkable." "The final rooftop fight is a pause-rewind-and-play-again masterpiece."

### *Police Story* (1985; Hong Kong, Ac, Cm) D: Jackie Chan C: Jackie Chan, Maggie Cheung, Brigitte Lin, Chor Yuen, Bill Tung

This landmark film was Jackie Chan's first contemporary martial arts film, and the first to cast him in the role of "supercop" Chan Ka Kui. It throws viewers into a whirlwind of jaw-dropping action from its opening, an incredible, "ecstatic" sequence which represents fifteen minutes of Chan's most inventive and eye-opening stuntwork—with ample thrills to come. After locking mob boss Chu Tu away, Chan is assigned to babysit the one witness who can ensure he gets sent to prison for good: Chu's gorgeous secretary Salina Fong (Lin). Chan's jealous girl-friend May (Cheung) reacts poorly to the news of his new duty, but not as badly as Chu, who orders a corrupt cop to kill both Fong and her reluctant bodyguard. Reviewers called this movie a "nonstop thrill ride" with "truly amazing stunts." "You'll see more breaking glass in this film than you'll ever see anywhere." Fol-lowed by two equally incredible sequels, *Police Story II* and *Police Story III: Super-cop,* the latter of which reintroduced Michelle Yeoh to action fans everywhere.

### Prison on Fire (1987; Hong Kong, Ac) D: Ringo Lam C: Chow Yun Fat, Tony Leung Kar Fai, Roy Cheung, William Ho, Tommy Wong

Lo Ka Yiu (Leung) is the "new fish" at a prison run by the nefarious "Scarface" Hung (Cheung), who rules the institution with an iron fist and a perpetual sneer. Clearly unprepared for the experience, Lo immediately starts off on the wrong foot by demonstrating both anxiety and a stiff, by-the-rules attitude that alienates both the corrupt guards and the entrenched Triad hierarchy. Luckily, "Mad Dog" Ching (Chow), an easygoing veteran convict, takes Lo under his wing. Reviewers called it "not just a great prison movie, but a truly great movie movie"; "a tense, under-stated melodrama" that's "Hong Kong's answer to *Cool Hand Luke.*" Ringo Lam won Best Director at the Hong Kong Film Awards for this picture. Followed by a lesser, but watchable sequel, *Prison on Fire II.*

### Project A (1983; Hong Kong, Ac, Cm) D: Jackie Chan C: Jackie Chan, Sammo Hung, Yuen Biao, Dick Wei, Tai Po

This film represented a milestone for director and star Jackie Chan in several ways. It was his first film set in an urban, twentieth-century setting (albeit the very begin-ning of the twentieth century); it was his first to showcase Jackie alongside his "Big" and "Little" brothers, Sammo Hung and Yuen Biao; and it was the first to fea-ture the "superstunts" that would eventually become his signature. Chan plays Sergeant Dragon Ma, an officer in the Hong Kong Coast Guard, which has been tasked with apprehending a gang of pirates. Despite Ma's best efforts, a double agent has been tipping off the cutthroats, allowing them to continually evade the Coast Guard's grasp. Frustrated with Ma's repeated failures, the British governor demotes him, forcing him and his men to report to the stone-faced head of the land police, Captain Chi (Kwan Hoi Shan) and his stiff-necked son Inspector Tzi (Yuen). Ma's unorthodox crime-fighting techniques have long been a source of irritation for the father-and-son duo, who are delighted to finally have the sergeant under their control. Faced with further career embarrassment, Ma turns in his badge and goes freelance, hunting down the raiders with the assistance of his shifty old friend Fei (Hung). As they close in on the pirate headquarters, they're joined by Tzi and the joint land and sea police forces, who have finally set aside their differences in order to battle the common enemy. Reviewers called it "constantly entertaining," with "one of the best scripts of any Chan film." The film's action sequences—like the intricate and mesmerizing back-alley bicycle chase, the knock-down fight between Tzi and Ma's men, and of course, the notorious clock-tower fall—are breathtaking showcases for Chan's inventiveness, humor, and willingness to risk life and limb for the sake of entertainment. "Arguably Chan's all-time best." Followed by a sequel, *Project A II,* that in some ways supersedes the original.

### Red Sorghum (1987; Mainland, Dr) D: Zhang Yimou C: Gong Li, Jiang Wen, Ten Rujun, Ji Cunhua, Liu Jia

The unseen narrator of this debut film by Zhang Yimou is a young man reminiscing about his grandmother's tales of her youth. The grandmother, nicknamed "Nine," since she was born on the ninth day of the ninth month, is played here by twenty-two-year-old Gong Li, also making her screen debut. As the story begins, Nine has been promised in an arranged marriage to a wealthy wine factory owner, and is traveling by palanquin to her new home. Because she has heard that the merchant is a hideously deformed leper, she has taken the precaution of hiding a small pair of scissors in her sleeve, to be used on him, or on herself, as the situation decrees. The bridal caravan is ambushed, but one of the bearers drives the bandits off. The heroic bearer, whom the narrator refers to only as Grandfather, later pulls Nine into a romantic tryst in the sorghum fields that leads to an affair. After the death of her husband, Nine inherits the factory, transforming it into an almost idyllic worker's oasis. All that changes abruptly when the Japanese invade. Reviewers called this first collaboration between Zhang and Li a "voluptuously visual" melodrama that "intoxicates the senses"; the "images and performances are so good you almost forget the film's structural shortcomings."

**_Rouge_** (1988; Hong Kong, Dr) D: Stanley Kwan C: Anita Mui, Leslie Cheung, Alex Man, Emily Chu, Irene Wan

Chan and Fleur are a star-crossed couple living in Hong Kong in the thirties; he's the earnest heir of a wealthy clan, while she's a beautiful "flower girl," or prostitute. Banned from seeing each other by Chan's family, they vow to end their lives together and reunite in the afterlife—but Chan loses heart at the last moment, leaving Fleur to die alone. Fleur is surprised not to see her lover on the other side, and heads back to the mortal plane to find him. But due to the slower passage of time in the spirit world, she arrives on Earth fifty years after her death—and completely lost in the chaotic environment of the eighties. Hoping to place an ad searching for Chan, she shows up at a newspaper classifieds office run by Yuan Ting (Man), but, being a ghost from another century, has no money to pay for the insertion. Knowing no one else in this era, she ends up following Yuan home, and finally explains to him her predicament. He and his journalist girlfriend Chu (Chu) agree to assist her in her search—and find themselves resolving their own relationship problems in the process. Reviewers called it "emotionally captivating" and "beautifully shot": an "essential purchase for anyone's collection."

**_Sandwich Man, The_** (1983; Taiwan, Dr) D: Hou Hsiao-hsien, Wan Jen C: Chen Bocheng, Yang Liyin, Cho Shengli, Jiang Hsia, Jing Ding

This adaptation of three short stories by author Huang Chun-ming features segments created by three different directors. Coming on the heels of the landmark anthology picture _In Our Time_, it established the New Taiwanese Cinema as a legitimate artistic movement, while giving Hou Hsiao-hsien in particular a venue to truly develop his directorial style. The film opens with his segment, "The Sandwich Man." Kunshu is a poor young man who takes a job as a clownish street promoter for a movie theater in order to support his family. He is mocked by passersby and snubbed by friends and relatives, who find his job embarrassing. But when he gets promoted to a position inside the theater and comes home without his clown makeup for the first time, his toddler does not recognize him, and bursts into tears. To his son, Kunshu's "sandwich man" face is his real face. The second segment, directed by Wan Jen (_Super Citizen Ko_), is entitled "Vicki's Hat." Wang Wu-hsiung, having finished his mandatory military enlistment, finds a job as salesman for a line of Japanese-made automatic rice steamers. The company sends him along with a partner, Li Tsai-fa, to a small town on the Taiwan coast. But upon their arrival, Wang and Li find themselves distracted from their original purpose— Wang by a precocious young girl named Vicki, who always wears a tight-fitting school uniform cap, and Li by a telegram that informs him his wife has miscarried and is asking him to come home. The third segment, by Tseng Chuang-hsiang, is called "The Taste of Apples." It follows a young country boy named A-fa who has come to Taipei with his family hoping to find his lucky break; the break comes in a literal sense, when an officer of the United States Army runs him down with his jeep and snaps both of A-fa's legs. Fearing international repercussions, the officer brings him to the military hospital and tells the nurses to treat him like a king. A-fa's wife and children come to visit him and marvel at the posh surroundings he's "earned" with his injury, and A-fa shares with them a gift he's received: crisp Delicious apples. The story and the film end with this symbolic consumption of American fruit. Reviewers called this a "creative milestone"; "watching it is like holding the seeds of greatness in your hand."

### *School on Fire* (1988; Hong Kong, Dr) D: Ringo Lam C: Fennie Yuen, Sarah Lee, Roy Cheung, Damian Lau, Lam Ching Ying

The last in director Lam's trilogy of "On Fire" films, the others being 1987's *City on Fire* and *Prison on Fire*. Though the three films share no common characters or situations, they have in common a bleakly cynical view of Hong Kong society, and this installment is perhaps the darkest of the three. Schoolgirl Chu Yuen Fong (Yuen) sees a brutal mob killing, and is compelled by conscience to tell the authorities. But no good comes of her noble gesture: Head thug Smart (played by eternal Triad Roy Cheung) demands that Chu pay the gang thirty thousand dollars for her impertinence or suffer the consequences. Chu's best friend, Kwok Siu Chun (Lee), prostitutes herself to earn the money her friend needs to avoid a horrible fate. The horrible fate happens anyway: Kwok's self-degradation spirals into self-destruction, and Chu, out of her mind on pills, sets fire to the school library. Everything comes to a head as teachers, students, and Triads are swept up in a deadly conflict, from which no one will emerge unscathed. Reviewers called it "gritty" and "unrelenting," with a "tone that would be documentary if it weren't so gut-wrenchingly harsh." "A powerful journey where all roads ultimately lead to a dead end."

***Seeding of a Ghost*** (1983; Hong Kong, Hr) D: Yeung Kuen C: Phillip Ko, Norman Tsui, Wong Yung, Maria Yuen, Chuan Chi Hui

When Irene (Yuen), the adulterous wife of cabbie Chau (Ko), is raped and killed by street thugs after being abandoned by her playboy lover Anthony Fang (Tsui), Ti is driven over the edge by rage and jealousy. Fortunately, if that's the word, he'd picked up a black magician in his taxi some time before the tragedy, and uses this connection to have a spell cast on his dead wife's corpse. She is transformed into an undead creature called a "Plazawa," which proceeds to exact horrible retribution on her two murderers, her callous lover, and just about every other person in the film. When the mayhem begins to flag, Chau feeds the Plazawa with his own blood, causing it to become spiritually impregnated with a killer embryo that implants itself in the womb of Fang's wife. Mrs. Fang gives birth to the grotesque fetus from hell while she and her husband are at a party. It proceeds to carry on Irene and Chau's mission of vengeance. Reviewers called it a "monumentally polarizing film." "You'll either be sickened or fascinated (or perhaps both in turns)—but you can't dismiss or ignore it." "Generous helpings" of gratuitous nudity, gore-drenched effects, and over-the-top supernatural violence make this a "cult favorite."

***Sentenced to Hang*** (1989; Hong Kong, CIII, Dr) D: Taylor Wong C: Tony Leung Kar Fai, Kent Cheng, Elvis Tsui, Tien Feng, Carrie Ng

A true-crime thriller that was the first film to receive the "Category III" adult rating, this film features Tony Leung as bank employee Wai, Kent Cheng as "Fatty" Ma, and Elvis Tsui as would-be casanova Tang—three childhood pals who vowed as kids to share sorrow and joy and even death together. When Wai is fired from his job as a bank assistant by his domineering and abusive boss (Tien), his buddies join him in plotting an act of revenge that almost immediately goes haywire. The story ends in tragedy, both in real life and in this film—the three were the last individuals to be hanged in Hong Kong. Reviewers called it "starkly realistic," with "melodrama to spare" and a "gripping climax." Though the film is violent, they agree that "this film would barely earn a IIB rating today."

**Shanghai Blues** (1984; Hong Kong, Dr) D: Tsui Hark C: Sylvia Chang, Kenny Bee, Sally Yeh, Loletta Lee, Shing Fui On

As Japanese bombs fall on Shanghai in 1937, an aspiring musician named Kwok (Bee) saves a young woman's life by pushing her into a safe nook under the Soo-chow Bridge. The two spend an evening huddled in one another's arms while explosions rock the landscape around them. Although they are separated before the arrival of dawn, the two make a pact to meet a decade later under the very same bridge—presuming that both survive the war. Once ten years have passed, Kwok returns to Shanghai, looking for his long-lost love. Unfortunately, his quest is hampered by the fact that, because of the darkness and chaos of their original meeting, he has no real idea what she looks like. A frustrated Kwok eventually rents a room in a lodging house above the apartment of a local cabaret singer named Shu Shu (Chang)—unaware that she is, in fact, the very woman he's look-ing for! By the time Shu Shu finally realizes Kwok's identity, a new complication has entered their lives: refugee Stool (Yeh), whose hapless naïveté prompted Shu Shu to take her in off the street. It isn't long before Stool becomes the unwitting third leg in their clue-challenged romantic triangle. Reviewers called it "classic screwball comedy," featuring a "wonderful, Lucy Ricardo–esque" turn by Yeh (who unveils here her command of a "jaw-dropping array of cartoon expressions," not to mention an "inspired talent for physical comedy"). "Watch as Hark tunes the comedic style that he perfects in *Peking Opera Blues*."

**Shaolin Temple** (1982; Mainland, Ac, Pd) D: Zhang Xinyan C: Jet Li, Yu Hai, Yu Xingwei, Ding Lan

This film, the first installment in what would become a trilogy, was Jet Li's debut as a cinematic lead; to many, it remains one of his greatest screen appearances. Li plays a young man whose father has been killed by Ching troops, with Li himself barely escaping. Badly hurt, he is taken in by Shaolin monks, who give him med-ical treatment, shelter, and eventually, training in the skills that will allow him to take revenge. Unfortunately, his first attempt at vengeance ends poorly, with Li hot-footing it back to the temple for more training. This time, however, the soldiers have marked Li's trail, and pursue him to the walls of Shaolin itself. A devastating siege begins, with Li joining forces with the other monks and novices in an attempt to prevent a massacre. Reviewers called it an "incredible display of real martial artists practicing real martial arts"—styles represented include drunken style, mantis, and Shaolin weapons styles, among many others. "Li shines here, and all without the assistance of wires." Followed by two equally brilliant sequels, *Shaolin Temple 2: Kids from Shaolin* (1984) and *Shaolin Temple 3: The Martial Arts of Shaolin* (1986), the latter offering a dream pairing of Li and master martial arts director Lau Kar Leung.

### Spooky Bunch, The (1980; Hong Kong, Hr, Cm) D: Ann Hui C: Josephine Siao, Kenny Bee, Olivia Cheng, Lau Hark Sun, Kwan Chung

This horror-comedy by director Ann Hui was a seminal entry in Hong Kong's New Wave of the eighties. A rich man named Ma invites a Chinese opera company to perform on Cheung Chau Island—long reputed to be haunted—at a time when tradition has it that ghosts are most active. Another catch: The lead role of the performance must be played by second-rate supporting actor Ah Chi (Siao). Despite their misgivings, the bankrupt troupe decides to accept the offer, only to discover Ma's hidden agenda: Many years ago, Ma's grandfather defrauded his old partner, Ah Chi's grandfather, and was cursed by him as a result. Ma hopes that his nephew Dick (Bee) will fall for and marry Ah Chi, assuming that this will appease her grandfather's spirit. But as the troupe begins its performance, strange things begin to happen: A female ghost, who announces that her name is "Cat Shit," possesses the body of the company's male lead, heralding the arrival of a literal army of spirits—who, as it turns out, are the *real* victims. Ma and Ah Chi's grandfathers made a fortune selling fake medicine to a military camp in the throes of an epidemic; the tonic poisoned the entire camp and prompted the spirits to spend eternity causing misfortune for the descendants of both clans. Reviewers called it a "quiet, almost reflective take on the Chinese ghost story" with the "deeper agenda of exploring the burden of history and tradition" and note that "Siao manages to be both remarkably charming and profoundly irritating at the same time."

### Summer at Grandpa's, A (1984; Taiwan, Dr) D: Hou Hsiao-hsien C: Chen Bocheng, Yang Liyin, Gu Jun

A young boy named Tung-tung is sent to the countryside with his little sister to live with their grandparents while their mother recovers from a serious illness. But a visit that initially promises a summer of fun and relaxation becomes increasingly complicated: Their uncle and their grandfather are at war, because of the latter's refusal to allow the former to marry the woman he loves; meanwhile, Tung-tung's little sister, excluded from the games played by the boys, befriends an unfortunate local madwoman. Then Tung-tung witnesses a mob murder. Although at first he hides his knowledge from the authorities, he's forced to come forward when his uncle is falsely accused of the crime. The two children return home a little less innocent, having learned unexpected lessons about life's harsh realities. Reviewers called it a "lyrical childhood remembrance" that "served notice of Hou's arrival as a major talent"; "a remarkably assured effort."

***Super Citizens*** (1985; Taiwan, Dr, Cm) D: Wan Jen C: Su Ming-ming, Guan Guan, Chen Bocheng, Li Zhiqi

The first in a pseudo-series of "Super Citizen" movies, whose later installments—Wan's *Super Citizen Ko* (1995) and *Connection by Fate* (1998)—are thematically, though not narratively, linked to this film. A country boy named Lee comes to the big city looking for his sister, who had come to Taipei months before to find a job. But as he searches, assisted by a vendor of counterfeit goods named Lo-lai, he encounters a variety of unusual characters—an insane professor, a teenage junkie, a war veteran, and a beautiful whore; all of them tell him their stories, and then either dismiss him, befriend him, or betray him. Reviewers called it an "effectively absurdist" portrayal of urban society that "generates sympathy for its working-class heroes." "A showcase for Wan's deft black-comedy touch."

***Taipei Story*** (1985; Taiwan, Dr) D: Edward Yang C: Hou Hsiao-hsien, Tsai Chin, Wu Nien-chen

Fellow Taiwanese New Cinema standout Hou Hsiao-hsien plays Ah Lung, the lead in this drama by Edward Yang (another of Yang's filmmaker colleagues, Wu Nien-chen, plays a supporting role). He's a former baseball star turned textile manufacturer, whose fiancée Shu-chen (Tsai) is an ambitious corporate executive. Although they've been together a long time, their relationship is far from ideal; Ah Lung is obsessed with the glories of his past and unable to express his feelings in the present. Meanwhile, Shu-chen is snarled in the problems of her family—her father is a bankrupt entrepreneur looking to her for assistance with his load of debt, and her little sister is a school dropout and budding delinquent. When Shu-chen loses her job and turns to

Ah Lung for support, he proves to be a less than adequate emotional prop. Reviewers called this, Yang's second feature, an "elegant tale of urban angst and alienation"; "refreshing and intelligent," with "absolutely superb" cinematography.

### Terrorizers, The (1986; Taiwan, Ac, Dr) D: Edward Yang C: Li Liqun, Cora Miao, Wang An, Jin Shi-jye

This psychological drama begins, innocently enough, with a harmless prank. Shu-an, a biracial girl with a rebellious streak, has been locked in her room by her mother to prevent her from looking for trouble on the streets. With nothing else to occupy her time, she decides to make random crank calls to strangers, and ends up dialing the home of a well-known author named Chou Yu-fen, who has not been able to write since marrying her dull but diligent husband, Li Li-chun. The call somehow causes Chou to break free from her emotional paralysis; not only does she begin writing again, penning a short, prizewinning story, but she begins to consider having an affair. Using the ersatz "stalker" as an excuse, Chou tells Li that she's going to move out and find her own apartment. Shu-an, meanwhile, has bolted her room by leaping off a balcony, just as the police are arriving to question her about her recently escaped convict boyfriend. Injured in her fall, Shu-an is brought to the hospital by a photographer who has been secretly taking pictures of her. She and the photographer have a brief fling, but Shu-an ultimately returns to her boyfriend and resumes the sex-and-blackmail con that had led to his original arrest. Li, meanwhile, has taken the collapse of his marriage badly; losing his grip, he steals the handgun of a police officer friend and murders his work supervisor and then his wife's lover. But the ambiguous climax of the film suggests that all may not be as it seems. Reviewers called this a "coolly intriguing intellectual thriller," "intensely cinematic" and "dazzlingly accomplished."

### Time to Live, a Time to Die, A (1985; Taiwan, Dr) D: Hou Hsiao-hsien C: You Anshun, Xin Shufen, Tien Feng, Mei Fang

This nostalgic, semiautobiographical drama by New Taiwanese Cinema master Hou tells the story of Ah Hsiao, a young boy growing up on the island in the early sixties, surrounded by a large extended family. Each of Hsiao's older relatives seems obsessed with the past—his parents constantly tell Hsiao and his siblings about their flight from the Mainland, while his grandmother reminisces endlessly about her lost home village; but to Hsiao, growing up in a rapidly changing Taiwan, these stories have little meaning. As he experiences the changes of adolescence, and as his father, mother, and grandmother each pass away in turn, he becomes increasingly emotionally isolated, and turns to juvenile delinquency as a result. Reviewers called it a film that was "lauded as Taiwanese cinema's greatest masterpiece upon its release," and that still ranks high in most critical estimations. "Hou's tribute to the passing of a generation, told with profound resonance and without sentimentality."

### *Yellow Earth* (1984; Mainland, Dr) D: Chen Kaige C: Liu Qiang, Tan Tuo, Wang Xueqi, Xue Bai

This film marked Chen's debut as a filmmaker, as well as the birth of the new Chinese cinema, whose influential proponents would eventually be dubbed the Fifth Generation. *Earth* is an adaptation of a novel by Ge Lan, telling the tale of a visit to a remote village by a Communist cadre named Gu Qing, whose task is to archive local folk songs for posterity. In the process, he becomes acquainted with his host's daughter, Cuiqiao, and son, the angelic but mentally handicapped Hanhan. The soldier's tales of female liberation under communism prompt Cuiqiao—betrothed at birth to a much older man—to flee her home for the big city, but tragedy strikes her before she reaches her goal. Reviewers laud cinematographer Zhang Yimou's "luscious location photography" and note that the film "remains Chen's most accessible work."

### *Zu: Warriors from the Magic Mountain* (1983; Hong Kong, Ac, Pd) D: Tsui Hark C: Yuen Biao, Adam Cheng, Damian Lau, Mang Hoi, Brigitte Lin

In creating this outrageous fantasy, Tsui set out to prove that Hong Kong cinema could embrace high-tech Hollywood special effects while keeping its essentially Chinese soul. Most reviewers agree that—despite its flaws—he succeeded to a remarkable degree. The film is set in a mythical prehistoric era ruled by might and magic; Yuen Biao plays a newly enlisted soldier who stumbles through a portal to the netherworld, where a variety of spectacular and gruesome beasts are preparing to invade the mortal plane. The only thing that can stop them is a pair of magical blades, the "celestial swords," which when combined can be transformed into an all-powerful mystic weapon. Reviewers have called this film the "Chinese *Star*

*Wars,"* and with some justice; both films have an epic feel anchored around a naïve Everyman protagonist who becomes drawn into a cosmic battle between good and evil; "still breathtaking" after many years of technological advance, *Zu* remains a "must see classic" for fans of period fantasy and Hong Kong cinema in general. Tsui was unhappy with the final cut as released by Golden Harvest; he went on to re-edit it after the fact, weaving in a freshly shot prologue and epilogue that change the movie's symbolism and backstory considerably. Even then he remained disatisfied. In 2001, Tsui addressed his concerns one more time by remaking the film from scratch, as *The Legend of Zu.*

# THE BEST OF TIMES, THE WORST OF TIMES: THE NINETIES

***All for the Winner*** (1990; Hong Kong, Cm) D: Corey Yuen, Jeff Lau C: Stephen Chiau, Ng Man Tat, Sharla Cheung Man, Sandra Ng, Paul Chun

This enormously successful satire on *God of Gamblers* (1989) achieved the unlikely feat of besting the film it parodied at the box office. Chiau plays Shing, a dim rural lad with remarkable psychic gifts; when he visits his Uncle Tat (Ng) in Hong Kong, the latter seizes upon Shing's abilities as an ideal means to strike it rich, parading the bumpkin through a series of casino contests and eventually drawing the unwanted attention of a pair of rival Triad families. Sharla Cheung Man plays a double agent working for (or against) both gangs who eventually becomes romantically involved with Shing. Reviewers called it "uneven" but "hilarious," with "brilliant chemistry between Chiau and his soon-to-be-omnipresent sidekick Ng." *God of Gamblers* producer Wong Jing subsequently snared Chiau and Ng for two sequels to the original film, causing a remarkable cross-breeding of the two lines.

***Anna Magdalena*** (1998; Hong Kong, Dr) D: Hai Chung Man C: Kelly Chen, Takeshi Kaneshiro, Aaron Kwok, Anita Yuen, Leslie Cheung

A romantic drama featuring three gorgeous people—Kwok, Chen, and Kaneshiro—tied up in a love triangle, whose conceit is that it is structured in the manner of Bach's famous musical composition "Minuet in G for Anna Magdalena." As a result, the film has four segments: two "movements," a "duet," and a segment entitled "variations." The minuet itself makes appearances throughout, both as part of the plot—Mok Man Yee (Chen) first makes herself known to roommates Chan Kar Fu (Kaneshiro) and Yau Muk Yan (Kwok) when she constantly and unsuccessfully tries to play it on her piano, entrancing mild-mannered piano-tuner Chan and driving the womanizing Yau to distraction. Yau and Mok start off on the wrongest of feet, but shy Chan recognizes the pattern: She will fall for him, because women always fall for him, despite or because of his flaws. Mok does, indeed, fall for Yau, and the romance ends badly—but even then, Chan can only consummate his love through fantasy. He subsequently writes a novel, a romantic adventure about characters named "X" and "O" that secretly features himself and Mok in the lead roles; this story is depicted in the film's fourth "variations" segment. Reviewers called this a "fun," "quirky," and "gorgeously shot" romantic drama, "winningly acted by its beautiful leads." "Watch for unexpected cameos by some very recognizable stars."

**Armour of God II: Operation Condor** (1992; Hong Kong, Ac, Cm) D: Jackie Chan C: Jackie Chan, Carol Cheng, Eva Cobo de Garcia, Shoko Ikeda, Aldo Sanchez

This film represents an act of phenomenal and nearly disastrous ambition by Chan, who decided to follow up his significantly smaller adventure picture *Armour of God* with a sequel that would be bigger in every way—more villains, more locations, more fights, more stunts, and more pretty girls. This time, Asian Hawk (Chan) is commissioned to find a trove of buried Nazi gold deep in the Sahara. He brings with him a historian named Ada (Carol "Do Do" Cheng) under the mistaken impression that she would prove useful; the pair subsequently come across two more women, an unfortunate Japanese tourist named Momoko (Ikeda) and Elsa (Cobo de Garcia) the granddaughter of the officer who originally secreted the stash. But as they bumble along toward their destination, it soon becomes clear that they're not the only ones looking for the gold. Reviewers called it an "awesome epic" that went "one hundred percent over budget"; "everything went wrong that could go wrong, but luckily, the film was one of Jackie's biggest hits." "The brilliant car-chase in the early going and the implausible, incredible wind-tunnel fight make it all worthwhile."

**Ashes of Time** (1994; Hong Kong, Dr) D: Wong Kar Wai C: Leslie Cheung, Tony Leung Kar Fai, Brigitte Lin, Jacky Cheung, Tony Leung Chiu Wai

This revisionist take on Jin Yong's *Eagle Shooting Heroes* has generated some of the most wildly polarized critical responses in contemporary Hong Kong cinematic history. Leslie Cheung plays the putative protagonist of the film, morose swordsman Ouyang Feng the "Malicious West," who is making his living as a killer for hire in the desert. Orbiting around Ouyang is a misfit constellation of alienated warriors, broken-hearted lovers, and vengeful victims. The interactions among these characters are languid and nearly devoid of traditional exposition; events and histories are painted gradually into existence through elliptical statements, flashbacks, and conflicting accounts. It is no wonder, then, that reviewers have responded with comments ranging from "confusing and inaccessible" and "heavy-handed, overwrought, and just plain boring," to "visually entrancing," with "incredible performances"; a "beautiful," "moving," and "undeniably powerful" work. Not a "must see" for all tastes, but a film that will be seen many times in sequence by those who appreciate its oblique intricacy.

### *Back to Back, Face to Face* (1994; Mainland, Dr) D: Huang Jianxin, Yang Yazhou C: Niu Zhenhua, Lei Luosheng, Li Qiang

This dark comedy by the director of *The Black Cannon Incident* (1985) is another satire of bureaucratic featherbedding, internal political intrigue, and socialist policies gone awry. A man named Li, the deputy director of a local culture office, has spent his career hoping for the opportunity to move from deputy to full director. Unfortunately, when that post finally opens up, a more politically appropriate candidate—a peasant with no experience or knowledge of what the office does—is appointed instead. An irritated Li finds small ways of making the new director's life miserable, and finally he leaves, giving Li hope yet again. This time, a friend of the first director is put into the job, but he turns out to be brutal and vindictive—even beating Li's aged father for accidentally ruining his shoes. The trauma of seeing his father's injuries sends Li to the hospital, where he has the sudden revelation that being precinct director of cultural affairs really has no value for him any longer. He decides instead to cherish his family and work toward getting a special waiver allowing him and his wife to work toward having a boy to join their young girl. Reviewers called it "subversively funny," although "one wonders how director Huang has avoided jail so far."

### *Be There or Be Square* (1999; Mainland, Cm, Dr) D: Feng Xiaogang C: Ge You, Xu Fan

Liu Yuan (Ge) and Li Qing (Xu) are Mainland immigrants doing their best to make it in LA—strangers in an incredibly strange land who turn to each other for emotional support. Carefree Liu does a little of everything, but nothing particularly well—he sells insurance, tries to break into the movie industry in a leisurely fashion, and takes on the occasional odd job to survive. Li, on the other hand, is ambitious and diligent, with little time for entertainment or even relaxation. It's obvious from the very beginning that this mismatched couple is made for each other.

Reviewers called it "pretty close to the perfect romantic comedy"—featuring a pair of "wonderful" actors with "remarkable screen chemistry," unencumbered by the "usual screen chestnuts" of meet-cute cinema or the "Chinatown clichés" of typical immigrant drama.

**Beijing Bastards** (1993; Mainland, Dr) D: Zhang Yuan C: Cui Jian, Li Mai, Wu Lala, Tang Danian

Sixth Generation standout Zhang takes a street-level look at the youthful bohemian underbelly of China's capital, exploring a world of aspiring novelists, starving artists, and substance-abusing rock stars. Cui Jian, China's best-known rock musician, plays the lead here, as a rock musician (naturally) around whom the turmoil and celebrations of a group of disaffected protagonists unfurl. Reviewers called it "edgy" and "unadorned," a "rare glimpse into the urban center of China."

**Blade, The** (1996; Hong Kong, Ac, Pd) D: Tsui Hark C: Zhao Wenzhou, Xiong Xinxin, Song Nei, Moses Chan, Valerie Chow

Tsui's reinvention of Chang Cheh's classic *One-Armed Swordsman* (1967) stars Zhao Wenzhou as On, the adopted son of a master bladesmith who has been told nothing of how his father died. The master's daughter, Siu Ling (Song), has long had her eye on both On and another worker named Iron Head (Chan), but can't decide between them; she decides she'll make them fight for her favor, not realizing that they are motivated by other obsessions. Her manipulations prompt a disastrous series of events, leading to On's disappearance and presumed death. Though he has survived, he has lost an arm, and must create a new style of swordplay that reflects his handicap. Meanwhile, Iron Head and Siu Ling travel the martial world seeking their lost friend—while trouble, in the form of the killer of On's father, awaits the blade factory and its workers. Reviewers called it "spectacular," if "flawed"; Tsui demonstrates a "captivating and eccentric new camera style here," as well as a "bleak, nihilist sensibility" that "lingers in the gut long after the film's shocking conclusion."

**Blue Kite, The** (1993; Mainland, Dr) D: Tian Zhuangzhuang C: Lu Liping, Pu Quanxin, Li Xuejian

This picture so incensed Chinese film ministry officials that it led to Tian Zhuangzhuang's virtual exile from film for years. Taking as its setting the years following the Communist Revolution, it follows the changes and challenges faced by every-day residents during repeated waves of politically motivated social upheaval. The film's young protagonist, Tietou, tells the story of the film in flashback, explaining how his parents, a librarian and a teacher, are targeted for abuse and harassment—despite their fervent belief in the party and the system. Reviewers called it "a brilliant journey through confusing and disquieting times"; "daring, yet subtle." In particular, Tian's "magical touch" with young performers is lauded as "refreshing." After completion, the film was banned from release, and Tian was excoriated for making a movie "without permission."

***Blue Moon*** (1997; Taiwan, Dr) D: Ko I-cheng C: Tarcy Su, David Wang, Leon Dai, Zhang Han

Most months in a year have just a single full moon—but every so often, circumstances (and our nonlunar calendar system) conspire to make a second full moon occur, an event unusual enough to inspire the expression "once in a blue moon," referring to something of astronomical rarity. This film is nearly such a rarity itself—a frustrated Ko had taken a six-year break from directing before making this picture, and only did so to experiment with a novel idea: a five-reel film composed of five interwoven stories of twenty minutes each, which could be shown in any order. Each combination ends up telling a different, yet comprehensible tale. The central characters—film producer A-gua (Wang), writer Cuen-shu (Dai), and Yi-fang (Su), the woman they both love—make up a romantic triangle whose resolution is different depending on which reel is shown last. Reviewers called it "appealing," "self-assured," and "surprisingly cohesive and satisfying, given its inherently random structure." "You'll want to watch it 120 times, just to see how the film differs each time." They also noted that the film being produced by A-gua in the movie is also titled *Blue Moon*, setting up an unsettling sense of recursion.

***Bodyguard From Beijing, The*** (1994; Hong Kong, Ac, Cm) D: Corey Yuen C: Jet Li, Christy Chung, Kent Cheng, Ngai Sing, Leung Wing Chung

Yet another uncredited Hong Kong remake, this film takes the storyline from the Hollywood Whitney Houston–Kevin Costner vehicle *The Bodyguard* and gives it a typical Hong Kong twist—adding wild action and goofy comedy to the basic plot of a mismatched pair falling in love. Chung plays heiress Michelle Yeung, a spoiled socialite threatened by mob killers after accidentally witnessing a Triad hit. Jet Li plays Hui, a Mainlander intelligence expert hired by Yeung's attorney boyfriend to keep her alive and out of trouble. At first, Yeung rebels against Hui's overprotective presence, but she grows to appreciate him when he repeatedly saves her from being gunned down in plain daylight. Eventually, of course, their relationship blossoms into love. Reviewers called it "thoroughly enjoyable" if "paper-thin," with "creative action sequences" captured in "stylish, glossy cinematography."

**Bride with White Hair, The** (1993; Hong Kong, Ac, Pd) D: Ronny Yu C: Brigitte Lin, Leslie Cheung, Elaine Lui, Yammie Nam, Francis Ng

Alongside Invincible Asia, Lin's turn here as Wolf Girl is perhaps her best-known and most cherished Hong Kong film role. Wolf Girl is a feral huntress in the sevice of the hermaphroditic/Siamese twin leaders of an evil cult, assigned to stalk and murder the members of the Wu Tang clan and its affiliated tribes. Wu Tang swordsman Cho Yi Hang (Cheung) becomes infatuated with the lovely warrior, despite the destruction she's wreaking on his comrades. Their romance blooms during an encounter in a lovely underground grotto, and Cho gives Wolf Girl her first human name: Lien Ni Chang. She agrees to abandon the cult and her twisted master/mistress, which results in painful physical abuse at the hands of the remaining members. But when Lien arrives at the Wu Tang hall to meet with Cho, she finds that the clan has been slaughtered—an attempt by the cultists to frame Lien for their massacre. When Cho arrives, he immediately assumes that Lien is to blame. Faced with this faithlessness, Lien loses her mind, her hair turning snow-white and becoming infused with supernatural power. Reviewers called it a "masterpiece of set direction," and a "deservedly beloved classic." Followed by an inferior sequel, showing the consequences of Lien's madness and how Cho finally (and tragically) brings her back to sanity.

**Brighter Summer Day, A** (1991; Taiwan, Dr) D: Edward Yang C: Chang Chen, Lisa Yang, Juan Wang, Elaine Jin, Zhang Guozhu

In this deceptively pop-savvy film, Yang subverts the "adolescent angst" genre of cinema by consciously placing it within the greater context of political change. S'ir (Chang Chen) is the teenage son of a KMT bureaucrat who, with his friends, is beginning to discover the twin joys of girls and rock 'n' roll. Unfortunately, as in adult society, access to such cherished commodities is dependent on social status, which among schoolkids depends on which faction you belong to and what faction is on top, as well as your family's wealth or power. The object of S'ir's affection, Ming (Lisa Yang), is a pretty young thing whose innocence belies a mastery of these rules. Although her family is poor, she maintains status within the student body by using her looks and sweet personality to cultivate the affections of faction leaders. Her flirtations with S'ir ultimately have chilling consequences. Reviewers called it "Yang's masterpiece"; a "Taiwanese *Rebel Without a Cause.*" The first of his films to gain widespread international attention, it has been called by some critics "the greatest modern Chinese-language movie."

### *Buddha Bless America* (1996; Taiwan, Cm) D: Wu Nien-chen C: Lin Cheng-sheng, Chiang Shu-na, Yang Tzong-hsien, Bai Ming-hua, Wu Ten-luo

Screenwriter Wu directs his sophomore effort here—another examination of the nature of Taiwanese identity, told through gentle but pointed humor. Brain (Lin) is a schoolteacher in a village that has seen multiple masters in a few short generations—the Japanese, the Nationalists, and, with a proposed occupation by American armed forces due to joint military maneuvers, the United States. Brain's fellow townsfolk consider protesting the "invasion," but Brain convinces them that the Americans will benefit the local economy. Secretly, he hopes to gain access to American medical technology for his brother, whose hand was mutilated in an industrial accident under Japanese rule. The GIs arrive and turn the area into a shattered wreck, ripping up farmland and converting the village into an R&R pitstop dotted with bars, brawls, and brothels. Enraged, the townsfolk put the blame on Brain. When the maneuvers end, the changes are permanent: Rock music fills the airwaves, and local kids now play at pretending to be soldiers and bar girls. Reviewers lauded the "flowering" of Wu's comic touch here, particularly praising the "enormously gifted" Lin Cheng-sheng, who plays Brain.

### *Bullet in the Head* (1990; Hong Kong, Ac) D: John Woo C: Jackie Cheung, Tony Leung Chiu Wai, Waise Lee, Simon Yam

This is the tale that John Woo intended to turn into the third installment of *A Better Tomorrow* (1986), resulting in his parting of ways with Tsui Hark, who found it too unrelentingly grim for commercial tastes. Ben (Leung), Paul (Lee), and Frank (Cheung) are a trio of childhood pals who flee to war-torn Vietnam on the night of Ben's wedding, after accidentally committing a street killing that forces them to go fugitive. They bring with them a cache of drugs that they hope to sell to buy off their enemies. But once in Saigon, Frank falls in love with a lounge singer being held captive by a local mob boss, and the three friends partner with a suave hitman (Yam) to save her. They succeed, and in the process, steal the boss's cache of gold—but are then captured by the Viet Cong and subjected to unimaginable physical and psychological tortures. Although the trio survive, the dynamics in their friendship shift unrecognizably. In their escape Ben is separated from the others, and Paul's selfishness drives him to shoot a wounded Frank in the head to prevent his screams from giving their position away. But Frank does not die from the betrayal. Now a brain-damaged, drug-addicted wreck, he becomes a mechanical killer for hire, earning money to buy heroin to ease the constant pain of the inextricable bullet in his skull. Ben finally finds Frank and helps him escape his misery, then goes to Hong Kong, where Paul has returned to become a successful businessman, bearing grisly evidence of Paul's crimes. Reviewers called it "shocking" and "ultraviolent"; "one of the most harrowing movie experiences ever," and "one of Woo's greatest achievements," although "you won't find subtlety here." They also noted that the "car-joust" scene that serves as the finale of the originally released cut was added against the wishes of Woo, whose "director's cut" edition ends with the grim confrontation between Ben and Paul in the executive boardroom.

### C'est La Vie, Mon Cheri (1993; Hong Kong, Dr) D: Derek Yee C: Anita Yuen, Lau Ching Wan, Carrie Ng, Carina Lau, Fung Bo Bo

A small film—loosely based on the classic Linda Lin Dai vehicle *Love Without End* (1961)—that unexpectedly captivated the hearts of Hong Kong filmgoers, becoming an enormous box office hit and rocketing the careers of Anita Yuen and Lau Ching Wan into the ranks of superstardom. Lau plays Kit, a morose musician who's lost his love of life, while Yuen plays Min, a fresh-faced gamine who helps him recover it—hiding the fact that she's had an early brush with death herself, as a childhood leukemia victim currently in remission. When Min's illness reemerges, the two switch roles, with Lau doing his best to buck up Min's spirits as her body weakens. Reviewers called it a "delightful little gem" with "great performances" and "genuine heart"; Yuen is "indescribably compelling" here, leaving no doubt about why the movie transformed her into Hong Kong's "It Girl." The film received nods for Best Picture, Director, Actress, Supporting Actress (Fung), Supporting Actor (Paul Chun), and Screenplay at the 1993 Hong Kong Film Awards.

**Cageman** (1992; Hong Kong, CIII, Dr) D: Jacob Cheung C: Kar Kui Wong, Roy Chiao, Kai Chi Liu, Teddy Robin Kwan, Michael Lee

This startling drama by Jacob Cheung is based on the real-life phenomenon of the "cage dwellers"—poor working men who, due to Hong Kong's outrageously expensive real estate, can afford no better home than rented beds in tenements separated into cubicles with chickenwire. When government-funded developers seek to tear down the ramshackle residence to build more tony condominiums, the building's owner Koo (Chiao), his mentally handicapped son Sam (Liu), and the cage-dwelling inhabitants unite to try to save their humble home. Reviewers called it an "astonishing" portrait of "Hong Kong class struggle," with "superb performances" by the "talented ensemble cast."

**Casino** (1998; Hong Kong, Ac) D: Billy Tang C: Simon Yam, Alex Fong, Kent Cheng, Ada Choi, Kenix Kwok

In a feat worthy of Bugsy Siegel, "Broken Tooth" Wan funded this film about his favorite subject—himself—and was actually arrested by Macanese authorities while watching the final product! If the screen version is to be believed, Wan (Yam) is a dashing and rather likable rogue who never hurt anyone who didn't deserve it—like Robin Hood, except with a better wardrobe and a penchant for karaoke. The film details Wan's rise in the Triads, from street thug to mob boss, not sparing in action (of the brawling-with-lead-pipes variety) but essentially representing the gangster as a kind of ass-kicking saint-slash-rockstar. Reviewers noted that "you get what you pay for"; "the fact that this ninety-minute Triad infomercial is actually rather entertaining is something of a miracle."

**Centre Stage** (aka *Ruan Lingyu: The Actress*) (1992; Hong Kong, Dr) D: Stanley Kwan C: Maggie Cheung, Tony Leung Kar Fai, Chin Han, Carina Lau, Lawrence Ng

In this experimental mix of documentary and biopic, Kwan explores both the life of tragic acress Ruan Lingyu—who committed suicide after being humiliated by endless media gossip—and the influence the twenties star had on later lights. Maggie Cheung essays the lead role, while a talented ensemble cast fills out the roles of Ruan's no-account husband (Ng), her married lover (Chin), and her friend and fellow performer Lily Li (Lau), among others. But Kwan also blends surviving footage from the real Ruan's works, as well as interviews with the cast discussing Ruan's legacy, into this complex mix. Reviewers called it a "breathtaking" work, with every element—in front of and behind the camera—"approaching perfection"; though "slow going," this is a "masterpiece" that "deserves its many honors," which include a clutch of Hong Kong Film Awards and a Berlin Golden Bear for Cheung as Best Actress.

### Chinese Odyssey, A, Part One: Pandora's Box and Part Two: Cinderella (1995; Hong Kong, Ac, Dr) D: Jeff Lau C: Stephen Chiau, Ng Man Tat, Karen Mok, Law Kar Ying, Yammie Nam

Lau, best known for his wildly ridiculous all-hands-on-deck farces, reins in his hyperactive humor gland here to craft his version of the epic *Journey to the West*, which tells the story of the Monkey King, Pigsy, Sandy, and the "Longevity Monk," tasked by the gods with bringing Buddhist sutras to the East. Lau begins the film with a preface set in Heaven, in which Monkey and the other characters of the story are sentenced to return to the wheel of incarnations for various indiscretions, and are unwillingly reborn as mortals. After half a millennium, the wheel's dials all line up once more, with Monkey's current incarnation, a rather hairy bandit named Joker (Chiau), getting in a scrape that sets him on the path back to paradise. But first, he must deal with a pair of witchy sisters (Nam and Mok)—one of whom falls in love with him and is then poisoned by her jealous sibling. He must also confront his growing realization that he isn't the man he thought he was—or, in fact, a man at all. To save his supernatural love interest from her sister's toxin, he uses the power of Pandora's Box, a time-travel device that he hopes will turn back the clock far enough that he'll be able to save her. Unfortunately, the device works too well, and he is propelled five hundred years into the past. The story picks up in Part II with Joker finding himself in an even crazier situation than the one he left behind. He meets and becomes enamored of the pretty Lin Zixia (Athena Chu), a goddess whose real identity is as half of the wick in Buddha's lamp; the other half is her nasty sister Lin Qingxia (the Chinese name of Brigitte Lin—two other individuals are referred to as Chin Han and Charlie Chin!). He also runs into the man who was Monkey's master—the Longevity Monk (Law Kar Yan)—and gradually and reluctantly finds himself embracing the immortal role he was always meant to play. Reviewers called this two-part epic "side-splitting"; "must-see movies" that are perhaps the "greatest parody ever." Chiau as Monkey and Ng Man Tat as Pigsy are a "casting coup, by anyone's standards."

**Chungking Express** (1994; Hong Kong, Dr) D: Wong Kar Wai C: Tony Leung Chiu Wai, Takeshi Kaneshiro, Brigitte Lin Ching-hsia, Faye Wong, Valerie Chow Kar Ling

The film that simultaneously introduced Wong Kar Wai to the Western world and served as a curtain call for screen icon Brigitte Lin Ching-hsia. Nominally the story of two policemen—neither of whom is shown actually pursuing any law-enforcement-related activities during the film—this definition-of-quirky Rorschach blot of a movie has been explained as an exploration of the connectedness of events and the disconnectedness of people; a tracing of parallel lives etched into the crowded urban landscape; a musing on the infuriatingly abstract nature of love and nostalgia; even as a love poem to Hong Kong before the handover. It is perhaps all of these things and nothing, and better enjoyed as a mirror for what reviewers bring to it than a portrait of what Wong may or may not have intended. The first policeman, 223 (Kaneshiro)—each is identified only by his badge number—is approaching his twenty-fifth birthday in a dazed and recursive state of obsession, having been dumped by his girlfriend May some weeks before. Since 223's birthday happens to be May 1, which also happens to be the ex-couple's anniversary, he's taken to commemorating each day until then by eating a can of pineapples that shares that "expiration date." The rest of his time is spent jogging, hoping to sweat off enough water and salt that he'll have "none left for tears." All of this is disrupted when he meets a mysterious woman in a blonde wig, sunglasses, and an unseasonable trenchcoat (Lin). Although the two share no words, 223 and the Blonde Wig Woman somehow bond enough for them to spend a night in a hotel room together, not talking and not having sex. (This is what passes for social congress in Wong Kar Wai's cosmos, a universe of ships missing each other in the night.) The Blonde Wig Woman, as it turns out, is a middleman in a drug deal that has come apart because of the betrayal of some of her "mules"; fearing that she'll be killed in retribution, she's silently turned to 223 for temporary sanctuary, which he's only too content to give. Leung's cop, 663, is equally heartbroken, and equally divorced from social interaction; having been dumped by his long-term girlfriend, an airline hostess played by Valerie Chow Kar Ling, he now spends nearly all of his time in his apartment, talking to inanimate objects, trying to convince them that she's going to come back home to them. (It's equally likely that he's hoping they'll convince him.) He has a secret admirer, a waitress at the snack shop he eats at every day named Faye (Faye Wong), but this fact is completely lost on him. A frustrated and curious Faye breaks into 663's apartment and begins a secret redecoration campaign—adding her spirit to his environment, hoping that it will cause him to love her by osmosis. Heartsick 663 takes all of the changes in stride, gently interrogating new pieces of furniture she has purchased and asking them about the reasons for their unexpected changes. Eventually, of course, he discovers Faye's role, and realizes that he's ready to begin his life again—perhaps too late, as Faye has taken a job that will finally bring her to her idealized paradise of California: She's become an airline hostess. A coda, in which 663 has quit the police force and purchased the old snack shop where Faye used to work, offers a "gently humorous and touchingly romantic" conclusion to their "remote-control flirtation." Reviewers called it a "real charmer" and a "minor classic," "almost in spite of itself," although some dissenters dismissed it as "overrated" and "repetitious." The film won a number of Hong Kong Film Awards, turned director Wong into a darling of the global cinema set, and mainland pop idol/actress Faye Wong into a Hong Kong "It Girl."

### Comrades, Almost a Love Story (1996; Hong Kong, Dr) D: Peter Chan C: Leon Lai, Maggie Cheung, Kristy Yeung, Eric Tsang, Christopher Doyle

This romantic drama depicts the intertwined fates of a pair of Mainland immigrants, Li Xiaojun (Lai) and Li Chiao (Cheung) as they begin new lives in the bustling metropolis of Hong Kong. Through their trials, triumphs, and tribulations, director Chan paints a muted, restless portrait of the city itself over a decade of wrenching change. In 1986, Xiaojun blinks himself awake on a train that has brought him from the staging ground of the New Territories into Hong Kong proper, grabs his bundles, and steps onto the platform with a half-puzzled wide-eyed look on his face that serves as his signature expression for the rest of the picture. Innocent Xiaojun soon encounters enterprising fellow migrant Chiao, who begins using Xiaojun as unpaid labor in a half-dozen jobs and entrepreneurial projects. Lonely Xiaojun is only too glad to pay for Chiao's company with free toil. But they soon develop into real friends, and then more—or at least, they should; obstacles seem to keep emerging to keep their relationship "almost." Reviewers called it "perhaps the most satisfying of the UFO films," and "Peter Chan's unquestioned masterpiece."

### Confucian Confusion, A (1994; Taiwan, Cm, Dr) D: Edward Yang C: Chen Xiangqi, Ni Shujun, Wang Weiming, Wang Bosen, Richie Li

A tale of young urban professionals in Taipei, struggling with persistent feelings of alienation despite, or more likely because of, their material success. Molly is the daughter of a wealthy family that dismisses her as worthless due to her sex; given little direction in her life, she has become the proprietor of a publicity agency that is mostly a vanity vehicle funded by her rich boyfriend, who is hoping that her urge to have a career "settles down" soon, so they can marry and she can become a suitable housewife. Meanwhile, Molly's employees, friends, and siblings struggle with their own problems, while inevitably getting involved with one another's; when Molly, as much for the sake of doing something as for any real reason, fires one of her more unproductive employees, wannabe actress Feng, a domino sequence of events occurs that will destabilize their fragile dynamic and challenge the characters to irrevocably alter their lives, for better or for worse. Reviewers called it a "sophisticated," "screwball comedy" about "cultural transition" in a "culture that has embraced Confucius more as a mascot than a philosopher"; "sleek, chic, and hysterical."

### *Crime Story* (1993; Hong Kong, Ac) D: Kirk Wong, Jackie Chan C: Jackie Chan, Kent Cheng, Law Kar Ying, Christine Ng, Chung Fat

An atypically dark Jackie Chan picture, due in large part to the grim-and-gritty sensibility of director Kirk Wong. Assigned to protect real estate mogul Wong Yat Fei from kidnappers, Detective Eddie Chan (Chan) comes to believe that his partner Hung (Kent Cheng) knows more about the conspiracy than he should. Reviewers called it a "remarkably fresh" treatment of a formulaic situation, and note that it was based on a true case of kidnapping. Although Chan "shows more dramatic chops here" than in any other film in his canon—winning a Hong Kong Film Award for his performance—the production was marked by disagreements between Chan and Wong, leading Chan to take over the direction of the film with a number of key sequences still to be shot.

### *Day the Sun Turned Cold, The* (1994; Hong Kong, Dr) D: Yim Ho C: Siqin Gaowa, Tuo Zhonghua, Ma Jingwu

Based on a true story, this film is about a twenty-four-year-old man's sudden discovery that his ten-years-deceased father did not die a natural death; indeed, evidence indicates that the most likely suspect for the murder is the man's mother, Fengying (Gaowa). Guan Jian (Tuo), torn between his loyalty to his father's memory and his love of his mother, decides that her crime cannot go unpunished and brings the evidence to the police. After Jian's accusation, Fengying is arrested and tried, and an autopsy discovers that the elder Guan died of poison. Fengying and her lover Liu, whom she has since married, admit conspiring to murder Guan, and are sentenced to death. On the eve of her hanging, Fengying attempts to leave a souvenir of sorts for her son—a sweater she has knitted; he takes it and then throws it away. "Remarkably effective" and "provocative," say reviewers, who compare its Oedipal dynamics to those of *Hamlet.* "Mongolian actress Siqin Gaowa is extraordinary."

### *Days of Being Wild* (1990; Hong Kong, Dr) D: Wong Kar Wai C: Leslie Cheung, Andy Lau, Maggie Cheung, Carina Lau, Jacky Cheung

An all-star cast enlivens Wong's followup to his hit gangster film *As Tears Go By,* which follows a group of young, alienated Hong Kong teens as they pair up, attempt to pair up, split up, and attempt to split up. Leslie Cheung is Yuddy, a no-account cad who lives off his aging aunt and sexually exploits, then disposes of, a series of women. Maggie Cheung is Su Lizhen, a pretty store clerk who was dumped by and now obsesses over Yuddy, while Carina Lau is Mimi, Yuddy's current lover, a dancer who refuses to accept his increasingly forceful rejections. Circling Yuddy and his women is Tide (Andy Lau), a young cop who has gotten to know Lizhen from her constant vigil outside Yuddy's apartment, and Zab (Jacky Cheung), Yuddy's idol-worshiping best friend. Tide falls for Lizhen and Zab falls for Mimi, but the women have no interest in either of them. Stung by Lizhen's rejection, Tide quits the force and becomes a sailor, and then runs across Yuddy in the Philippines, where the latter has gone in search of his birth mother. After Yuddy prompts an altercation by stabbing a passport forger, Tide shoots him, and then, as Yuddy dies, attempts to determine whether he is the man who broke Lizhen's heart. The film ends with the introduction of a mysterious man, played by Tony Leung Chiu Wai, dressing himself and preparing to go out into the world; although critics have postulated various symbolic rationales for Leung's sudden, brief, and anonymous entrance, the truth is that Leung was to be the star of a followup to this film, which never materialized due to its commercial failure. Critics called it "moody," "starkly beautiful," but "langorously slow." The film, obsessed with the passage of time, is filled with representations of clocks and watches; reviewers note that the title of this film was the Hong Kong title for Nicholas Ray's classic *Rebel Without a Cause.*

***Dragon Inn*** (1992; Hong Kong, Ac, Pd) D: Raymond Lee C: Maggie Cheung, Tony Leung Kar Fai, Brigitte Lin, Donnie Yen, Lau Shun

This remake of King Hu's classic *wuxia pian* is, as a result, sometimes referred to as *New Dragon Inn*. Although Raymond Lee is the nominal director here, producer Tsui Hark, as usual, played a significant role in envisioning and shaping this project. The storyline is similar to that of the original: During the Ming Dynasty, an evil eunuch named Tsao (Yen) has eliminated one of his greatest rivals, sending the dead official's supporters fleeing. In hopes of flushing them out of hiding, Tsao orders the exile of the official's children, thinking correctly that someone will come to save them. His hope is that it will be the dead man's aide de camp Chow Wei On (Leung), who is the eunuch's current greatest threat; instead, it turns out to be Chow's lover and second in command Yau Mo Yin (Lin), who brings the kids to the notorious Dragon Inn for temporary safekeeping while she waits to rendezvous with Chow. But the proprietress of the inn, Jade (Cheung), is a tough girl with an eye for the main chance, whose money-hungry tactics include having her barbarian chef shred the dead bodies that often litter the inn and its immediate surroundings into fillings for her "pork buns." Not interested in supporting either the rebel cause or the tyrannical eunuch, Jade ends up selling information to both sides of the conflict—until her growing attraction for Chow overcomes her greed. Chow, Jade, and Yau then take on Tsao and his army in an all-out battle that will determine the future of the empire. Reviewers called it a "graceful blend" of "precision swordplay," "dizzying acrobatics," and "political intrigue"; "consistently engrossing," with "terrific performances from the entire cast," particularly "poised and gorgeous" Lin and "sly and sexy" Cheung.

***Drifting Life, A*** (1996; Taiwan, Dr) D: Lin Cheng-sheng C: Grace Chen, Lee Kang-sheng, Vicky Wei, Wang Yu-wen, Chen Shi-huang

In this debut film by Taiwanese "Next Wave" filmmaker Lin Cheng-sheng, a young man named Kun-cheng loses his adored wife to the birth of their second child. No longer able to face the daily pressures of living with his weak father and shrewish mother, he leaves the household and his young children behind and heads for another town, where he takes odd jobs and begins a listless relationship with an equally rootless young woman. But when his mother collapses with a stroke, he is called back to face his responsibilities. Reviewers called it a "superb" first outing, with the casting of frequent Tsai Ming-liang collaborator Lee Kang-sheng in the lead role an "unlikely but brilliant choice." "Intensely moving."

**Drunken Master II** (1994; Hong Kong, Ac, Cm, Pd) D: Lau Kar Leung, Jackie Chan C: Jackie Chan, Anita Mui, Ti Lung, Felix Wong, Lau Kar Leung

A decade and a half after *Drunken Master*, Chan returns to the role that first turned him into a superstar, playing a young Wong Fei Hung in this big-budget sequel. Wong is still a lazy, irresponsible lout, more fond of brawling than studying. Complicating matters this time is Master Wong's young second wife, played by Anita Mui, whose misguided attempts at providing maternal support and guidance end up getting both her and Fei Hong in hot water. The story begins with Wong literally running into a Manchu official (played by director Lau) while on a train home to Guangdong; Wong is ferrying a piece of valuable ginseng back to the family medical clinic, but in the collision, he accidentally mixes up his package with one being carried by the official, General Fu, leading to a memorable battle between the two on, around, and under the moving train. Unable to retrieve his father's ginseng root, Wong opens up the official's package to find that it contains a rare ancient seal. Wong soon finds himself ensnarled in General Fu's attempt to bust a ring of antiquities thieves, masterminded by none other than the British ambassador. Reviewers said that "once you overlook the fact that Jackie is very obviously a forty-year-old man—about the same age as his father, and a decade older than his stepmother—it's remarkable how easily he slips back into Fei Hong mode"; "Mui is hilarious," "Ti Lung is splendid," and "Lau proves that he hasn't lost a step." The extended, climactic battle at the iron factory that caps the film is "one of Chan's most incredible achievements." Sadly, Chan clashed with Lau during shooting and ended up firing him from the production, "leading reviewers to wonder what might have been," but "what's there is pretty spectacular already."

**Eagle Shooting Heroes, The** (1993; Hong Kong, Cm, Pd) D: Jeff Lau C: Leslie Cheung, Tony Leung Chiu Wai, Tony Leung Kar Fai, Jacky Cheung, Brigitte Lin

This film was shot by Wong Kar Wai's production company partner Jeff Lau back to back with Wong's own *Ashes of Time*; it features the same cast and source material as the former film but takes them in an utterly different (and typically Jeff Lau-

town's residents—particularly Ermo's hated neighbor Fatty, who resents Ermo's youth and beauty, and the fact that she has given birth to a son. Ermo decides to get the last laugh on Fatty and the town's other residents by earning enough money to buy the largest color TV set in the county—a feat that would take most villagers a year's salary or more. Reviewers called it a "lovable classic," offering a "similar brand of subtle, naturalistic humor as Zhang Yimou's *Story of Qiu Ju* (1992)"—a common comparison work. "Alia shows once again that she's one of the best actresses in contemporary Mainland cinema."

### *Eternal Evil of Asia, The* (1995; Hong Kong, CIII, Hr, Cm) D: Chin Man Kei C: Ellen Chan, Lily Chung, Chan Kwok Bong, Elvis Tsui, Ben Ng

Referred to by reviewers as "a prototypical 'only in Hong Kong' film," this out-of-control schlockfest combines low-budget horror, lowbrow comedy, and tasteless sexual situations in nearly equal proportions. Bon (Chan Kwok Bong) and a trio of his male buddies are on vacation in Thailand. Although Bon is happily engaged, his friends are eager to find some prostitute action. Having no luck with the local bars, they naturally wander out into the jungle, where they encounter a weird shaman (Ng) named "Laime" (just as it sounds). Laime proves his powers are real by turning Elvis Tsui into a literal "dickhead." This causes some consternation among the pals, but they still give the shaman a helping hand when he is "attacked" by a sexually voracious naked sorceress named "Chusie." (Tsui is actually not that helpful, as he is busy ogling Chusie and rubbing his neck. Think about it.) Laime is grateful enough for their assistance that he invites them home to his lair, where they meet Laime's gorgeous younger sister, who promptly falls for Bon. Attempting to feed him a love potion, she ends up accidentally dosing herself and Bon's three pals instead; a wild orgy ensues, with Bon looking on in consternation. When the girl comes out of it, she is understandably dismayed. Trying to calm her down before she alerts her big brother, the three guys accidentally kill her. The quartet decides that this is a good time to head back to Hong Kong. But Laime quickly figures out what happened, and—going quite insane—vows revenge. Bon's pals begin to die in terrible ways—one falls off a building and is impaled by a fluorescent light fixture; another is afflicted with cannibal frenzy, and eats himself—and Bon soon realizes that he's likely to be next. Worse yet, Laime has decided to do to Bon's fiancée May (Ellen Chan) what his pals did to his sister—by astral remote control, if necessary. Some reviewers called it "recommended to those who are game for this sort of demented sleaze"; others called it "a symptom of a desperately sick mind."

### *Fallen Angels* (1995; Hong Kong, Dr) D: Wong Kar Wai C: Leon Lai, Takeshi Kaneshiro, Charlie Yeung, Michelle Lee, Karen Mok

A sequel-in-sensibility to *Chungking Express* (1994), this stylish Wong effort looks at the flip side of the cops-in-love stories of that film, taking as its protagonists a pair of criminals. Leon Lai is Ming, a hitman whose "controller" (played by the lovely Michelle Lee) passes assignments on to him but has never actually met him; he has, in fact, become a kind of anonymous object of fantasy for her. Ming is rapidly tiring of his profession, and when one job nearly kills him, he hangs up his gun for good. Free of the burden of his lifestyle, he encounters a frenetic young woman in a blonde wig named Baby (Mok), and the two establish a strange connection. Meanwhile, Takeshi Kaneshiro plays He Qiwu, whose father owns the boarding house where Ming used to live. He Qiwu has been mute since childhood (he ate a can of expired pineapple, and never spoke again); his hobby of breaking into and operating shops after they've closed for the day is his primary enjoyment in life, until he meets and falls for Charlie (Yeung)—a pretty girl obsessed with finding the blonde woman who stole her ex-boyfriend. Reviewers noted that the film's subtle references to *Express* are "part of what make it so joyful to watch and rewatch"; "darker" than its predecessor, it still manages to "capture the first film's magic."

### *Farewell My Concubine* (1993; Mainland, Dr) D: Chen Kaige C: Leslie Cheung, Zhang Fengyi, Gong Li, Ann Mui

In this work tracing the chaotic history of China from the twenties through the Cultural Revolution, Leslie Cheung and Zhang Fengyi play Cheng Dieyi and Duan Xiaolou, a pair of top opera stars who have been friends since their childhood days, when they trained at the same academy. Cheng, smaller and slighter of frame, has been forced to take on female roles; Duan, meanwhile, has been given masaculine roles, such as that of the king of Chu in the opera *Farewell My Concubine,* which—partnered with Cheng, who plays the role of the concubine Yu Ji—becomes his signature. Over the years, despite Cheng's painfully suppressed crush on his costar, the two men remain friends. But when Duan meets and marries a prostitute named Juxian (Li), Cheng becomes wildly jealous. Their partnership splits, and then, as they are drawn into the chaos of the Cultural Revolution, degenerates into mutual betrayal. Years later, after the Revolution's end, the two prepare to stage a reunion performance of their most famous work; at the climax of the production, Cheng takes Duan's sword and commits suicide, ending his life in fact and fiction. Reviewers called it "Chen's acknowledged masterwork," "an epic in every sense, yet grounded by the career performances of Cheung and Zhang." The film won the 1993 Palme D'Or, the top prize at the Cannes Film Festival.

### *Fight Back to School* (1991; Hong Kong, Cm) D: Gordon Chan C: Stephen Chiau, Cheung Man, Ng Man Tat, Roy Cheung, Gabriel Wong

Wisely using the comic repertory group assembled around Stephen Chiau in his three hugely successful *God of Gamblers* parody-followups, this undercover cop comedy features Chiau as Detective Sing, a cop whose chief, Scissor Legs Wong (played by coscripter Barry Wong), despises his smartass personality and lackadasical attitude toward police work. When the chief's gun is stolen by young punks operating out of a local high school, he decides to kill two birds with one stone—getting Sing out of his hair and retrieving his weapon—by assigning him to enroll at the school as a student. Sing is appalled at the assignment, since the reason he joined the force to begin with was to get out of school, but he has little choice in the matter. Reluctantly reporting to campus, he checks in with his contact, Uncle Tat (Ng), who is already ensconced at the school as a janitor, and then begins his first day as a student. Within three days, he's become the laughingstock of the school, made enemies of the class's resident bullies, been pounded with dozens of thrown erasers, and is on the verge of getting thrown out—all without having made any headway on his case. The only bright spot in Sing's student life is the guidance counselor, Miss Ho (Cheung Man), who provides him with the gentle support he needs to find his confidence as a pupil and as a policeman. Reviewers called this "Chiau at his best," with Cheung Man "never looking better" as the beautiful facultymember/love interest; some dissenters found this "a little too pat" for their tastes, and noted their preference for the two followups to this effort. This film launched a mini-trend of campus comedies, as well as the career of Gabriel Wong, who turns in a likably nerdy performance as Sing's bespectacled student sidekick "Turtle" Wong (his resemblance to the reptile really is remarkable). Two official sequels followed, as well as blatant ripoffs like Wong Jing's 1992 *Truant Heroes* (which replaced Chiau with Alfred Cheung but preserved much of the rest of the cast) and Chu Yen-ping's 1992 *To Miss With Love* (which keeps Cheung Man, Ng Man Tat, and Gabriel Wong, and adds a handful of Taiwanese pop stars).

**First Strike** (1996; Hong Kong, Ac) D: Stanley Tong C: Jackie Chan, Jackson Liu, Annie Wu, Bill Tung, Jouri Petrov

Stanley Tong takes the helm here for a semi-sequel to Chan's trilogy of "supercop" films, *Police Story 1, 2,* and *Supercop* (1985–1992). This time, Chan's character (called simply "Jackie") is recruited by the CIA to assist them in an operation that takes him around the globe, to frozen Ukraine and sun-drenched Australia, among other fabulous locations. The tissue-thin plot involves Jackie tracking down a missing missile and the former intelligence officer who stole it, Tsui (Liu); it turns out that Tsui is just a puppet for the real brains behind the theft—blackmailed into cooperating to protect his pretty younger sister (played by Taiwanese actress Annie Wu). The real attraction here is Jackie's stunts, which are bigger and more impressive than ever: An insane snowboard chase that ends with a leap onto a hovering helicopter, and then a fall into a frozen lake; an incredible battle in a warehouse involving props like a push-broom and a stepladder; a fight on giant stilts in which Jackie kicks a villain unconscious while he's standing on a second-story balcony; and an oxygen-deprived duel in a tank full of (obviously mechanical) sharks. The comic sequences (like Jackie in koala underpants) are "just clutter," say reviewers, who are divided between those who appreciate the "straight, uncut action" and those who found this "Bond ripoff" to be a "soulless mess."

**Fist of Legend** (1994; Hong Kong, Ac, Pd) D: Gordon Chan C: Jet Li, Shinobu Nakayama, Chin Siu Ho, Yasuaki Kurota, Ada Choi

A "taut" and "respectful" remake of Bruce Lee's classic *Fist of Fury* (1972), this film seamlessly inserts Jet Li into the legendary shoes of the Dragon, playing kung fu student Chen Zhen, who returns to his Shanghai martial arts academy to find his master Huo dead and the school in ruins. He rightly suspects foul play, and after challenging and defeating the master who killed his *sifu*, he requests an autopsy of Huo's body, which shows traces of poison. Tension between Li's school and its Japanese rival rises toward a breaking point—which arrives when the Japanese master, Akutagawa (Jackson Liu) turns up dead. The culprit behind the second murder is a scheming Japanese general, Fujita (Billy Chow), who is seeking to cause an international incident, allowing him to crush the Chinese power to fight once and for all. It all leads up to a climactic battle between Chen and Fujita, which is "appropriately fantastic, with choreography that brings the brutal and direct combat of Bruce Lee into a new acrobatic dimension." Reviewers noted that the original *Fist of Fury* was highly dependent on Chinese nationalism for its emotional thrills, repeatedly depicting Japanese characters as "crude cartoon villains"; "this version is significantly more balanced, with more depth provided to the enemy team—and the added twist that Chen's girlfriend is Japanese." "One of Li's best to date, and it'll stay that way. A true must see."

### *Flirting Scholar* (1993; Hong Kong, Cm, Pd) D: Lee Lik Chi C: Stephen Chiau, Gong Li, Natalis Chan, Cheng Pei Pei, James Wong

In this rollicking costume farce, based on a classic Ming Dynasty comic tale, Chiau plays Tong Pak Fu, an eminent member of the scholarly class who is "blessed" with eight good-for-nothing wives, who spend their days gossiping and playing mah-jongg, with little time for or interest in their husband and his literary pursuits. One day, Master Tong catches sight of the beautiful Chen Heung (Li), a servant girl at a household that unfortunately happens to be presided over by Madame Wah (Cheng), the jilted ex-girlfriend of Tong's father. In order to get closer to her, he goes undercover as a servant in Wah's household. Ultimately, however, the plot here is just a skeleton on which Chiau hangs a vast array of comic set-pieces. Reviewers called it "high on the list of Chiau's finest works," with his "signature *mo lei tau* humor in full sail." "A plus is the casting of 'queen of swords' Cheng Pei Pei as Chiau's nemesis; she shows that she has plenty of martial arts left in her, as well as surprisingly sharp comic timing."

### *Flowers of Shanghai* (1998; Taiwan, Pd, Dr) D: Hou Hsiao-hsien C: Annie Shizuka Inoh, Shuan Fang, Michiko Hada, Tony Leung Chiu Wai, Carina Lau

An atypical film for Taiwanese New Cinema master Hou Hsiao-hsien, in that its setting is not contemporary Taiwan (his chosen milieu), but rather nineteenth-century Shanghai. Framed as a series of vignettes, the film dreamily examines the lives of a set of "woman flowers"—elite prostitutes—and the men upon whom they depend. Tony Leung Chiu Wai plays one such gentleman, Master Wang Liansheng, while Michiko Hada plays his longtime favorite Crimson. As the film opens, it seems that Wang has recently dallied with another "flower"—Jasmine (Vicky

Wei), leading to turmoil within the pleasure-house's ranks. This is but one of the threads of tension, competition, and conspiracy that runs through the weave of the courtesan society; given Hou's naturalistic, one-take-one-setup camera technique, audience members feel uncomfortably like keyhole voyeurs, which is certainly Hou's intent. Reviewers called it "perhaps the most beautiful film of the decade," "a near-mystical reverie" that explores the "cruelty of sexual commerce."

***Fong Sai Yuk I and II*** (1993; Hong Kong, Ac, Cm, Pd) D: Corey Yuen C: Jet Li, Josephine Siao, Michelle Lee, Sibelle Hu, Chen Sung Yung, Amy Kwok Oi Ming

The "other" great Cantonese folk hero of the silver screen, Fong Sai Yuk, was a turn-of-the-century patriot whose exploits, like those of Wong Fei Hung, have been regularly portrayed in film and television since the dawn of Chinese cinema. This revisionist take on the legend focuses on Fong in his youth, before he went to the Shaolin Temple for his final training, and before he joined the rebel patriots of the Red Flower Society. The central conceit of this film is that Fong's role model and martial arts teacher wasn't his father, but his mother—played here by Josephine Siao, in a stroke of brilliant casting. In the first film, Fong (Li) wins the heart of a gorgeous Manchu girl named Lui Ting Ting, despite his mother's "assistance" (she enters a competition for Lui's hand as Fong's "elder brother," Fong Tai Yuk—and ends up winning a female admirer of her own). He also joins the rebel Red Flower Society and defends the organization against Manchu champion Governor Oryeetor (Zhao Wen Zhou). The rushed-into-theaters sequel picks up shortly after the events of the first, with Fong Sai Yuk (Li) now a full-fledged member of the Red Flower Society, albeit one currently in the doghouse, due to his running hostilities with obnoxious fellow rebel Yu (Chi Chen-hua). Assigned by Red Flower leader Master Chen (Adam Cheng) to steal a box containing secret documents—which turns out to be in the possession of Manchu princess Angie (Kwok)—Fong ends up a contestant in a competition to win Angie's hand in marriage. Fortunately for the rebel effort—and unfortunately for his relationship with Ting Ting—he succeeds. Reviewers called the first "one of the best mixtures of comedy and traditional kung fu yet," and "undoubtedly one of Jet Li's best," although "the true scene-stealer, of course, is 'supermom' Josephine Siao." The second was called "slapdash compared to the original," but "still great fun"; the "characters and situations are so engaging that you forgive the 'perfunctory' storyline."

***For Fun*** (1992; Mainland, Dr) D: Ning Ying C: Huang Zungluo, Huang Wenjie, He Ming, Han Shanxu

Mainland China's foremost woman filmmaker directs this initial installment in what she calls her "ordinary people" trilogy, attempting to capture the personality of Beijing society before its inevitable total slide into modernity. Based on a novel by Chen Jiangong, this film follows Old Han, a recently retired custodian at a Beijing opera theater who finds himself not quite ready to slide into a life of rest and relaxation. While walking through the park, he runs into a group of senior citizens who gather to perform amateur Beijing operas "for fun." He decides that their performances could be improved if only they organized themselves, and he begins to provide them with the benefit of his experience—completely against their will. Reviewers called it a "truly wonderful portrayal" of a disappearing facet of Beijing society.

***From Beijing with Love*** (1994; Hong Kong, Cm) D: Stephen Chiau, Lee Lik Chi C: Stephen Chiau, Anita Yuen, Pauline Chan, Law Kar Ying, Wong Kam Kong

A spit-take parody of Bond, this film offers up Chiau as Ling Ling Chai (whose name translates to "007"), a member of Chinese intelligence's backup backup reserve unit whose full-time job is pork vendor. Agent Ling has been waiting for a call to action for years, but the division chief (Wong) has his own agenda in finally bringing Ling in from the cold—he's secretly the one behind the crime in question (the theft of a rare dinosaur fossil) and he wants to assign the least competent agent the bureau has to the case. After giving Ling a perfunctory briefing, he sends him off to meet his contact, Siu Kam (Yuen), who is actually working as one of the chief's paid assassins. (Siu Kam's parents and grandparents were traitors, so she's been brainwashed into thinking that she must be a traitor too, to carry on the family tradition.) Despite the chief's hopes that Ling will get himself killed or allow himself to be killed by Siu Kam, the dense butcher-turned-spy gets closer and closer to solving the mystery—forcing the chief to don his suit of superarmor and his high-tech golden gun to hunt down Ling himself. The spy genre is so ripe with opportunities for parody that Chiau is like a kid in a candy shop here, gleefully gunning down such clichés as the "naked woman in silhouette" opening credit sequence; the "unveiling the spy accessories" scene (rather than being a series of deadly devices, all of Ling's secret tools are convertible into either hair dryers or electric shavers); and the "escaping certain death" scene (in which, faced with execution, Ling discovers a remarkably simple means of dodging the bullet). Reviewers called it "a textbook-perfect spy satire" that will "make you laugh until whatever you're drinking comes out of your nose." "Anita Yuen doesn't have much to do here, but her wide-eyed, deadpan reactions to Chiau's equally deadpan idiocies are part of what make the film work so well." Chiau adapted his secret agent spoof for dynastic-era China in an almost as brilliant semi-sequel, *Forbidden City Cop* (1996).

### *Full Contact* (1992; Hong Kong, Ac) D: Ringo Lam C: Chow Yun Fat, Simon Yam, Anthony Wong, Ann Bridgewater, Bonnie Fu

Nightclub bouncer and expert marksman Jeff (Chow) agrees to take on an illicit mission in order to save the life of his pal Sam (Wong), who owes thousands to a local loanshark. The job, involving the hijacking of a truck delivering stolen arms, teams up Jeff, Sam, and another of their friends, Chung (Chris Lee) with a bizarre team of bandits led by murderous gay stereotype Judge (Yam). Judge proceeds to betray the three pals during the mission, leading to Chung's death and Jeff's presumed fatality. As it turns out, Jeff survives, but with several of the fingers on his shooting hand blown off. Recovering from his injuries and nursing his desire for revenge, Jeff returns home some months later fit and ready for action (having learned how to shoot with his left hand), only to find that his pal Sam is now married to Jeff's longtime girlfriend Mona. Rather than blame Sam, he enlists his help in taking down real villain Judge, in a sequence that is among the most memorable shootouts in Hong Kong action cinema. This film is famous for Lam's innovative use of the "bulletcam," which seems to ride projectiles into their eventual (and usually human) targets. Reviewers called it "campy" but "undeniably entertaining"; "high-class exploitation" with a "memorably over-the-top turn by Yam."

### *Full Moon in New York* (1990; Hong Kong, Dr) D: Stanley Kwan C: Sylvia Chang, Maggie Cheung, Siqin Gaowa, Josephine Koo

Three women—one from Hong Kong, one from Taiwan, and one from the Mainland—become friends in New York City, sharing their different Chinese and American experiences. Reviewers called it "interesting," with "consistently good performances" from the "great lead actresses," but "slow and uneven," with "implausible plot twists marring the story's flow."

***Gen-X Cops*** (1999; Hong Kong, Ac) D: Benny Chan C: Nicholas Tse, Stephen Fung, Sam Lee, Daniel Wu, Grace Yip

Produced in partnership with Jackie Chan's JC Group and starring a slew of the industry's fastest-rising young actors, this actioner was developed with Western crossover possibilities firmly in mind; much of the dialogue is even spoken in English. Eric Tsang plays a nebbishy cop assigned to investigate an apparent partnership between the Triads and the Yakuza, led by a ruthless young ganglord named Daniel (Wu). Realizing that the landscape of crime has changed for the twenty-first century, he decides that the only solution is to field a team of twenty-first century cops—Gen-X Cops. He recruits the three academy rookies whose attitudes have been judged the most idiosyncratic, uncooperative, and rebellious—Jack (Tse), Match (Fung) and Alien (Lee)—and offers them two options: be expelled from the academy or join his team. Reviewers were divided over whether this film was a "breakneck thrillride combining Hong Kong attitude and Hollywood effects" or a "misbegotten hybrid mess" with a "way too self-consciously hip sensibility." Followed by the inferior sequel *Gen-Y Cops,* which replaces Nicholas Tse with Edison Chen.

***Gigolo and Whore*** (1991; Hong Kong, Cm, Dr) D: Terry Tong C: Simon Yam, Carina Lau, Alex Fong, Angile Leung

In this inversion of *Pretty Woman,* Carina Lau plays Chung Siu Hung, a frumpy Mainland hick who comes to Hong Kong to stay with her cousin Kiki (Leung), but has her money and belongings stolen from her minutes after arrival. With no cash for food or transportation, she's rescued by Sam, an amused gentleman in the kind of outfit that shouts "professional sex worker." It turns out that Sam is a gigolo—and one known quite well by Kiki, who happens to be a whore herself (and doing quite well by it). After Chung is fired from her job as waitress at the club where Kiki is a "hostess," she encounters Sam once again, and asks him to train her to become a call girl. He tells her that it is not a profession for the faint of heart, but she's determined to follow through, so Sam agrees, giving her instruction in everything from how to satisfy a man orally (that is to say, screaming and moaning with convincing ecstasy during sex) to the most important skill of all: how not to fall in love. This last lesson is of course the most critical, since Chung has fallen for Sam in the process. When he breaks her heart to prove his point, she gets the picture, and soon becomes the most sought-after whore in town. Eventually, of course, Sam realizes that he's failed to take his own critical advice. Reviewers called it "fairly entertaining," although it "completely dismisses the uglier aspects of the sex trade, making prostitution look like a great career move." Followed by an unrelated but watchable sequel, *Gigolo and Whore II* (1992).

### *Golden Girls, The* (1995; Hong Kong, Cm, Dr) D: Joe Ma C: Lau Ching Wan, Anita Yuen, Ada Choi, Francis Ng, Paulyn Suen

This nostalgic look at the sixties heyday of Hong Kong cinema features Anita Yuen as Mei Ball, a pretty and talented aspiring actress whose career has been confounded by her refusal to sleep with her directors. Meanwhile, Ada Choi plays her friend Lulu—more glamorous, less talented, and somewhat less scrupulous about her sexual habits. Lau Ching Wan is Chun Wai, a screenwriter hopelessly in love with Mei, but whose affections are mostly ignored, until Mei decides to take a lengthy retreat from the film industry to consider her future options. Returning from her vacation, she finds that Lulu and Chun have moved in together—but that Chun still clearly has his heart set on her. Things get more complicated when Chun gets his breakthrough chance to direct an adaptation of the opera classic *The Butterfly Lovers,* and casts Mei as one of the leads—the male lead. This stroke of genius transforms Mei into a huge star, albeit one with more swooning female fans than male ones. It also threatens to end several relationships at once, disrupting friendships that have lasted for half a decade. Reviewers called it a "dazzling" "little gem," with a "brilliant screenplay" by Joe Ma (whose directing talents here are not as consistently praised). "Anita Yuen is wonderful," and her "chemistry with Lau Ching Wan is perfect."

### *Good Men, Good Women* (1995; Taiwan, Dr) D: Hou Hsiao-hsien C: Lim Giong, Annie Shizuka Inoh, Jack Kao

Annie Shizuka Inoh plays Liang Ching, an actress preparing for her part in a film (also called *Good Men Good Women*) that takes as its subject a Taiwanese couple who went from being heroes and patriots for their resistance against the Japanese to being terrorized by the Nationalist government for their leftist leanings in the fifties . But Liang is being terrorized herself as well, by an anonymous blackmailer who faxes her revealing pages from her missing personal journal that detail her tawdry past, as a junkie bar girl with a Triad ex-boyfriend. Slowly, Liang sees a pattern of similarities between her own experiences and those of her character in the film—which both excites her, as an actress seeking a "way in" to her performance, and frightens her, as a woman being stalked by a strange and presumably dangerous individual. Reviewers called it a "masterful weaving" of "past and present, fiction and history"; "slow, but hypnotic," this film "demands multiple viewings" to fully understand its "full measure of riches."

### *Goodbye, South, Goodbye* (1996; Taiwan, Dr, Cm) D: Hou Hsiao-hsien C: Lim Giong, Annie Shikuza Inoh, Xu Guiyin, Jack Kao

This was Hou's conscious attempt to fashion a more commercially appealing picture, although it retains his idiosyncratic stylistic touches and camera techniques. The film, something like a "road movie" focusing on a pair of small-time hoods and their molls, proved to be quite popular with Taiwan's visibly tattooed set. Xiao Kao (Kao) is a gangster turned restaurant manager whose young sidekick, Flathead (Lim), is constantly getting into trouble with both other thugs and the law. Kao, meanwhile, is beginning to realize that he's heading into middle age with little in the bank and less by way of prospects, so, prompted by the domestic desires of his girlfriend Ying (Xu), he decides to run a big final scam, strike it rich, and retire. He hustles a deal involving the transfer of a large herd of pigs, and prepares to travel south to complete the transaction. Meanwhile, Flathead goes along as well, since he's being pursued by a group of very angry Triads, to whom he owes a fortune in gambling debts. With them goes Pretzel (Inoh), Flathead's equally no-account girlfriend. While down south, Flathead goes to visit his family in hopes of getting a handout, and ends up in an altercation with his older cousin, a police officer. An enraged Flathead swears his revenge, but before he can do something rash, he, Kao, and Pretzel are captured by the gangsters who've pursued him all the way from Taipei. In the end, it's Flathead's cop cousin who gets them off the hook—but as they head back toward Taipei in defeat, greater tragedy awaits. Reviewers called it a "knife-edge look at contemporary Taiwan" that "inspires both tears and laughter"; a "subdued" comedy of "existential inertia and frustrated ambition."

### *Happy Together* (1997; Hong Kong, Dr) D: Wong Kar Wai C: Tony Leung Chiu Wai, Leslie Cheung, Chang Chen

A drama about the longing and waiting and the emotional distance between people who spend every moment of their days in close proximity. The gay angle of this film is both critical to the film's integrity and yet not a factor central to its impact; in short, Wong creates this as a gay story that is also a universal story. Ho Po Wing (Cheung) and Lai Yiu Fai (Leung) are lovers who live together in Buenos Aires, but whose relationship is slowly evaporating. Ho is a sexually voracious, emotionally manipulative hustler; Lai is a steadier sort, but has his own deep-seated problems, notably represented by the fact that as much as he wants Ho out of his life, his continued custody of Ho's passport means his ex can never go farther away from him than the border. After the two separate, Ho takes up prostitution to support himself; when Ho is battered by a trick, Lai takes him in and cares for him, but refuses to allow their relationship to rekindle. Eventually, Lai's interaction with a young Taiwanese tourist (Chang) leads him out of Argentina, out of Ho's life, and into a new direction of his own, liberated from his role as Ho's constant other. Reviewers called it "luminous," and "perhaps the most accessible of Wong's recent films"; "engrossing and deceptively simple," with a triad of "superb performances."

### *Hard Boiled* (1992; Hong Kong, Ac) D: John Woo C: Chow Yun Fat, Tony Leung Chiu Wai, Teresa Mo, Phillip Chan, Phillip Kwok

After making this film, John Woo headed to Hollywood for good; it is also the last film that Woo has made to date in collaboration with his chosen avatar, Chow Yun Fat. Here Chow plays Detective Tequila, a jazz-loving, hard-drinking cop; after Tequila's partner is murdered by a vicious gang of arms traffickers, he decides to stage a commando raid on the perpetrators' headquarters—almost taking out undercover operative Tony (Leung) in the process. Tequila realizes that something is going on that he, the officer assigned to the investigation, has not been informed about, driving him to storm into the office of his superintendent, Teresa (Mo), who also happens to be his sometime girlfriend. The truth comes out: Tony has been under the deepest of covers for months to gain the trust of Hui, the head of the gunrunning gang; he's almost at the point of finding out where the thugs are hiding their vast trove of ordnance, and when he does, the force will be ready to move in. Tequila's maverick attack has jeopardized Tony's position, since one of his rivals in the organization is curious to know why he's the only one to have survived. As a result, plans are changed and timetables are moved up, and Tony is barely able to get the message out to the force about the location of the cache in time: beneath a public hospital. The final forty minutes of this thriller involve the attempts by Tequila, Teresa, and other members of the force to simultaneously stop the criminals and prevent the patients from being harmed in the crossfire—possibly the longest "finale" in the history of action cinema. Reviewers called it "a study guide to Woo's entire previous canon"; the "apocalyptic" "final firefight has been compared to the bombing of Dresden"—although it's "mildly damaged by an unnecessary baby-related potty-joke that comes at Chow's expense."

**He's a Woman, She's a Man** (1994; Hong Kong, Cm) D: Peter Chan C: Anita Yuen, Leslie Cheung, Carina Lau, Jordan Chan, Eric Tsang

Yuen plays idol-worshiping Wing, a young woman whose life is dedicated to "supporting" superstar couple Rose (Lau) and Sam (Cheung)—the former a top pop diva, the latter a morose and enigmatic producer who writes all of Rose's hit songs. Although to the rest of the world Sam and Rose are a fairy-tale fantasy, the truth is that Sam's interest in her is starting to fade: Sam first met Rose years ago as a young, unknown singer and transformed her into a big star, and now that she's made it, his restless Pygmalion complex has gotten the better of him. To reignite his creativity, Sam decides to look for a fresh talent—but is careful to stipulate that his new find must be male. To get the chance to actually see Sam in person, Wing recruits her goofy roommate Fish (Chan) to school her in the ways of walking, talking, and acting like a man. During Wing's audition, a jealous Rose dares Sam to sign the pitifully untalented "boy" on the spot, and Sam accepts, declaring that he can turn anyone into a star. After Wing moves into a spare room in Sam's apartment, some awkward dynamics ensue, as Rose at first believes Wing has a crush on her, and then that Wing is gay; meanwhile, to his horror, Sam has begun to suspect that the old pattern is beginning to recur, his new protégé's sex notwithstanding. Reviewers praised its "delightfully barbed humor at the expense of the Hong Kong music industry, its fans, and its performers," including Cheung himself, whose sexual preferences have become a tabloid fixture. The film is slightly marred by Eric Tsang's cartoonishly swishy gay character, "Auntie," but "it's all so good-natured that it's hard to imagine anyone truly finding it offensive." Followed by a worthy but somewhat less stellar sequel, *Who's the Woman, Who's the Man* (1996), which brought in Anita Mui as Fan Fan, an ambisexual temptress who sleeps with both Sam *and* Wing.

### *Hero Never Dies, A* (1998; Hong Kong, Ac) D: Johnnie To C: Leon Lai, Lau Ching Wan, Fiona Leung, Yoyo Mung

Jack (Lai) and Martin (Lau) are a pair of killers who work for opposing gangs. Although Jack and Martin are deadly enemies, out of professional courtesy, in their off hours the two hitmen socialize, introduce their respective girlfriends to each other, and exchange the kind of arm-punching gibes that rival golf players might offer in the clubhouse. But buddy-talk ends at the muzzle of a gun, and while on assignment in Thailand, the two end up dealing each other crippling injuries; meanwhile, their respective bosses, at the advice of a fortune teller, have decided to join forces—sealing the deal by agreeing to eliminate their two assassins. This turns out to be a bad idea for all concerned, but especially the bosses. Reviewers called it "bleak, contemporary," and "certainly worth seeing," both for the "sterling performances of its leads" and its "coherently off-kilter script."

### *Heroic Trio, The* (1993; Hong Kong, Ac) D: Johnnie To C: Michelle Yeoh, Maggie Cheung, Anita Mui, Damian Lau, Anthony Wong

Three of Hong Kong's brightest femmes fatale join forces for a science-fiction-action-fantasy with comic-book zip. Wonder Woman (Mui) is a masked crusader who uses her kung fu skills to secretly assist the efforts of her husband, Inspector Lau (Lau). Chat the Thief Catcher (Cheung) is a cat-suited bounty hunter who has escaped the mind control of a dark supernatural overlord referred to only as the Demon (Yam Sai Kwoon). Aided by henchman Number 9 (Wong) and a similarly brainwashed superwoman known variously as the "Invisible Girl" and "Number 3" (Yeoh), the Demon is kidnaping babies in search of the child destined to rule all of China after the coming of the apocalypse. Reviewers called it a "visually stunning" "Hong Kong cinema insider's favorite" with "incredible mood and atmosphere"; "the plot doesn't make much sense, but the trio of female leads drive this bus merrily along at 60 m.p.h." Followed by an even darker sequel reuniting the three superheroines, *Executioners* (1993).

### *High Risk* (1995; Hong Kong, Ac, Cm) D: Wong Jing C: Jet Li, Jacky Cheung, Chingmy Yau, Valerie Chow, Kelvin Wong, Charlie Yeung Choi-Nei, Yeung Chung Hin

This "devastating" satire so infuriated Jackie Chan that it was rumored he'd vowed never to work with any of its participants again. Frankie Lane (Cheung) is an immature, lecherous, cowardly clown of an action star who boasts that he "always does his own stunts," when in reality he never does *any* of them—his loyal body-guard Kit Li (Li) takes the real risks. When a priceless jewelry collection is scheduled to be unveiled on the penthouse floor of Hong Kong's highest skyscraper, superstar Lane is invited, as are Lane's father (Wu) and his manager (Cho). Kit tags along in case anything happens, and of course, something does, in a plot torn from the script of *Die Hard.* Swept up in the chaos are an intrepid reporter determined to expose the true secret behind Lane's stunts (Yau), and a couple of young lovers (Charlie Yeung Choi-Nei and Yeung Chung Hin), all of whom manage to get in the way of Kit's attempts to save the day. Reviewers called it "funny enough," with some "potent action sequences"; however, the "Chan-bashing quickly moves from humorous to just plain cruel," and "Jacky Cheung's rubbery mugging is too annoying to be effective."

*Hitman* (1998; Hong Kong, Ac, Cm) D: Stephen Tung C: Jet Li, Eric Tsang, Gigi Leung, Simon Yam

As this thriller opens, an aging Japanese gangster named Tsukamoto threatens his anonymous assailant with a warning: He has set aside a "revenge fund" of $100 million in the event that he is ever murdered. The killer whacks him anyway, and Hong Kong transforms into a hitman's convention, with the world's most notorious gunmen arriving to compete for the gigantic bounty. Among them is Tai Feng (Li), a rookie killer who has so far proven too kind-hearted to take out even a single victim. Still, Tai's obvious fighting skills lead Sam (Tsang), a self-styled "hitman contractor," to stake him the $5 million needed to enroll him in the contest. Meanwhile, the competition fans out to search for the mysterious man called the "King of Killers," while a dogged cop (Yam) does his best to put a halt to the deadly game. Things become complicated when Sam's beautiful daughter Kiki (Leung) enters the picture—and more complicated still when the nested secrets surrounding the identity of the King of Killers begin to unravel. Reviewers called this film—Li's last before moving to Hollywood—a "stylish" "last hurrah," with a "fantastic story premise" and "dazzling, sophisticated action."

*Hole, The* (1998; Taiwan, Dr) D: Tsai Ming-liang C: Lee Kang-sheng, Lin Hui-chin, Miao Tian, Tong Hsiang-chu, Yang Kuei-mei

This typically strange film by Malaysian-born Taiwanese "Next Wave" filmmaker Tsai is set in the premillennial year of 1999, in which a strange virus has been afflicting residents of Taipei; the symptoms of the disease are an unusual compulsion to emulate cockroachlike behavior. Infected blocks of the city are cordoned off, with those residents who have not yet been stricken asked to evacuate for designated "safe zones" while a cure for the disease is found, but some holdouts refuse to abandon their homes—including a young man (Lee) who owns a small market and the woman who lives immediately downstairs from him (Yang). A visit by a plumber one day results in the creation of a large hole between the two apartments, which initially provides the young man with some minor voyeuristic pleasures, but eventually becomes like something of an emotional conduit between these two islets of humanity. Reviewers noted that the film is punctuated with musical interludes inspired by sixties movie songstress Grace Chang Ge Lan, which inject a "campy energy" into the otherwise "spare, impersonal texture of the film"; an "original and clever" musing on the "primal need for human connection."

### Holy Virgin vs. the Evil Dead, The (1991; Hong Kong, Hr, CIII) D: Wong Chun Yeung C: Donnie Yen, Pauline Yeung, Ben Lam, Kathy Chow, Sibelle Hu

The title alerts viewers up front to the fact that this is not high art cinema, and indeed, this trash-opus is far from ashamed of its origins and its objectives; nudity is gleefully presented under its opening credits, followed by more nudity in the film's opening scene, followed by a gory sequence of violence. Teacher Shiang (Yen) is on a nighttime outing with five of his female students when the group is attacked by a bizarre creature with neon-green eyes; although Shiang survives the attack, no one else does, and he awakes in a clearing surrounded by corpses and body parts. Shiang and the local police determine that the killer creature originates in Cambodia, and is the object of veneration of a cult whose goal is either to rule the world, or, failing that, to rip the clothes off as many young women as possible. Shiang, the cops, Shiang's ex-wife (who's sleeping with the chief investigator), and various comic-relief types then go to Cambodia to assist the "holy virgin," a priestess of the High Wind Tribe, in defeating the monster and its nefarious worshipers. Reviewers called it a "sleazefest" with "few adequate comparisons" for its "fundamental strangeness," its "total abandonment of logic early in its plot," and its cast, which is "head and shoulders above the performers in most such outings."

***Hu-Du-Men*** (1996; Hong Kong, Dr) D: Shu Kei C: Josephine Siao, Anita Yuen, Daniel Chan, Chung King Fai, Waise Lee

Based on a play by Raymond To, this film features Josephine Siao as Lang Kim Sum, the middle-aged star and owner of a Chinese opera company who must confront both the advance of time and the march of progress as she prepares to retire from the stage at the top of her profession (reviewers note that the screaming, fainting antics of her fans are a clear dig at the idol-driven Hong Kong pop scene). Lang specializes in playing cross-dressed male roles, yet has trouble accepting the facts of her daughter's relationship with another woman. Meanwhile, she's been assigned an apprentice to train, so as to preserve the secrets of her craft for the next generation—an enthusiastic young Singaporean woman named Yuk Sheung, played by Anita Yuen. And her husband, whose business is failing, wants all of them to emigrate to North America. Reviewers called it a "delightful experience" with "outstanding performances" by all concerned, most notably Siao, whose "brilliantly deadpan" turn is the "undoubted soul" of the film.

***In the Heat of the Sun*** (1995; Mainland, Dr) D: Jiang Wen C: Jiang Wen, Xia Yu, Ning Jing, Tao Hong, Siqin Gaowa

This directorial debut by Jiang Wen, one of China's most popular actors, triggered a wave of controversy for its subversive, revisionist take on the Cultural Revolution. His conceit is to explore the period from the perspective of a group of wild and rather spoiled adolescents, for whom the era's breakdown of discipline and freedom from supervision means simply the chance to do anything they please. Led by an enterprising boy named Monkey (Xia), a gang of youths terrorize teachers, fight with rival gangs, ride the chaotic streets of Beijing on their bicycles, and chase after girls, knowing that the adults around them have bigger problems to worry about. The film's screenwriter is Wang Shuo, one of the Mainland's most popular punk novelists, and he presents these delinquent youths in a carefree, yet deeply ironic light: They're like Peter Pan's lost boys in a socialist Never Never Land. Reviewers called it one of the "ten best Chinese films of the nineties," and lauded Xia Yu's "simply astonishing" performance. "Jiang presents a kind of jubilant *Lord of the Flies*"; "imagine anyone thinking of the Cultural Revolution as the 'good old days'!"

***Iron Monkey*** (1993; Hong Kong, Ac, Pd) D: Yuen Woo Ping C: Yu Rongguang, Donnie Yen, Jean Wang, Tsang Sze Man, Yam Sai Kwoon

Made in the midst of early-nineties Wong Fei Hung mania. The fim's titular hero,
played by Yu Rongguang, is a masked martial arts master who steals from wealthy
and corrupt Ching officials and distributes his loot to the poor. After being victimized one time too many, the governor of the province, Cheng (James Wong),
decides to fight fire with fire—kidnaping the son of another local martial arts master and blackmailing the latter to assist in capturing the Monkey. The master happens to be Wong Kei Ying (Yen), and his son, played by acrobatic female martial
artist Tsang Sze Man, is the young Fei Hung. Wong and the Monkey end up joining
forces to thwart Governor Cheng, but when a traitor Shaolin monk named Hin
Hung (Yam) comes to Guangdong to end the Monkey threat once and for all,
even the duo's combined might may not be enough. Reviewers called the film
"smart" and "fast," with "dazzling" action sequences; nearly a decade after its
Hong Kong run, and on the heels of *Crouching Tiger, Hidden Dragon*'s triumph,
the film had a highly successful release in the United States.

***Justice, My Foot!*** (1992; Hong Kong, Cm, Pd) D: Johnnie To C: Stephen
Chiau, Anita Mui, Ng Man Tat, Carrie Ng, Paul Chun

The first of Chiau's unofficial "legal trilogy" (of which 1994's *Hail the Judge!* and
1997's *Lawyer, Lawyer* are the others), this film was one of the biggest box office
hits of 1992, confirming Chiau's status as Hong Kong's most consistent cinematic
draw. Here he plays a lawyer named Sung Shih Chieh—a fast-talking hustler
whose dazzling verbal gymnastics enable him to sway the sternest of judges to his
side. Although he has retired from the legal profession due to his wife's pregnancy, when a rich tycoon offers him an enormous fee to defend his murderous
son, Sung decides to unretire for one last case—against the wishes of his wife
(played with acrobatic grace by Anita Mui). Shortly after he wins the case, his wife
has a miscarriage. Seeing this as a punishment for his ethically questionable
actions, Sung decides to retire for good—until a woman (Carrie Ng) asks him to
represent her in prosecuting her brother-in-law, whom she (correctly) accuses of
killing her husband. Unfortunately, her brother-in-law's massive bribes quickly sub-
orn the local magistrate (Ng Man Tat), with the result that Sung not only loses the
case but is thrown in jail as a possible alternative suspect. It will take all of his con-

siderable wit and wiles just to get himself free: Will he successfully be able to appeal his client's case as well? Reviewers called it a "showcase for Chiau's lightning *mo lei tau* verbal wizardry," which "unfortunately does not translate well to English." However, even Anglophones will enjoy scenes of an "agile Anita Mui booting her hangdog husband around the room," as well as the "requisite toilet humor and goofy slapstick."

### *Keep Cool* (1997; Mainland, Cm) D: Zhang Yimou C: Jiang Wen, Qu Ying, Li Baotian, Ge You, Zhang Yimou

The setting, style, and genre of this film mark it as a pointedly atypical work for director Zhang; his canon has primarily consisted of melodramas, usually set in the past, and always backdropped by lovely, languorous images of the Chinese countryside. Here Zhang adapts a comic novel by Shu Ping starring Jiang Wen as Xiao Shuai, a bookseller in love with a gorgeous young woman named An Hong (Qu). Sadly, An is already spoken for, being the girlfriend of a cabaret owner named Lao Zhang (Li). The situation rapidly spins into chaos, and a police officer (Ge You) is ultimately forced to intervene and mediate. Reviewers praised the film's "fantastic" cast, starring as it does Mainland China's three most popular male actors, along with top Mainland supermodel Qu. "Zhang rolls the dice on this one—even adopting a trendy but appropriate handheld-camera technique"; "anyone who thinks Zhang is capable only of directing soggy potboilers must see this." *Keep Cool* never received much Western attention, as it was barred from participation at Cannes as part of a scheme to prevent Zhang Yuan's audacious *East Palace, West Palace* (1996) from being shown abroad. "A sadly overlooked classic."

### *King of Beggars* (1992; Hong Kong, Cm, Pd) D: Gordon Chan C: Stephen Chiau, Sharla Cheung Man, Ng Man Tat, Norman Tsui, Lam Wai

In this big-budget martial arts comedy spectacle, Chiau plays So Chan, illiterate layabout son of an equally worthless but influential father, a general in the Qing army (Chiau's regular sidekick Ng Man Tat). General So has brought his boy up as a chip off the old block, and the two spend their time frequenting brothels and living the good life, with no particular goals or ambitions—until So Chan meets the beautiful prostitute Yu Shang (Sharla Cheung Man) and falls instantly in love. She rejects his advances, telling him that he must prove his worth to her by becoming the country's top kung fu scholar if he wants her love. So Chan vows to do just that, and enlists his father's help in preparing for the examinations. Unfortunately, although So succeeds handily in the martial arts segment of the tests, he can't even write his own name and is forced to cheat on the written segment. Discovering this, General So's evil rival Chiu (Tsui) exposes So Chan and urges the emperor to make an example of father and son. The emperor announces that as a penalty, he is stripping the Sos of their rank, riches, and privilege, and sentencing them to live as beggars for the rest of their lives. The dirty, hungry, and pathetic duo nearly die of exposure before they are found by none other than Yu Shang, who invites them to join the "Beggars Association," of which she herself is a member. But the sight of lovely Yu Shang sends So Chan into a deep depression, and he ends up spending much of his time sleeping off his misery—until he has a vision of his old *sifu,* who suggests to him a way in which he can restore his honor and regain face in Yu Shang's eyes. So Chan takes the advice to heart, and becomes a leader among the beggars; when Yu Shang is kidnapped by Chiu, he leads his smelly crew against the evil warlord and saves not only his love but the emperor himself, using a new and potent martial arts technique: "sleeping fist" kung fu! Reviewers called this film—the number-one box office hit of 1993—an "impressive" "combination of kung fu, drama, and comedy," although the climactic final battle is "a bit cheap"; others said it "lacked the heart" of his best work. Still, "fun and weird," with "more kung fu" than most of Chiau's efforts.

### King of Comedy (1999; Hong Kong, Cm) D: Stephen Chiau, Lee Lik Chi C: Stephen Chiau, Karen Mok, Ng Man Tat, Cecilia Cheung, Lam Chi Sin

After a number of disappointing outings, Chiau returned to form with this film, which also marked a new, sophisticated direction for the man who rightly deserves the title "King of Comedy." The film features Chiau as Wan Tin Sau, a struggling actor whose estimation of his own dramatic ability is exponentially greater than it probably should be. Nevertheless, Wan puts everything he has into his performances, which to date have been limited to stints as a crowd-scene extra. Wan's day job is serving as the supervisor for a ramshackle community center. However, his love of acting is so great that it intrudes even into this setting, with Wan running "drama classes" for local Triad kids who want to learn how to act intimidating, and staging low-budget theater productions (including a hilarious adaptation of the classic 1972 Bruce Lee film *Fist of Fury*). One day, lovely, foulmouthed club girl Piu Piu

(Cheung, in her film debut) wanders into one of Wan's classes and spends most of the period heckling him. This puts a dent in Wan's normally unshakable confidence, but after Piu Piu successfully uses one of his moronic pieces of acting advice to earn a huge tip from a client, she ends up returning convinced that there's something to his techniques after all. Meanwhile, Sister Cuckoo (Mok), Hong Kong's top female action star, has become curiously fond of Wan, despite the fact that his bungling has put her latest production in jeopardy. When her producers tell her that her usual leading man is unavailable, she suggests Wan as a substitute—eventually requiring Wan to choose between his developing romance with Piu Piu and fame and fortune with Cuckoo. The ending essentially "resolves Wan's dilemma by ignoring it," but reviewers still call the film a "breathtaking achievement" that shows "Chiau's increasing maturity as an actor and as a filmmaker." The "real triumph" here, however, belongs to Cecilia Cheung, who was catapulted into "It Girl" status by her "incredibly charming and obnoxious" performance here. Watch for "dead-on" parodies of John Woo films, Japanese schoolgirl romances, and even Hong Kong cinema groupie Quentin Tarantino.

***King of Masks, The*** (1996; Mainland, Dr) D: Wu Tianming C: Zhu Xu, Zhou Renyin, Zhang Ruiyang, Zhao Shigang

Wu Tianming, head of the influential Xi'an Studio and "godfather of the Fifth Generation," takes his own turn behind the camera here, filming a "wonderfully rich" tale of an itinerant street performer, Bian Lian Wang (the "King of Masks"), and his quest to find an heir for his "face-changing" storytelling technique, in which he rapidly switches silken masks to adopt a range of fantastic characters. Wandering into an "adoption market," Wang thinks he's found the son of his dreams in "Little Doggie." Only later does he discover that his precious male-child is actually a "useless" female. Reviewers called it "quiet" but "hugely emotional," with an "absolutely astonishing performance by Zhou Renying, a young member of the Xian Acrobatic Troupe, as Doggie."

***Legend of the Mad Phoenix, The*** (1996; Hong Kong, Dr) D: Clifton Ko C: Tse Kwan Ho, So Yuk Wah, Poon Tsan Leung, Ng Yee Lei

This film, another adaptation of a successful Raymond To play, stars young stage actor Tse Kwan Ho in the role of real-life author and composer Kiang Yu Kou, an eccentric but brilliant thirties screenwriter whose pride, arrogance, and oddball behavior got him blackballed from the film industry, leading him to turn back to his first love, Chinese opera; under the name Sap Sam Lung, or "Mr. Thirteen of the South Sea" (Kiang was his father's thirteenth child), he became the foremost opera playwright of the forties and fifties, before succumbing to schizophrenia and dying homeless on the streets. Reviewers called it a "fascinating" and "entertaining" movie that uses Sap Sam Lung as a window on the "turbulent changes that affected Chinese society over the past half-century," as well as, perhaps, a "symbol of Hong Kong itself."

### Life on a String (1991; Mainland, Dr) D: Chen Kaige C: Liu Zhongyuan, Huang Lei, Xu Qing

Adapted from a bleak short story by Shi Tiesheng, this film about a street performer's shattered dream of a magical cure to his blindness has been called director Chen's "most thought-provoking work." Itinerant banjo player Old Master (Liu) has lived for decades without sight, but retains hope in his heart, because a fortuneteller has told him that his vision will return when the thousandth string has broken on his sanxian (Chinese banjo). His simple songs are so enchanting that even warring clans lay down their weapons upon hearing them. When the Master's thousandth string finally breaks, and the piece of paper that is supposed to contain the cure to his blindness falls out, it turns out to be blank. The fortuneteller was a fraud, and the Master's hopes have been for nothing. Reviewers called it a film whose "images and score will linger with you long after it ends," but whose "glacial pace may cause your attention to drift."

### Lifeline (1997; Hong Kong, Dr) D: Johnnie To C: Lau Ching Wan, Alex Fong, Carman Lee, Damian Lau, Ruby Wong

This drama about Hong Kong firemen starts out slowly, but finishes with a forty-minute climax set within a blazing textile factory inferno that is "among the most incredible extended sequences in recent Hong Kong history." Lau Ching Wan plays Yau Sui, a hard-headed but warm-hearted maverick, whose team has been dubbed the "jinxes" by their fellow firefighters, due to the frequency with which they find themselves in death-defying situations. His comrades on the squad include Cheung (Fong), the tough supervisor, and squad leader Madam (Wong);

away from the firehouse, he finds companionship with a depressed young doctor, Annie Chan, whose lover has been neglecting her. But the most memorable character in this film is fire itself—the raging blaze that the "jinx" team goes in to battle, which then traps them within its belly. Although *Lifeline* is clearly inspired by the Ron Howard film *Backdraft,* reviewers note that, "in Hollywood, 10 percent is real, while 90 percent is special effects; in Hong Kong, the ratio is reversed"; they called the film's fiery endgame a "glorious spectacle" with "perfect pacing"; the "finale saves the film from its insipid, soap-operatic first half."

**Longest Summer, The** (1998; Hong Kong, Dr) D: Fruit Chan C: Tony Ho, Sam Lee, Jojo Kuk

This film, director Chan's followup to his surprise sensation *Made in Hong Kong,* follows ex-soldier Ga Yin (Ho) as he searches for a career after being discharged due to Hong Kong's "Reunification" with China. Unable to find work, he and several of his former army comrades end up joining his little brother Ga Suen (Lee) as low-level thugs for the Triads. But the military experience of the new recruits leads Triad boss Siu Wing (Kuk) to conceive of the dangerous idea of using their combat skills by sending them out to rob a bank. Reviewers called it "affecting" and "oddly comic," with "strong performances from the unknown cast," most of whom are nonactors "discovered" by Chan for this film (save for Lee, whom Chan first cast in 1997's *Made in Hong Kong*).

**Lost and Found** (1996; Hong Kong, Dr) D: Lee Chi Ngai C: Kelly Chan, Takeshi Kaneshiro, Michael Wong, Hilary Tsui, Josie Ho

A girl facing terminal illness runs into a mysterious problem-solver and asks him to fulfill a final request, in a movie that prompted both inordinately strong praise and vehement criticism when it was released. Kelly Chan plays the role of Chai Lam, a wealthy girl who has been diagnosed with what is likely to be a fatal case of leukemia. When she sees a young man leave a cellphone behind after unearthing a wallet in a garbage bin, she follows him to return it, and then asks him his name and his business; giving her his business card, he tells her that he is known as That Worm, and runs an "agency" that specializes in "finding lost things." Intrigued, Chai Lam hires Worm (Kaneshiro) to find something she has lost: her sense of hope. Some reviewers found it "maudlin," "heavy-handed," and "pretentious," with an "excess of 'Handover millennialism' in its symbolism"; others, taking it at face value, thought it "incredibly affecting," with "brilliantly quirky characterization," drawn "vividly and with grace" by its trio of leads, particularly Takeshi Kaneshiro's "memorably offbeat" finder of lost things. A "genuinely heartwarming" film that is a "must-see," even for those who aren't fans of melodrama.

### *Love Go Go* (1997; Taiwan, Cm, Dr) D: Chen Yu-hsun C: Tang Na, Liao Huei-jen, Chen Ching-shin, Ma Nien-hsien, Shih E-li

This sophomore effort by Chen Yu-hsun, whose first feature was the acclaimed *Tropical Fish* (1995), is a quartet of quirky, interwoven love stories set in modern Taipei. The first features an affable and portly baker named Ah Sheng (Chen), who is shocked when his long-lost childhood friend Li Hua (Tang) walks into his store and becomes a regular, apparently not recognizing him at all. He begins baking her cakes with secret love messages and including them with her orders, but she becomes puzzled rather than curious. Finally, Ah Sheng—a karaoke buff—sends her an anonymous letter that tells her of his lifelong infatuation, which he will declare in public by singing a love ballad on a national "open mike" television show that night. Ah Sheng's roommate Lily (Liao) has her daily tedium punctured by the discovery of a lost pager, which is urgently flashing a number. She calls it, and is enthralled by the sexy voice of the man who answers. The two begin a phone relationship that culminates with the man asking to meet her in two weeks. This prompts overweight Lily to begin a crash diet, which fails miserably. When she meets her mystery man, he turns out to be complete jerk. Meanwhile, Ah Sung (Shih E-li) is a shy salesman, recently discharged from his mandatory military service, who has been assigned by his brother-in-law to sell "personal defense products" for women. Searching for a good place to find prospects, Ah Sung visits his local beauty salon, where, using one of his products, he saves the proprietor—none other than Li Hua—from a beating by the angry wife of her married boyfriend. After the woman flees, Li Hua and Ah Sung spend the afternoon together. Li Hua heads home, where she finds a letter from her lover telling her the relationship is over. She bursts into tears and turns on the TV set as a distraction. There, on screen, is tubby Ah Sheng, singing her an off-key love song. Reviewers called it a "light" and "inventive" "comic-romantic rondelay" that "gets to the heart of the absurdity of modern romance."

**Love in the Time of Twilight** (1995; Hong Kong, Dr) D: Tsui Hark C: Nicky Wu, Charlie Yeung, Eric Kot, William Ho, Cheung Ting

Re-pairing Charlie Yeung and Nicky Wu after their successful outing in *The Lovers,* this time-traveling romantic comedy features the duo as Yan Yan and Kong, two handsome young people who annoy each other on sight, and are thus obviously meant for each other. Perky Yan Yan runs into Kong on "Affinity Day," a traditional matchmaking holiday, but the duo merely manage to irritate each other before parting ways—Yan Yan to her family's opera theater, Kong to the bank where he works. Later that day, Kong runs into a beautiful woman, who seduces him and then tricks him into assisting her boss, a Triad known as the "Devil King" (Ho), in robbing his bank. When Kong realizes what's going on, the King strangles him with an electrical wire and leaves him to die. That night, Yan Yan flips the light on in the theater, only to have a ghostly Kong appear in front of her. It seems that his murder-by-wire led to his spirit being trapped in the electrical circuitry, and Yan Yan has released him. Kong begs Yan Yan go back in time with him to prevent his murder from taking place; she agrees, but the duo repeatedly fails. Their struggles are compounded when the Devil King accidentally dies as well and turns into a vengeful spirit seeking his own sort of payback. Even after defeating the King, Kong begins to suspect that returning to the mortal world may be impossible, since he and Yan Yan have changed virtually every variable they could, with the same results. As this sinks in, Yan Yan goes to Kong's grave in tears to mourn him, which makes the one variable they didn't change suddenly obvious. Reviewers called it "tremendously enjoyable," due in large part to the "unparalleled chemistry of the two young leads."

**Love Will Tear Us Apart** (1999; Hong Kong, Dr) D: Nelson Yu C: Wang Ning, Tony Leung Kar Fai, Lu Liping, Rolf Chow

This "small jewel" of a film was coproduced by Stanley Kwan and Tony Leung Kar Fai, who also stars; its first-time director, Nelson Yu, is a prominent cinematographer who shot Jia Zhangke's *Xiao Wu* (1997) and Ann Hui's *Ordinary Heroes (1999)*. Here he examines the grim world of a trio of immigrants residing in the slums of Hong Kong's Reclamation Street, whose lives are changed forever when they each encounter Ying, a hard-living prostitute and fellow Mainlander. Reviewers called it a "haunting portrait of a floating world" that "points the way to a new kind of fusion of Hong Kong and Mainland aesthetics," marked by a "stunningly original visual style."

**Lovers, The** (1994; Hong Kong, Dr, Pd) D: Tsui Hark C: Charlie Yeung, Nicky Wu, Carrie Ng, Elvis Tsui, Lau Shun

Tsui claims the age-old tale of the "Butterfly Lovers" for himself in this retelling, starring—in a break with opera tradition—a male and a female as its two leads, Liang Shanbo (Wu) and Zhu Yingtai (Yeung). Although the story is ultimately true to its tragic source, Tsui infuses it with lighthearted humor and a sense of awareness regarding the sexual orientation issues inherent in the plot (Liang worries that he is gay as he finds himself rapidly falling for his ostensibly male classmate), and makes a legendary love story feel "remarkably contemporary." Reviewers called it a "showcase for its terrifically endearing young leads," and an example of Tsui's "inventive touch with the classics."

**Made in Hong Kong** (1997; Hong Kong, Dr) D: Fruit Chan C: Sam Lee, Neiky Yim, Wembers Lee, Chung Siu, Amy Tam

This "incredible" breakthrough feature by Fruit Chan, whose rookie effort *Finale in Blood* (1993) showed little of the potential delivered here, won dozens of awards in Hong Kong and around the world. Serving as the first installment of Chan's "Handover trilogy," the film follows slacker youth and unambitious novice gangster Moon (Sam Lee) and his big, slow-witted pal Sylvester (Wembers Lee) as they make their way through life in Hong Kong's squalid public housing tenements. One day, Sylvester comes across a pair of suicide notes, written by a girl named Susan (Tam) who recently killed herself. He brings them to Moon, who is suddenly beset with visions of the dead girl that give him nocturnal emissions, even as he meets and falls in love with Ah Ping (Yim), a lovely but sickly girl whom Moon's Triad boss Wing is forcing into prostitution to pay off her mother's debts. Together, the three friends decide to exorcise the ghost of Susan by delivering the suicide letters—the first, to Susan's physical education teacher and hopeless crush, who destroys the message without reading it; the second, to her parents, who turn out to be away from home. Reviewers called this independent film, filmed on a "minuscule" budget, the "antidote to *Young and Dangerous*," a "gritty, nihilist drama" in which "everything rings true."

***Mahjong*** (1996; Taiwan, Dr) D: Edward Yang C: Virginie Ledoyen, Tang Congsheng, Ke Yulun, Chang Chen, Wang Qizan

The "players" of this offbeat gangster film are a quartet of young men, tough-guy Red-fish (Tang), sensitive Luen Luen (Ke), smooth-talking Hong Kong (Chang), and fake fortuneteller Toothpaste (Wang). While Redfish is the group's acknowledged leader, each is running his own individual scams. Their side interests end up colliding when Redfish's womanizing lout of a father bolts home, leaving behind a huge Triad debt. This prompts Redfish to seek a means of earning quick cash; when he encounters pretty French teenager Marthe (Ledoyen), he targets her as a potential "escort" for local brothel-owner Ginger (Diana Depuis). As the stakes of the game rise higher, tragedy becomes inevitable, the only question being which of the players will win, which will lose, and how much. Reviewers called it an "intricately structured" yet "emotionally out of control" "masterpiece," "dense with hidden rage."

***Mistress, The*** (1999; Hong Kong, CIII, Dr) D: Crystal Kwok C: Jacqueline Peng, Vicky Chen, Ray Lui, Moses Chan

This directorial debut from actress Crystal Kwok received accolades from astonished critics, who were astounded that someone of her youth (early thirties), background (former beauty pageant contestant turned B-actress), and, ultimately, sex could create a film marked by such "sophistication" and "searing insight." Newcomer Jacqueline Peng plays Alex, an overseas student who has returned to Hong Kong seeking work. With nothing else available, she accepts a position as the English teacher of a married executive's Mainlander "kept woman," Michelle (Chen). Her initial contempt for her charge soon turns to friendship and respect. But Michelle is unhappy in her gilded cage, and when Michelle's patron Henry (Lui) makes a pass at Alex, Michelle bolts, leaving Alex to pick up where she left off. But Alex soon finds that being a mistress isn't as easy as it appears. Reviewers called it "confident" and full of "wit, intelligence, and honesty." The "flamboyant" cinematography, featuring bizarre fantasy sequences intercut with equally lurid reality, "works remarkably well."

***Moment of Romance, A*** (1990; Hong Kong, Ac) D: Benny Chan C: Andy Lau, Wu Chien-lien, Ng Man Tat, Tommy Wong, Lau Kong

This "iconic" film, featuring Andy Lau as young gangster Wah Dee and Wu Chien-lien as his rich-girl hostage, Jo Jo, has become a part of the essential vocabulary of

Hong Kong cinema; Johnnie To even parodied the movie's memorable motorcy-cle-riding sequence in his 2000 hit *Needing You*—which stars an older Andy Lau as a middle-aged businessman, cursing his inability to keep up with a gang of carefree street-biker youths. Wah Dee is recruited by vicious thug Trumpet (Wong) to serve as the getaway driver for an attempted bank heist, but when the robbery goes bad, Wah Dee takes Jo Jo hostage in order for the gang to escape. Trumpet demands that Wah kill her to eliminate any witnesses, but he refuses. Though Jo Jo, who has fallen for the very cool Wah Dee, refuses to identify the gang when she's brought in by police, Trumpet still wants her dead. Wah Dee and Jo Jo have no choice but to go on the run together, although both know that their romance is doomed from the start to exist only in the "moment." Reviewers called it a "sur-prising gem," with a turn by Lau that became his signature performance, and is still perhaps "his best." "Wu Chien-lien charms in her Hong Kong screen debut."

### *Murmur of Youth* (1997; Taiwan, Dr) D: Lin Cheng-sheng C: Rene Liu, Tseng Jing, Tsai Chin-hsin, Lin Li-hsiu, Lien Pi-tung

Chen Mei Li (Liu) is the daughter of an affluent but dysfunctional family and lives in a highrise tower in downtown Taipei; Lin Mei Li (Tseng) lives in a ramshackle old house on the outskirts of the city with her loving father and grandmother. The two Mei Lis encounter each other when both end up working at the same theater ticket counter, much to the confusion of everyone around them. The girls become close friends and confidantes, with Chen Mei Li slowly becoming infatuated with her like-named friend. One evening, when they accidentally get locked into the theater box office, she makes a move on her pal, who tentatively responds. But the day after their night of passion, Lin Mei Li experiences pangs of guilt and shame. Reviewers called it "daring," and "perhaps Taiwan's first open and sympathetic depiction of a lesbian rela-tionship"; "explores taboo topics with depth and delicacy."

### *My Father Is a Hero* (1995; Hong Kong, Ac) D: Corey Yuen C: Jet Li, Anita Mui, Xie Miao, Blackie Ko, Yu Rongguang

Mainland cop Kung Wei has a sickly wife and a tiny dynamo of a son named Kung Ku, but having a loving family doesn't prevent him from going deep, deep undercover as a Triad thug working for insane mobster Po Kwong (Yu). After a weapons deal goes wrong, leading to a standoff with Hong Kong police, Kung Wei takes policewoman

Fong Yat Wah (Mui) hostage; but after he saves her life and sets her free, she suspects that there's more to Kung Wei's story than meets the eye. Fong travels to the Mainland to investigate—but in doing so, accidentally blows Kung Wei's cover, leading to a wild final battle between the father and son Kung team and Po and his heavily armed men. Reviewers called it "fantastically entertaining," with "pint-size minimaster Xie Miao [showing] that he's a worthy chip off Jet Li's block."

### *Naked Killer* (1992; Hong Kong, CIII, Ac) D: Clarence Fok C: Chingmy Yau, Simon Yam, Carrie Ng, Kelly Yiu, Madoka Sugawara

This "relentlessly stylish" softcore actioner film launched dozens of knockoffs and inspired a burgeoning cult of fans in both Asia and the United States. Chingmy Yau plays Kitty, a juvenile delinquent recruited to join a gang of scantily clad female assassins led by Sister Cindy (Yiu). But Cindy isn't the only one who has an eye on Kitty; a former member of the group, murderous lesbian Princess (Ng), has also taken a fancy to the rookie and is willing to do anything to have her. Meanwhile, Princess's hobby—which involves luring male victims into compromising positions, then shattering their limbs and harvesting their gonads—is putting the entire gang in jeopardy. After the latest discovery of a broken, castrated corpse, the Hong Kong police finally move into action, with sexually dysfunctional detective Tinam assigned to the case. It's just a matter of time before Kitty and Tinam meet cute (if you can call any hookup between an obsessive detective and a serial killer in training "cute")—making both of them instant targets for Princess's wrath. Reviewers called it "one of the greatest trashy films ever," full of "irresistible," if "politically incorrect" sequences that are "beyond adequate description." One scene in particular, where a dumb cop accidentally consumes a piece of evidence thinking it's a "sausage," is often cited as being typical of the film's "irresistible" "baseline humor." Wong Jing stepped into the director's seat for a series of unrelated "sequels" to this film, the repugnant 1993 *Raped by an Angel* and its four equally sleazy sequels.

### *92 Legendary La Rose Noire* (1992; Hong Kong, Cm) D: Jeff Lau C: Maggie Siu, Tony Leung Kar Fai, Teresa Mo, Fung Bo Bo, Wong Wan Si

In this satire of sixties-era television, a pair of women (Siu and Mo) witness a killing; to avoid getting called in for questioning, they leave a note behind declaring that the crime was committed by the "Black Rose," a swashbuckling old-school TV character. This leads the less-than-bright cop assigned to the case to begin hunting down the heroine in question, who, it turns out, is very much a real individual, and not too happy about being falsely charged with murder. However, her attempts at gaining revenge are hampered by her advancing senility. Reviewers praised Tony Leung's turn as "nerdy," "mincing policeman Keith Lui," as well as Fung's "superb" turn as the "addled action queen," for which she won Best Supporting Actress at the Hong Kong Film Awards. Others note that, like many of Jeff Lau's over-the-top farces, "it's an acquired taste." Followed by a pair of sequels, *Rose Rose I Love You* (1993) and *Black Rose II* (1997).

### *Not One Less* (1999; Mainland, Dr) D: Zhang Yimou C: Wei Minzhi, Zhang Huike, Tian Zhenda, Gao Enman, Sun Zhimei

The rural village of Shuiquan undergoes a crisis when the only instructor at its ramshackle primary school, Teacher Gao (Gao), must leave town to take care of his sick mother. Already facing a profound dropout trend among its students, the town's mayor (Tian) realizes that a monthlong shutdown of the school would mean an end to education in Shuiquan. Tian recruits the only substitute he can find, thirteen-year-old Wei Minzhi (Wei), telling her that she will receive a special bonus of ten yuan (about $1.25) if the month goes by without another student dropping out. The determined Wei—who is just a few years older than her charges—all but locks her unruly kids in the schoolhouse, instructing them to copy phrases she's written on the blackboard. Then, when ten-year-old hellion Zhang Huike (Zhang) runs away, Wei heads to the big city to bring him back—by any means necessary. One reviewer called it "an adolescent retelling of *The Story of Qiu Ju*," "simple, unadorned, and direct"; "Zhang elicits terrific, naturalistic performances from his players, all of whom are nonactors playing characters bearing their own names, and in some cases based on their real identities." They also noted that Zhang withdrew this film from Cannes after it went unselected for the competition portion of the festival, blasting the judges for their inherent bias regarding Chinese film: "To Westerners, Chinese film is all either antigovernment or it is 'propaganda.'"

### *Now You See Love, Now You Don't* (1992; Hong Kong, Cm) D: Alex Law C: Chow Yun Fat, Carol Cheng, Teresa Mo, Carina Lau, Anthony Wong

In this Lunar New Year offering, Chow Yun Fat plays Ng Shan Shui, the headman of a rural New Territories village, who discovers that his fiancée Firefly (Cheng), just returned from three years of overseas study in London, has become a hip, sullen poseur with a love of big-city life. The two immediately and understandably clash, with Firefly accusing Ng of being a bumpkin, and Ng calling Firefly an impostor. Firefly breaks off their engagement and heads to Hong Kong, where she gets a waitressing job and prepares to start a brand-new life. Ng follows her, but is told—in a memorable monologue—to step off, and take his chauvinistic attitudes about women with him. He decides, in turn, that perhaps he could use a little "self-improvement," and informs the villagers that he'll be taking a leave of absence from running the town to learn how to be a modern man. With that, he and his pal Dunno (Wong) are off to Hong Kong, where Ng starts a business and begins a romance with a kooky evangelistic Christian (Lau). Firefly, meanwhile, is beginning to have second thoughts about life in the metropolis, dreaming of the huge dream house Ng promised to build her. Since this is a New Year's film, the ending is as inevitable as the sun going down in the West: After a mutual brush with death, Ng and Firefly renew their love, while all the other plausible couples couple up as well. Reviewers called this a "gentle little comedy" with "remarkably appealing leads, whose chemistry is evident in every scene." "Little details stand out, like the 'family portraits' in Shan Shui's house—a classic now-pay-attention sight gag!"

**Odd One Dies, The** (1997; Hong Kong, Ac) D: Patrick Yau C: Takeshi Kaneshiro, Carman Lee, Byun Woo Nin, Kenneth Choi, Tin Man Chuk

Takeshi Kaneshiro is a poverty-stricken and not-too-bright street thug who out of desperation accepts a hit assignment from the local Triad boss. Figuring he has nothing more to lose, he takes the advance payment and goes to a casino, where he ends up winning a fortune. No longer interested in killing anyone (or risking his own life, for that matter), he decides to "subcontract" the job to someone else. The only person interested in his offer is a slightly unhinged young woman, played by Carman Lee, who has just been released from prison. Takeshi (neither character is given a name) is initially hesitant about hiring her, but she proves her seriousness quite effectively, and he agrees to take her on. But as they explore the setup to the hit, two things become clear: The first is that the assignment is almost certainly a kamikaze mission. The second is that they are beginning to fall in love. Reviewers called this oddball Milkyway Image film "eminently compelling" and "completely original," with "exceptional" performances by the leads (who nevertheless have never looked "more in need of a shower and a new wardrobe").

**On the Beat** (1995; Mainland, Cm, Dr) D: Ning Ying C: Yang Guoli, Wang Lianggui, Zhao Zhiming

The second installment in Ning's "Beijing Trilogy," which began with 1994's *For Fun,* takes as its protagonists the members of a police precinct in a somewhat crime-free section of the city, where the cops spend most of the day riding around on their squad bicycles answering complaints by old grandmothers and rousting the occasional drunk. Not that they aren't serious about their job: Among the law-breakers they apprehend are a family with an unregistered, and possibly rabid, dog, as well as the dog itself; a man who has been caught selling "dirty pictures" of bikini-clad women; a card hustler; and other such serious criminals. The film is structured as a ride-along with veteran cop Yang Guoli showing rookie cop Wang Liangui the ropes. Reviewers called it a "drily comic" and "subtly subversive" portrait of contemporary Beijing.

**Once Upon a Time in a Triad Society** (1996; Hong Kong, Ac) D: Cha Chuen Yee C: Francis Ng, Loletta Lee, Spencer Lam, Michael Chan, Jamie Luk

A "twisted" and "venomous" satire of the Triad Boys genre, in which Francis Ng revisits his most famous villain role: that of Ugly Kwan, from 1996's first *Young and Dangerous* film. Here Kwan is shown dying on a hospital gurney, as a voiceover indicates that he is about to re-examine his evil life from its beginnings. The subsequent flashback shows how he was first pulled into the Triad world as a child by a local boss named Sheung Yee (Lam), who betrayed him to the police to save his own hide. Kwan then joined a rival boss, Brother Lone (Chan), only to be stabbed in the back again. Finally forsaking the world of *"jiang hu,"* Kwan moved to Japan and turned over a new leaf, starting a business and getting married, until a Triad assassin gunned his bride down, prompting Kwan to dedicate his life to villainy. Of course, things are not as simple or as straightforward as they seem, and a narrative twist midway through the film is guaranteed to throw viewers off guard. Reviewers called it "exceedingly clever," a "shaggy dog story that will leave you angry and then shaken and then, possibly, inspired." Followed by the unrelated, but equally worth watching sequel, *Once Upon a Time in a Triad Society II* (1996).

***Once Upon a Time in China*** (1991; Hong Kong, Ac) D: Tsui Hark C: Jet Li, Rosamund Kwan, Yuen Biao, Kent Cheng, Jacky Cheung, Jonathan James Isgar, Yam Sai Kwoon

With this "cleverly original" and "wildly entertaining" film, director/producer/cowriter Tsui revisited the tale that stands at the heart of the Hong Kong motion picture industry—the legend of the great physician and martial artist Wong Fei Hung—reinventing and updating it for a new generation of moviegoers. By recruiting Mainland *wushu* champion Jet Li to play Master Wong, he ensured that the fighting skills depicted would be legitimately impressive; by adding a romantic subplot (in which Wong awkwardly expresses his attraction to his "Thirteenth Aunt" Yee, played by Rosamund Kwan), he ensured that the film would appeal to both sexes; and by focusing the storyline on the tensions between Western and Eastern culture, modernism and tradition, he ensured that the film would be both resonant with present-day audiences and historically authentic. In short, Tsui stacked the deck in hopes of creating a cinematic landmark, and largely succeeded. Here Wong is asked by the retreating general of the Black Flag Army to form a militia to keep order in Guangdong, a city occupied by multiple factions of Westerners and beset by organized criminal activity. Wong agrees to help, out of civic duty, but when his militia gets into a nasty brawl with the members of the Sha Ho organization, the region's most powerful Triad group, Wong is accused by the police of engaging in gang warfare and his volunteers are arrested. Meanwhile, vengeful Shao Ho members burn down Po Chi Lam, Wong's medical clinic. All of this is mere prequel for the larger story that follows: It turns out that the Sha Ho gang is secretly working with Jackson (Isgar), an American railroad representative, to ship Guangdongese women to the United States as prostitutes for the company's coolie laborers. Meanwhile, "Iron Vest" Yim (Yam), a powerful but unscrupulous martial arts master, has decided to challenge Wong as the reigning champion of the region, hoping to win students to his rival kung fu academy. When he is approached by the Sha Ho gang with an offer to join forces, he agrees. The Sha Ho gang abducts Wong's secret love, Aunt Yee, hoping to use her as leverage against him—while Yim leads a frontal assault against Wong himself. The final conflict between Yim and Wong is an incredible spectacle of virtuoso fighting technique and canny wirework. Reviewers called it a "millennial epic" that "launched a golden age in Hong Kong cinema." "Stunning visuals," a "stirring theme song," and a "career-reviving performance by Jet Li" make this an "undisputed classic." Followed by two sequels featuring Jet Li, and then—after Li and Tsui Hark had a dispute about pay—

two additional sequels with fellow Mainlander *wushu* champion Zhao Wenzhou donning the robes. Li returned to the series for its final installment to date, *Once Upon a Time in China and America* (1997), which brings the characters to the American West.

**Peach Blossom Land** (1993; Taiwan, Dr) D: Stan Lai C: Brigitte Lin, Jin Shi-jye, Lee Lichun, Ismene Ting, Ku Paoming

A "tour de force" by director Lai, a notable dramatist and the artistic director of the Performance Workshop Theater Company. This movie—based on his stage play—was his cinematic debut. The conceit of this film is that, due to a scheduling error, two plays are being staged in the same space; the first, *Secret Love,* is a contemporary drama about two lovers, Chiang Bin-liu (Jin) and Yun Chih-fan (Lin), apart for nearly four decades. The two had believed they were tragically separated due to the Nationalist retreat to Taiwan, but then learn that both of them in fact made it to the island, and actually live rather close to each other, a fact that puts a new face on their long-simmering feelings of sentimental yearning. The second, *Peach Blossom Land,* is a period tale of a fisherman named Tow (Lee), afflicted with impotence and jealous suspicions regarding his wife's fidelity. As the two plays progress, and the camera's attention shifts between them, they begin to fuse together, as lines overlap, staging intersects, and stagehands attempt to battle for space by moving props back and forth. Soon it becomes clear that the two dramas are merging strangely into one, providing different but complementary viewpoints on the nature of loss, separation, and home. Reviewers called it "marvelous theater," "enhanced by the immersive quality of cinema"; "Lin is a wonder, both 'in character' as Yun Chih-fan and in the scenic breaks where she plays the actress playing Yun."

**Personals, The** (1998; Taiwan, Dr) D: Chen Kuo-fu C: Rene Liu, Jin Shi-jie, Gu Baoming, Niu Chengze, Chen Chao-jung

Chen's followup to 1995's *Peony Pavilion* is a "whimsical," "sparklingly entertaining" film about the ambiguity of human relationships, and about the ultimate truth: that to love someone else, you first have to love yourself. Liu plays Chia-chen Tu, an ophthalmologist who suddenly quits her job and begins placing personal ads stating that she is "open to friendship followed by marriage." Love is neither promised nor required—perhaps because she is already in love, with a married man named Wu, who has ceased returning her calls or even acknowledging her existence. Still, since Tu has Wu's home phone number, she has taken to leaving him a running diary of her life, out of frustration as much as anything else. In her interviews of prospective mates, she calls herself "Miss Wu," hiding her identity as she drinks in the eccentricities of a series of boors, lechers, and losers. Reviewers called it "deceptively thoughtful," leaving you with "plenty to mull over after it's done"; nevertheless, "it doesn't skimp on entertainment."

### *Police Story III: Supercop* (1992; Hong Kong, Ac, Cm) D: Stanley Tong C: Jackie Chan, Michelle Yeoh, Maggie Cheung, Kenneth Tsang, Yuen Wah

Although Jackie Chan has the above-the-title billing on this third installment to the *Police Story* trilogy, viewers will readily note that Chan is matched and in some ways surpassed by his female costar Yeoh, who used this film to unretire with a bang. Here she plays Chief of Security Yang, a stoic Mainland supercop assigned by the PRC to work with her Hong Kong counterpart, Chan Ka Kui (Chan), in breaking a drug ring that threatens to flood both territories with cheap and powerful heroin. To get inside the ring, Chan is sent undercover as a convict in a Mainland prison camp, where Panther (Yuen), the brother of the gang's boss Chaibat (Tsang), is incarcerated. Chan assists Panther in breaking out of prison, winning his trust; Panther invites Chan and his "sister" Yang to go with him to Thailand, where Chaibat's headquarters are located. Chan and Yang are recruited to join the gang, and even asked by Tsang to take on a special mission: breaking his wife (the only person with the code to unlock Chaibat's secret Swiss bank account) out of a Malaysian prison. As it happens, Chan's long-suffering and disgruntled tour guide girlfriend May (Cheung) is in Kuala Lumpur as well, leading a group of tourists through the area. When she happens to spot Chan with Yang, her incensed reaction blows their cover; learning of Chan's real identity, Chaibat turns May into a hostage (par for the course in this series) against the safe return of his wife. The result is a set of sequences that has few, if any, rivals in action cinema. Chan and Yang are forced to rescue the kingpin's spouse from jail, but then turn the tables in a chase that involves nearly every imaginable means of risking one's life—with Yeoh performing a crazy motorcycle jump up a ramp and onto the top of a moving locomotive, and Chan matching that stunt by dangling from a speeding helicopter's rope ladder hundreds of feet above the city, dodging billboards and the tops of buildings. Reviewers called it an "astounding," "fast and furious" "action classic" with a "can-you-top-this" chemistry propelling the two leads to ever greater heights." Followed by a spinoff film featuring Yeoh's character, *Project S* (1993).

**Postman, The** (1995; Mainland, Dr) D: He Jianjun C: Feng Yuanzheng, Liang Danni, Pu Cunxin, Huang Xin

The sophomore effort of Sixth Generation filmmaker He, this film is a "devastating portrait" of life in a run-down Beijing slum, where Xiao Du (Feng) lives with his sister. The area is ironically known as the "Xingfu" or "Happiness" District, and its residents tend to be the outcasts of Chinese society. Xiao is hired as a postal worker when the district's previous letter carrier was found to be opening and reading the mail. Soon, however, in an effort to break out of the mindless tedium and repetition of the job, he finds himself emulating his predecessor, and is fascinated to voyeuristically read about the private lives of his neighbors, until he uncovers secrets that he is better off not knowing. Before this film's release, He was banned from filmmaking in China; *Postman*'s print was smuggled out of the country and delivered to supporters of the director in Europe.

**Puppetmaster, The** (1993; Taiwan, Dr) D: Hou Hsiao-hsien C: Li Tien-lu, Lim Giong, Yang Liyin, Ming Hwa-bai, Hung Liou

This second chapter in Hou's unofficial "Taiwanese History Trilogy" is a dramatized biopic of eighty-four-year-old Li Tien-lu, a performer who has been named a "living treasure of Taiwan"; Li appeared as an actor in several of director Hou's earlier works, leading a mesmerized Hou to call him a "library of Taiwan's past." The film covers the first thirty-six years of Li's life, alternating interview-style segments showcasing Li's own storytelling with acted sequences featuring Fue Choung Cheng as the child Li and Lim Giong as the young adult Li. Reviewers called it "astonishingly rich in amosphere" and "layered with multiple strata of meaning and emotion." A "challenge" to watch, but "worth the time and effort."

**Queen of Temple Street** (1990; Hong Kong, Dr) D: Lawrence Ah Mon C: Sylvia Chang, Rain Lau, Lo Lieh, Ha Ping, Josephine Koo

Although this film is set in Temple Street's underworld of sex workers and Triad thugs, it offers a stark contrast to standard works of genre exploitation tied to that milieu. Sylvia Chang here plays Big Sister Wah, a madam hoping desperately for a better life for her daughter Yan (Lau, making her screen debut). Unfortunately, Yan seems determined to make the same mistakes as her mother. Reviewers called it one of the "most effec-tive" and "least glamorous" depictions of the sex trade in Hong Kong history; notably, however, it "humanizes prostitutes and their johns, rather than humiliating them," avoiding the "patronizing air" that afflicts many of the better films in this genre.

### *Raise the Red Lantern* (1991; Mainland, Pd, Dr) D: Zhang Yimou C: Gong Li, Ma Jingwu, He Caifei, Cao Cuifeng, Jin Shuyuan

Based on a novel by Su Tong, this "eerie" tale of concubinage in feudal China features Gong Li as Songlian, the newest wife of a wealthy man, who designates which of his wives he will grace with his presence for the night by raising a red paper lantern in front of her bedchamber. At first, beautiful, educated Songlian reacts to her fate with rage—she has been raised to believe that life has more to offer than a kind of game-show competition for spousal attention—but with no other options, she eventually succumbs to the pressure to live by the strange rules of her new existence. She meets the other three women of the household—stoic, dignified First Wife (Jin); pampered and flighty Third Wife (He); and Second Wife (Cao), seemingly the most friendly and open of the three. But the agendas of the three wives are more complex and dangerous than they may seem, and seeming ally Second Wife soon reveals herself as a venomous and Machiavellian player in the game—destroying her opponents with subtle and deadly behind-the-scenes maneuvers. The foreordained finale is "wrenchingly tragic." Review-ers called it a tale of "sensuous, almost overripe beauty," and a "defining moment in Chinese cinema of the nineties."

### *Rebels of the Neon God* (1992; Taiwan, Dr) D: Tsai Ming-liang C: Chen Chao-jung, Li Kang-sheng, Wang Yu-wen

The debut film of Malaysian-born Taiwanese "Second Wave" filmmaker Tsai Ming-liang, this is the story of a high-school student named Hsiao Kang (Li) who ditches his parentally mandated cram-school sessions in order to spend time at a local video arcade. There he runs into a delinquent named Ah Tse (Chen), whom he recognizes as the thug who smashed up his father's taxi; he is inexplicably drawn to stalk Tse, watching as he engages in petty theft and entertains his brother's girl-friend Ah Kuei. Finally, something in Kang snaps. When Tse's prized motorcycle is left unattended so he can make out with Ah Kuei, Kang "avenges" his father by slashing the tires of the bike and painting "AIDS" in large letters on its gas tank. Reviewers called it full of "haunting" and "repetitive" images (running water is a frequent theme in this and other Tsai works); an "irreplaceable classic" that "tenderly unwraps" "young male angst."

### Remains of a Woman (1993; Hong Kong, CIII, Ac) D: Clarence Fok C: Carrie Ng, James Pak, Loletta Lee, Jacqueline Law, Melvin Wong

Based on a true and gruesome account, this "relentlessly grim" procedural explores the strange charm of a charismatic psychopath, Billy Chan (Pak), which allows him to seduce first Judy Yu (Ng), a racetrack clerk who ends up pilfering funds to feed Chan's drug habit, and then flight attendant Lisa Wong (Law), who ends up the unfortunate victim of the other two members of the triangle—murdered and dismembered into small, easy-to-dispose-of pieces. At the beginning of the film, both Chan and Yu are in custody, but Chan is about to receive a retrial, as he has claimed that the murder was committed solely by Yu, and furthermore that he has converted to Christianity through the efforts of social worker Annie Cheung (Lee), whom he intends to marry. The prosecutor who tried the duo's first case, played by Melvin Wong, decides to interview Yu to get her side of the story, and she tells him a tale of lurid debauchery and Chan's Svengalilike power over women. But Chan's hold over Yu remains—when brought into court, she exonerates him and takes the blame fully on herself, setting an "innocent" Chan free to wed his new love. Reviewers called it "wildly unpredictable," and "extremely difficult to watch" for the "faint of heart."

### River, The (1997; Taiwan, Dr) D: Tsai Ming-liang C: Lee Kang-sheng, Tien Miao, Luh Sheau-lin, Chen Jaw-rong, Chen Shiang-chi

An "off-kilter" portrait of dysfunctional family values, in which Tsai's regular screen avatar Lee Kang-sheng plays Xiao Kang, the teenage son of a pair of parents who have drifted to opposite emotional poles and no longer communicate in any fashion. Kang's mother (Luh) is an elevator operator who is having an affair with a porno entrepreneur, while Kang's closeted father (Miao) seeks out the comfort of anonymous young men (which later leads to one of the film's most "dangerous and controversial" sequences). After soaking in the vile, discolored water of the Tanshui River, playing a corpse as an extra in a movie, Kang wakes up the next day with a terrible ache in his neck, which nothing seems to cure. His father—who is battling a persistent water leak in the ceiling of the bedroom he shares with Kang's mother—takes him to various physicians and healers. None of them help. Finally, they set off together to a remote temple hoping that religion can do what science could not. They stop at a hotel to stay the night, and both father and son independently decide to visit the hotel's health spa—the father to cruise for a pickup, and the son hoping to find a means of alleviating his pain. Both end up in the steam room, with zero visibility, with predictable results. Upon discovering what has happened, Kang's father slaps him across the face, and the two end up going to sleep in silence. The next morning, Kang's ache is gone. Reviewers called it "strange and shocking" but "monumental."

### Road Home, The (1999; Mainland, Dr) D: Zhang Yimou C: Zhang Ziyi, Sun Honglei, Zheng Hao, Zhao Yuelin, Li Bin

A "small" and "charming fable" from a director known more for vivid melodramas than "simple, sensitive love stories." A successful entrepreneur, Luo Yusheng (Sun), is called back to the remote village where he grew up when he hears that his father has died. The problem is that his father died far away from the village, and his mother, Di (played by Zhao Yuelin as an old woman, and the remarkable Zhang Ziyi as a young girl), demands that he be provided with the traditional custom of "walking back the dead"—in which friends, coworkers, and volunteers carry the deceased's body on foot back to his native village so that his spirit will remember the road home. At first, Luo tells his mother that the weather and distance make this impossible, but as he spends time with her and other older folk in the village, hearing the story of how the two met and fell in love, he comes to understand the reasons for the depth of her devotion. Eventually, the problem solves itself, as dozens of volunteers who have been touched by his father's kindness offer to walk his coffin back home. Reviewers called it "romantic," without Zhang's traditional "underlying fatalism." Zhang himself calls it a paean to "true Chinese values."

### Royal Tramp I and II (1992; Hong Kong, Cm, Pd) D: Wong Jing C: Stephen Chiau, Cheung Man, Ng Man Tat, Chingmy Yau, Damian Lau, Brigitte Lin

A two-part epic farce, loosely based on Jin Yong's legendary novel *Duke of Mount Deer*, whose protagonist Wei Xiaobao (called here "Wilson Bond") was a trickster and conman who ended up becoming best friend of the emperor and the husband of eight beautiful wives. The film begins with Bond (Chiau) at work, as a whorehouse storyteller who specializes in heroic tales about Chan Kan Nam (Lau), the leader of the rebel Heaven and Earth Society, which is dedicated to overthrowing the Ching Dynasty. When Manchu soldiers suddenly raid the house of ill repute, it becomes clear Chan is actually there at the brothel undercover! In the fight, Chan is temporarily blinded, and a star-struck Bond assists him in escaping; grateful, Chan deputizes Bond as a member of the Society, and gives him the mission of somehow infiltrating the Forbidden City and stealing a secret text with instructions on how to find an ancient treasure. Bond wanders over to the palace and, not knowing how else to get inside, stands on a queue that he thinks will take him to the entrance. It turns out instead to be the application line for would-be eunuchs. Before Bond is snipped, however, he manages to get the ear of the chief eunuch (Ng), who agrees to keep him out of the corps of the castrated in return for Bond accepting a secret assignment to watch over the dowager empress (Cheung), who the eunuch thinks has been acting a little strangely. As Bond leaves the eunuch quarters, he runs into a small and irritating eunuch, with whom he gets into a verbal battle. The eunuch is not a eunuch at all—but the imperial princess, the emperor's sister. After the two prove to each other that neither is a eunuch, Bond is introduced to court, and quickly becomes a trusted confidant of the emperor himself. He proves his "loyalty" to the throne, as well as his "faithfulness" to the Heaven and Earth Society, by exposing the dowager empress as actually being an impostor, sent to take over the reins of power by the dreaded Dragon Sect. Everyone is happy with Bond, and the princess is quite taken with him. In Part II, things pick up where the first film left off—with the caveat that Lone-er (the undercover agent played by Cheung Man) has returned to Dragon Sect headquarters to report in, and been transformed in the process to her true form: that of Brigitte Lin! She is warned, however, that she must at all times preserve her virginity, or else lose 80 percent of her powers to the man she sleeps with. It should be easy to predict who this ends up being. She vows to assassinate Bond, but ends up getting poisoned; on the verge of death, she reveals that her only hope is to diffuse the poison by having sex with someone else. After Bond does the honors, he finds out that he now has 80 percent of Lone-er's incredible powers. With these in hand, and Lone-er at his side, he must ward off a threat to China not from within, but without, as the king of a neighboring land has declared war on the empire, and recruited an all-powerful martial arts master to lead his troops. Reviewers called both films a "Chiau-powered blast," with "more action than many 'straight' martial arts films," and a "bevy of beautiful and talented women"; "Bond is a cowardly nerd who gains superhuman powers and sleeps with every attractive girl in sight. What's not to like?"

**Rumble in the Bronx** (1995; Hong Kong, Ac, Cm) D: Stanley Tong C: Jackie Chan, Anita Mui, Francoise Yip, Bill Tung, Marc Akerstream, Garvin Cross, Kris Lord

In the film that first proved Jackie could make it in the States (the film earned over $80 million at the United States box office), Chan plays Keung, a Hong Kong cop who has come to America to attend the wedding of his Uncle Bill (Tung). Meanwhile, since Bill is retiring to travel the world, he's selling his supermarket business to a somewhat naïve Chinese immigrant named Elaine (Mui). As a favor to the new owner, Bill asks Keung to stay around a few extra days to give her any help she might need. The help turns out to be of a very different variety than either Bill or Keung expected: A gang of thugs begins terrorizing the store, vandalizing the property and stealing goods. Keung is forced to defend both the market and its owner using his kung fu skills—which leads the gang to target him for abuse instead. After Keung is brutalized by the gang in a nighttime torture session, he stumbles back up to his apartment, and on the way runs into a young, wheelchair-bound kid named Danny (Morgan Lam), who turns out to be the brother of Nancy (Yip), the cycle-racing Chinese girlfriend of gang boss Tony (Akerstream). It turns out that Nancy isn't bad, just misunderstood—and after a little bit of smacking around, most of the rest of the gang turns out to be okay as well, with the exception of bleached-blond punk Angelo (Cross), whose theft of a bag of diamonds from a very deadly gang of Mafia killers—and his decision to hide said diamonds in Danny's wheelchair cushion—leads to a climactic showdown between Keung and mob chieftain White Tiger (Lord). Reviewers called it "all over the place," but "if you let your mind drift and focus on the action, you can't miss." "Anita Mui is wasted in a promising role here; it's as if Jackie decided to cast both her and Francoise Yip, and then forgot her two-thirds of the way through the movie." "They should have just called it *Rumble in Vancouver*—the obvious fakeness of the setting is distracting, as are the cheesy 'Warriors come out and play' outfits the gangsters wear." "Love those scenic New York mountains!"

## *Running Out of Time* (1999; Hong Kong, Ac) D: Johnnie To C: Andy Lau, Lau Ching Wan, Yoyo Mung, Waise Lee, Hui Siu Hung

This "intricately plotted," "magnificently clever" thriller stars Andy Lau as Wah, a mysterious surveillance whiz and master of disguise with an unknown agenda, and Lau Ching Wan as Ho, the dogged, sharp-witted cop intent on bringing him down. The film begins with Wah plotting what seems to be a bank heist that leads to an apparent hostage situation; Wah gets away with the goods—except that the police, led by ace hostage negotiator Ho, soon realize that the "goods" are . . . nothing. The entire setup seems to have either been an elaborate prank, or a test of the cops' capabilities. Given the brilliance of the criminal in question, Ho suspects the latter. His suspicions are confirmed when Ho receives a phone call from Wah, telling him that he wants to "play a game with him for the next seventy-two hours." But Wah won't tell Ho the rules of the game, or the objective. And he also isn't about to let him know that, diagnosed with terminal cancer, he has just fourteen days left to live—which means that he doesn't have anything left to lose. The remainder of the movie is all "terrific cat-and-mouse tactical maneuvering" between the master criminal and the unrelenting detective, until the final sequence—which leads reviewers to wonder what's real, what's not, and whom or what to believe. Yoyo Mung, as the innocent bystander whom Wah uses to get out of a jam, and whom he subsequently develops an odd bond with, plays a "small but charming role." Followed by a lesser but still worthwhile sequel, 2001's *Running Out of Time 2,* with Ekin Cheng as Lau Ching Wan's new tormentor.

## *Sex and Zen* (1991; Hong Kong, CIII, Pd) D: Michael Mak C: Lawrence Ng, Kent Cheng, Elvis Tsui, Amy Yip, Carrie Ng

Based on a classic text of moral instruction known as *The Carnal Prayer Mat,* this film features Lawrence Ng as Mei Yan Ching, the scholar who decides that life should be all about lust, has a horse penis transplanted onto his body, and subsequently goes off for a series of carnal misadventures, with tragic consequences. Much of the draw here is the mostly naked and wildly debauched shenanigans, including the infamous "two-girl flute scene" (which is better left undescribed here, and can easily be filled in by the imagination). Ultimately, this "over-the-top pornfest" falls "somewhere in the gray area between period sex flick and prop comedy." Amy Yip, Hong Kong's "Queen of Bust," became a cult icon after this film, which certainly shows her talents off to good measure. Followed by two unrelated sequels directed by Wong Jing, with all that implies. Yu Pui Tsuen offers a somewhat less addled take on the same source material.

### *Shower* (1999; Mainland, Dr) D: Zhang Yang C: Zhu Xu, Pu Cunxin, Jiang Wu, He Zeng, Zhang Jinhao

Daming and Erming (Pu and Jiang) are the sons of Master Liu (Zhu), the owner of one of the last public bathhouses in Beijing. Although Daming has long since left home to pursue a non-hygiene-related career in Shenzhen, when he receives a cryptic but ominous postcard from his mentally retarded brother, he goes home, fearing that his father has died. Relieved but irritated when he finds that his father is alive and well, he decides to stay for a few days to catch up with his family. The gap between Daming, an entrepreneur with a permanent cellphone fixation, and his gentle brother and humble father, is enormous, and is best illustrated by Daming's preference for quick, efficient showers rather than the languid and relaxing tradition of the bath. While Daming is visiting, his father falls sick, and Daming is forced to step in to manage the business; in the course of running the bathhouse, Daming begins to see that his father serves as a combination of therapist, physician, and guru to his clients, who do not visit merely for baths, but for comfort, wisdom, and warmth. Reviewers called it "somewhat predictable," but "uplifting," and "definitively commercial"—an adjective not applied to too many Mainland movies.

### *So Close to Paradise* (1998; Mainland, Dr) D: Wang Xiaoshuai C: Wang Tong, Shi Yu, Guo Tao, Wu Tao

Wang's followup to his critically acclaimed *The Days* (1993) was held up from release for three years by government censors, who critiqued it as "negative" (Wang admits it is a "not so happy" film) and had problems with its inclusion of a Vietnamese prostitute as one of its central characters. Two friends from the countryside come to the big city to find their fortunes; sharp Gao Ping becomes a small-time con artist, while his quieter friend Dongzi ends up as a "shoulder pole," a bearer who carries people's belongings in exchange for tips. When one of Gao Ping's hustles goes wrong, he goes searching for information about the man who stiffed him and in frustration ends up kidnaping a Vietnamese bar girl named Ruan Hong—not knowing that she is the mistress of the region's most vicious crimelord. The boss's vengeance on Gao Ping is swift and terrible, and Dongzi is left alone with Ruan Hong, whom he has gradually fallen in love with, wondering what his next move should be. Reviewers praised its "brilliant visual style" and its "terrific performances" from a group of first-time actors.

### Soong Sisters, The (1997; Hong Kong, Dr) D: Mabel Cheung C: Maggie Cheung, Michelle Yeoh, Vivian Wu, Wu Xingguo, Winston Chao, Niu Zhenhua

This film by Mabel Cheung, a coproduction between Hong Kong and the Mainland, tells the story of the so-called "Soong Dynasty"—the three sisters who ended up marrying three of the most important and powerful men in contemporary Chinese history. The eldest, Ai Ling (Yeoh) married H. H. Kung (Niu), the financier who was widely reputed to be the nation's wealthiest man. The youngest, Mei Ling (Vivian Wu), married Chiang Kai-shek (Wu Xingguo), the general who would eventually place the entire republic under his iron fist. The middle sister, Ching Ling (Cheung), married Sun Yat-sen (Chao), the idealistic revolutionary who toppled the Ching and became the father of modern China. Because it tackled so many hot-button issues in recent Chinese history, the film faced numerous obstacles to its final release, including a year-long holdup by censors that almost led to it losing its financing. Ultimately, Mainland censors cut almost twenty minutes from the film—minutes that Cheung called "critical" to the narrative. Reviewers called it "technically outstanding," but "almost textbookish in its chapter-and-verse presentation of history," which limits the performers' ability to draw complex characterizations.

### Sorry Baby (1999; Mainland, Cm) D: Feng Xiaogang C: Ge You, Wu Chien-lien, Fu Biao, Ming He, Got Chengsheng

Ge You, the most popular actor in China, here plays Han Dong, a kind-hearted doormat of a cabbie who has been placed under personal contract to a wealthy businessman named Ruan Dawei (Fu). Ruan owns a travel agency and enjoys showing off his affluence by having Han on call, but somehow can never remember to pay him. An increasingly desperate Han pleads, begs, wheedles, and demands the nearly 100,000 RMB that he's owed from his employer, only to get the constant chorus "OK, OK, OK, OK"—and no actual payment. Finally, Han loses it and kidnaps Ruan's lover, Liu Xiaoyun (Wu) from Beijing hospital, where she's recuperating from tuberculosis. Upon discovering Han's reckless act, Ruan tells him that he can go ahead and kill her, knowing full well that Han would never do such a thing. But hearing this statement does make Liu very angry, causing her to throw her lot in with Han to plan a means to get the money Han is owed—as well as a modicum of revenge. Reviewers called it an "extremely funny" film, with "great chemistry between the leads." Upon its release in 1999, it instantly became Mainland China's biggest hit.

***Spicy Love Soup*** (1998; Mainland, Dr, Cm) D: Zhang Yang C: Pu Cunxin, Lu Liping, Xu Fann, Guo Tao

This film weaves together five discrete love stories between different residents of contemporary Beijing, beginning with the story of a boy's sonic infatuation with a female classmate, which he consummates by editing together the phrase "I love you" from different sentences he's recorded her saying. Then, a widowed woman turns to the magic of broadcast to find a new husband, making an appearance on TV that produces three aggressive respondents, whom the woman is ultimately able to satisfy by turning to the great Chinese tradition of mah-jongg. A couple tries to keep the sizzle in ther relationship by purchasing toys—and not the kind of toys that might immediately spring to mind among reviewers in the decadent West. A young boy tries to "heal" his parents' relationship by cooking an herbal meal that has cure-all properties. The final story, which is also a kind of frame for the film, is a story of the accidental meeting, courtship, and blossoming of romance between two young people, now headed for the altar. Reviewers called it a "tasty dish" that ended up becoming the second-biggest box office hit of 1998, after the juggernaut *Titanic,* while its soundtrack became the second-highest-selling soundtrack in Chinese history. "Incredibly simple, universal, captivatingly funny."

***Storm Riders, The*** (1998; Hong Kong, Ac, Pd) D: Andrew Lau C: Ekin Cheng, Aaron Kwok, Sonny Chiba, Kristy Yeung, Shu Qi

A cryptic prophecy informs Lord Conqueror Hung Ba (Chiba), leader of the Tin Ha Sect, that he will rise to power over the martial world, if he commands the power of Wind and Cloud. Conqueror decides that the prediction relates to children who will grow up to become the land's greatest fighters. To ensure that these warriors will be his own, he uses astrological charts to find two babies of the right age named Wind and Cloud, kills their families, and raises them as his own alongside his son, Frost (Michael Tse), and his daughter, Charity (Yeung). Wind (Cheng) and

Cloud (Kwok) grow up to become Conqueror's greatest lieutenants, with Wind becoming the gentle master of the Wind Kick, and Cloud the brooding master of the Cloud Palm. But as time goes on, Conqueror's paranoia expands along with his empire; he decides to call in a mystic for a full explanation of the original prophecy. It turns out that Wind and Cloud are destined to be critical to both Conqueror's rise and fall. He decides to eliminate the two young superheroes before they can turn on him, with disastrous consequences. Reviewers called this special-effects blockbuster, based on the Hong Kong comic book series of the same name by Ma Wing Shing, "hyperkinetic" "eye candy." They noted, however, that the "over-large cast" and "wooden performances by the leads" effectively made the effects the star of the show. "Worth watching to see the 'future of Hong Kong cinema,' but you may not be too pleased by what the future holds." It was the top-grossing film in Hong Kong history, until the release of Stephen Chiau's *Shaolin Soccer* (2001).

### *Story of Qiu Ju, The* (1992; Mainland, Dr, Cm) D: Zhang Yimou C: Gong Li, Liu Peiqi, Lei Luosheng, Yang Liuchun

Gong Li plays Qiu Ju, a tremendously pregnant, tremendously persistent young woman seeking justice for her husband, who has been kicked in the testicles by a village elder, demanding that the elder provide a formal apology. The elder refuses, and Qiu Ju subsequently demands the help of a local magistrate, then higher officials in turn, getting rebuffed repeatedly and simply going up to the next level of authority as a result. It's a "study in bureaucratic meandering" and an "effective, subtle parody." The film is an interesting visual departure for Zhang as well—both because he hides his lovely star Gong Li under layers of thick quilted coats and scarves (not to mention an almost-to-term pregnant belly) and because he adopts a cinematographic style that is more "unadorned and realistic" than his usual "rich, painterly look." Reviewers called it a "shaggy dog story" that "may wear away at your patience."

### *Summer Snow* (1995; Hong Kong, Dr) D: Ann Hui C: Josephine Siao, Roy Chiao, Law Kar Ying, Helena Law, Allen Ting

A "muted but lovely" vehicle for Siao as May Sun, a middle-aged clerk at a toilet paper importer who must juggle her job, her family, and her Alzheimer's-stricken father-in-law (Roy Chiao, in a "truly wonderful" turn), who has regressed into a childlike state. Soon he no longer recognizes even his son, mistaking him for a thief and beating him up. Indeed, May is the only person he seems to know and respond to, increasingly turning him into her burden. Driven to distraction, May finds a nursing home for the elder Sun, but when he runs away and returns to their home, she relents and tells him he can stay forever. Reviewers were divided between those who thought it was "excellent," a "warm and unmaudlin look at a sad illness," and those who found it a "TV movie of the week."

***Super Citizen Ko*** (1995; Taiwan, Dr) D: Wan Jen C: Lin Yang, Chen Chiou-yen, Su Ming-ming, Ko I-cheng

This is a "potent," "subversive" tale of a man's persecution during the White Terror of the fifties, in which the government arrested and detained anyone suspected of political activity against the Kuomintang, while cultivating a dark atmosphere of anticommunist hysteria. Here, Lin Yang plays Ko I-sheng, a man who is jailed for belonging to a political discussion group. In the course of his interrogation, he names the organizer of the group, Chen, and the latter is arrested and executed. Ko's imprisonment lasts for sixteen years, but due to his feelings of guilt for having caused the death of his friend, he refuses to return to his home, living for another decade in a nursing home, until he nearly dies of a cardiac arrest. Realizing that he won't live forever, Ko decides to reach out to his estranged daughter Ko Hsu-chin (Su), who has stayed away from him ever since his arrest, his divorce from her mother, and her mother's subsequent suicide. I-sheng's overtures to his daughter are met with bitterness, and he can't find words to answer her accusations. Meanwhile, his friends have forgotten him and tried aggressively to forget the past as well. Finally, he decides to seek out Chen's grave, to seek out forgiveness from the dead. Reviewers called it "introspective" and "somber," and a "deeply absorbing drama" about the "fading of history from memory."

***Swordsman*** (1990; Hong Kong, Ac, Pd) D: King Hu C: Sam Hui, Cecilia Yip, Cheung Man, Jacky Cheung, Lau Shun

***Swordsman II*** (1991; Hong Kong, Ac, Pd) D: Ching Siu Tung C: Jet Li, Brigitte Lin, Michelle Lee, Rosamund Kwan, Fennie Yuen

***Swordsman III: The East Is Red*** (1992; Hong Kong, Ac, Pd) D: Ching Siu Tung, Raymond Lee C: Brigitte Lin, Joey Wang, Yu Rongguang, Eddy Ko, Lau Shun

This trilogy, based loosely on Jin Yong's *The Laughing and Proud Warrior*, began as producer Tsui Hark's attempt to stage a comeback for classic *wuxia* director King Hu.

During the filming of the first installment, disagreements emerged between Tsui and Hu, and the latter quit (or was fired)—leaving the film to a series of substitutes, including Ann Hui, Andrew Kam, and Raymond Lee; finally Tsui and action director Ching Siu Tung went ahead and finished fthe film themselves. The first film introduces good-natured, wine-loving student warrior Ling (played here by Sam Hui), as he and his tomboy sidekick Kiddo (played by Cecilia Yip) travel to meet a besieged nobleman who has stolen a sacred martial arts scroll. The message they bear: Their master, the powerful chief of the Wah Mountain Sword Sect, isn't coming to save the day. The surprised nobleman and his small force of loyalists are murdered by an army led by the chief eunuch's henchman Zhor (Yuen Wah). Ling and Kiddo barely escape themselves, and are sheltered from Zhor's troops by the Sun Moon Sect, a gypsylike band of Highlanders. But their survival may be moot, given the number of people who want to kill them in order to obtain the Sacred Scroll—including their own master Ngok. Reviewers called it "convoluted" and "murky," which stems from the fact that its source material is itself rather convoluted and murky, and attempting to assemble a movie from such a source using a tag team of directors doesn't help. "Sets up interesting situations, but is generally something of a mess." The second installment, directed by Ching, is better in all aspects—replacing the cast wholesale, with the introduction of Jet Li as Ling particularly key to the film's success. But the cunning twist that makes *Swordsman II* worthwhile is Brigitte Lin's iconic portrayal of Invincible Asia, a male warrior who castrated himself in obedience to the instructions of the Sacred Scroll, and was granted unimaginable power as a result—at the expense of his sex. Ling, who does not know that Asia is a man, engages in a strange flirtation with the enigmatic transsexual, setting the stage for an epic confrontation that understandably comes as quite a shock to the laughing warrior. Reviewers called it a "virtuoso piece of fantasy" that nearly stimulates "sensory overload" through its series of ever more flamboyant action set-pieces—showcasing such wild techniques as Chief Wu's "Essence Absorbing Stance," Asia's deadly embroidery needle and thread, and Ling's "wavering sword" stance. It also serves as "remarkably fertile ground for interpretation"—inspiring avalanches of analysis from political, feminist, and gay and lesbian perspectives. "A landmark of the golden age of Hong Kong cinema." The third and final installment in the *Swordsman* trilogy is less a climax than a coda—taking the plot well away from its Jin Yong origins and bringing it decades forward into the future. After the events of *Swordsman II*, Asia the Invincible (Lin) has been presumed dead. But his/her legend has inspired dozens of impostors to create Invincible Asia cults, whose members see him/her as the savior of a China beset by foreign invaders. When a Chinese official named Koo (Yu) seeks out the site of Asia's death and discovers that the master is still alive, he informs her about the impostors—and, enraged, she sets about eliminating those who have taken her name in vain. Filled with "outlandish" visuals (such as Asia riding a huge swordfish into battle, and defeating a giant ninja master who turns out to be an automaton controlled by a tiny dwarf), this segment "verges on self-parody"; still, reviewers call it "essential viewing" for fans of Lin's gender-bending antihero.

**Temptress Moon** (1996; Mainland, Dr, Pd) D: Chen Kaige C: Leslie Cheung, Gong Li, Kevin Lin, He Saifei, Zhang Shi, Zhou Yemang

Reviewers call Chen Kaige's followup to *Farewell My Concubine* (which reunites hiim with Gong Li and Leslie Cheung, two of the stars of that epic) a "potboiler of the first water," with "ravishing images" but "little heart or substance." Zhongliang is a young boy summoned to the palatial estate of the wealthy and decadent Pang family, to whom he is related by marriage—his older sister Xiuyi (He) is the wife of the Pang heir, Zhengda (Zhou). Upon arrival, he realizes that he hasn't been invited as a guest, but rather as a servant, whose primary responsibility is to prepare pipes of opium for the heir, the old Master, and his own sister Xiuyi. Years later, an adult Zhongliang (Cheung) is now working as a gigolo, hustling lonely women. Satisfied with his "progress," his pimp assigns him a special new mission: Return to the Pang estate and seduce the new heir to its fortune—Zhengda's sister, Ruyi (Gong Li). Zhongliang is faced with the decision of whether to follow his heart or his thirst for revenge; the choice he ultimately makes sends all concerned spiraling into tragedy. Due to its depictions of opium-fueled decadence and the vague suspicion among censors that its plot involves some kind of subversive political allegory, this film was never released in China.

**To Live** (1994; Mainland, Dr) D: Zhang Yimou C: Ge You, Gong Li, Niu Ben, Guo Tao, Jiang Wu

In 1947, after World War II but a few years before total Communist victory, a weatlhy merchant's heir named Fugui lives a life of easy leisure. He has all the money he could need, a beautiful wife, a lovely daughter and another child on the way, and nothing better to do with his time than fritter away his cash at local gambling dens. When Fugui actually succeds in losing everything on a single impetuous dice roll, his horrified father dies of a heart attack, and his wife Jiazhen (Li) abandons him. Fugui visits the man who beat him out of his inheritance in hopes of some kind of mercy, and the man gives him a set of shadow puppets. Fugui takes the puppets and hits the road as an itinerant street performer. But while giving a show one day, he's drafted by a Nationalist press gang and forced to join the losing side of the great civil war. Through his native wit and adaptability, however, he manages to find his way home to Shanghai, and back into the arms of Jiazhen, who has decided to give him a second chance. As the years roll on, the family faces trial after trial, yet perseveres. When Jiazhen first returns to Fugui, she tells him that all she asks for is a quiet life together; by the end of the film, they have had an extremely unquiet life—but at least it was together. Reviewers called it "marvelously textured, by turns funny and touching," and praised Ge and Li's "rare chemistry." Zhang Yimou was banned from making films in China for two years after directing this picture.

### *Too Many Ways to Be No. 1* (1997; Hong Kong, Ac) D: Wai Ka Fai C: Lau Ching Wan, Francis Ng, Carman Lee, Cheung Tat Ming, Elvis Tsui

Frequently compared to Tom Tykwer's *Run Lola Run* (although this film came out several years earlier!), *Too Many Ways* takes the same basic scenario and runs through it multiple times, showing how even minor decisions can lead to enormously different results. As the film begins, hoods Wong Ah Kau (Lau) and Matt Chan (Ng), along with the rest of their miserably incompetent comrades in the Hung Lok Gang, are trying to run a scam involving a fleet of hot vehicles, but somehow manage to kill their boss before the deal can be done. To get rid of the body, they decide to brick it up in the wall of a bathroom—but realize when they hear a beeping noise that the customer for their merchandise was supposed to page their boss with contact info, and the pager is still on his body, which is now behind the wall. Further complications ensue . . . and then, like a reset button being hit, Wong is shown choosing a slightly different path, leading to a wildly different set of circumstances, a conceit that happens again and again, at different points in the narrative, which constantly converges, cycles, and forks again. At the end of each road: over-the-top violence, personal humiliation, hairbreadth escape, and other flavors of "inspired looniness." Reviewers called it "one of the strangest and most remarkable Hong Kong films ever," "provocative and amusing," with "aggressive, experimental camera techniques that you'll find either brilliant, or annoying, or both."

***Untold Story, The*** (1993; Hong Kong, CIII, Hr, Dr) D: Herman Yau C: Anthony Wong, Danny Lee, Emily Kwan, Julie Lee, Shing Fui On

This true-crime stomach turner is based on the account of a Macanese murderer/restaurant owner who apparently used Sweeney Todd's patented method of disposing of surplus corpses. Anthony Wong plays Wong Chi Hang, who is tabbed as a suspect in the disappearance of the original proprietors of the Eight Fairies Restaurant. Danny Lee plays Inspector Lee, whose police unit is assigned to sort out Wong's story. After a bit of judicious torture, the story comes out: Wong acquired the restaurant by killing its owners and grinding the juicy bits up into stuffing for his "roast pork buns," thus displaying the waste-not-want-not attitude that any successful small businessman should have. It's at this point that several of the cops realize that they've eaten and enjoyed Eight Fairies pork buns quite a bit in the past few months. From there, the film spins into a lurid set of flashbacks that leaves no gross-out stone unturned. Reviewers called it "really violent," and "quite disgusting," but apparently seminal; it essentially launched the exploitation subgenre of the true-horror flick, many of whose entries would involve actor Wong, director Yau, or both.

***Viva Erotica*** (1996; Hong Kong, CIII, Cm) D: Derek Yee, Law Chi Leung C: Leslie Cheung, Karen Mok, Shu Qi, Law Kar Ying, Elvis Tsui

A "pointed" and "sporadically witty" satire of the lurid world of Category III softcore erotica, this film features Leslie Cheung as Sing, a director of earnest but pretentious art cinema, whose films have been so unpopular that he's forced to accept a porn-directing gig just to survive. Unfortunately, there's a hitch: The film has to star Mango (Shu), the lovely but certified talent-free girlfriend of the "executive producer," a gruff Triad heavy named Boss Wong (Paul Chun). Ultimately, Sing reconciles his desire to create art with his need to make a living, and by the film's end, he's overcome his contempt for the pornography genre—telling his cast and crew to "make me think it's real." Reviewers called it "amusing," but unsure of its tone; still, the parody is "effective" and the overall effect is to "humanize a secretive industry."

***Vive l'Amour*** (1994; Taiwan, Dr) D: Tsai Ming-liang C: Yang Kuei-mei, Chen Zhaorong, Lee Kang-sheng

This "startlingly brilliant" sophomore effort by Tsai explores some of the same territory as his debut film, *Rebels of the Neon God* (1992), with a slightly older (but no wiser)

set of characters. May (Yang) is a real estate broker who spends most of her time in empty buildings, talking with potential clients on the phone, and picking up strangers for sexual interludes in her listed properties. Ah Rong (Chen) is an arrogant, handsome street vendor whom May meets and efficiently seduces. Closeted and awkward Hsiao Kang (Lee) markets crematorium slots. While riding his scooter, Hsiao Kang notices a "for sale" sign on a building, and decides on a whim to enter it and take a bath. When May and Ah Rong enter to consummate their tryst, Kang is nearly trapped inside, but manages to escape without being discovered. Kang finds himself strangely attracted to Ah Rong, but unsure of how to approach him, especially given the fact that he's having a sexual fling with May. Encountering him wandering in another of May's empty houses, Kang introduces himself; later, he tucks a pair of porn magazines into Ah Rong's briefcase. All of this culminates with a scene in which Kang finds himself underneath the bed as Ah Rong and May make love, furtively masturbating, which is as close to closure as this odd triangle gets. Reviewers called it "mature and precise," beyond expectations for a sophomore effort; the minimalist cast and general lack of dialogue contribute to the film's sense of "restless alienation."

### Wedding Banquet, The (1993; Taiwan, Dr) D: Ang Lee C: Sihung Lung, Gua Ah-leh, Winston Chao, Mitchell Lichtenstein, May Chin

Wei-tung (Chao) is an immigrant from Taiwan living in Manhattan who has adopted most of the trappings of yuppie life, including a promising job in the real estate business, a beautiful townhouse, and a loving significant other. What his parents don't know is that his other happens to be male—gentle, supportive Simon (Lichtenstein), who is torn between wanting to protect Wei-tung from the possibility that his parents will discover the truth and wishing that the truth could just come out, once and for all. Meanwhile, Wei-tung's mother, played by Gua Ah-leh, persists in trying to set him up with eligible women, driving him to distraction. The perfect solution seems to arrive in the form of Wei Wei (Chin), an artist from Mainland China seeking permanent residency. Wei-tung offers to marry Wei Wei to kill two birds with one stone: getting Wei Wei her green card and getting Wei-tung's parents off his back. But the path to the perfect solution has its own pitfalls. Mr. Kao (Lung) demands that Wei-tung and Wei Wei have a traditional Chinese wedding banquet to "give him face"—which ends with a drunken Wei-tung and Wei Wei being forced to spend the night together, with the unexpected result that Wei Wei gets pregnant. Reviewers called it a "nontraditional family drama based on traditional family values."

**Wooden Man's Bride, The** (1993; Mainland, Dr, Pd) D: Huang Jianxin C: Wang Lan, Wang Fuli, Wang Yumei, Chang Shih

A young woman is hijacked by bandits while being brought to the remote desert estate of her husband, with disastrous results, in this melodrama that "brings to mind Sergio Leone westerns." The Young Mistress (Wang) is being ferried to her future family, the Liu household, by Kui (Chang), a bearer and servant. Although she has no desire to be taken so far away from her home, she has no choice: Her father owes a great deal of money to the Lius, and they have agreed to erase his debts in exchange for his daughter. While on the journey, a hot and irritated Mistress takes off her traditional red veil, breaking the custom that a bride not reveal herself to strangers before her marriage day; from that point on, nothing but misfortune occurs, as the Whirlwind Gang attacks the bridal caravan and carries off Young Mistress. Hearing this bad news, her future husband heroically decides to grab the family rifle to go after her; stumbling, he shoots himself dead by accident. But Young Mistress is saved due to the efforts of Kui, who confronts the bandit chieftain in order to gain her return, and carries her to the Liu household, now decorated not for celebration but for mourning. However, despite the absence of a bridegroom, Madame Liu (Wang) is not willing to release Young Mistress. Instead, she unveils her plan to marry the Mistress off to a carved wooden symbol of her son, thereby guaranteeing that she wiill stay and take on the responsibilities of caring for Madame Liu and the rest of the household. The lonely wooden man's bride is soon embroiled in an illicit affair with Kui—one that can no longer be hidden when it results in her pregnancy. Reviewers called it "visually stunning" and "emotionally powerful."

**Xiao Wu** (1997; Mainland, Dr) D: Jia Zhangke C: Wang Hongwei, Hao Hongjian, Zu Baitao

A two-bit burglar is the protagonist in this debut film by director Jia, which uses a cast of nonactors to "powerfully naturalistic effect." (Wang Hongwei, who played the lead role, was also the film's production manager!) Xiao Wu may be a rogue and a thief, but he has his own strange sense of values—he refuses to do anything that may be seen as "going with the flow." He won't carry a state ID card. He refuses to get a "legitimate" job, unlike his old comrade Xiao Yang (Hao), who has given up robbery to open a karaoke club (e.g., a brothel and illegal cigarette sales operation), and is now considered a fine, upstanding entrepreneur. As a result, he's an outcast, dismissed and ignored by all of his former petty-crook friends, each of whom has moved on to socially acceptable careers and lifestyles. The only individual willing to show him kindness is Mei Mei, a hostess girl at Yang's club, and Xiao Wu responds to her small gestures by stealing an ever-increasing number of wallets to provide her with gifts, until one day she simply goes away without warning, and he is left alone once more, holding the ring that he has so painstakingly procured for her. His devotion to Mei Mei has led him to a grudging acceptance of his only "leash" (a pager she has given him so that she can track him down at any time); ironically, it is this that ultimately brings him down, when it goes off just as he is attempting to pick a pocket. The message isn't even from Mei Mei; it is an automated weather-report page. And so, the man who refuses to be tied down to the system ends up shackled to a pole, subjected to public humiliation. Reviewers called it "gleefully nihilistic"; an "incredible debut."

**Young and Dangerous** (1996; Hong Kong, Ac) D: Andrew Lau C: Ekin Cheng, Jordan Chan, Gigi Lai, Francis Ng, Simon Yam, Jerry Lamb, Jason Chu

A blockbuster hit that defined an entire category of cinema: the *"goo wak jai"* or "Triad Boys" subgenre, which would dominate much of the latter half of the nineties. (Indeed, the *Young and Dangerous* series, with its five sequels and multiple spinoffs, would dominate theaters all by itself.) Based on a comic book by the evocatively named Cow Man, the film follows the recruitment and initiation of a quintet of young hoodlums—soulful Chan Ho Nam (Cheng); his brash friend Chicken (Chan); brothers Pou Pan and Chow Pan (Lamb and Chu); and energetic Dai Tin Yee (Michael Tse). The five prove themselves loyal members of the Hung Hing Triad under Brother Bee (Francis Ng), by infiltrating a bathhouse and whacking a thug who has failed to pay his debts; unfortunately, this act enrages another Hung Hing leader, the psychotic Ugly Kwan (Francis Ng). It seems the same thug owed Kwan quite a bit of money as well, and is not likely to be able to pay it as a corpse. Kwan subsequently lays a trap for Ho Nam and his boys, setting them up for an ambush with a fake job in Macau, and then inciting a drugged Ho Nam to sleep with Chicken's girlfriend. This "disloyalty" toward his brother leads to Ho Nam's humiliation and resignation from Hung Hing and Chicken's departure for greener pastures in Taiwan. But Kwan is far from done: He goes on to have

Brother Bee murdered, and then takes control of the Hung Hing organization itself. It's up to Ho Nam to come out of retirement and take Kwan down—with help from an unexpected quarter. Reviewers called it a "watershed" film, influencing most of the popular films that came after with its MTV-style freeze-frames, motion blurs, and snap cuts, as well as its garish, neon aesthetic and its pretty-boy take on criminal enterprise. The film is "not critically acclaimed" but "undoubtedly entertaining." "Ng's portrayal of Ugly Kwan steals the show"; "one of the most memorable villain turns in recent memory." Followed by five sequels (2 through 4 and the finale *Born to Be King* [2000]), tracking the rise of Ho Nam and Chicken to Triad leadership, as well as a prequel looking at their young, pre–Hung Hing days.

# EPILOGUE: 2000 AND BEYOND

*Beijing Bicycle* (2001, Mainland, Dr) D: Wang Xiaoshuai C: Cui Lin, Li Bin, Zhou Xun, Gao Yuanyuan

Guei (Cui) is a country boy who has come to Beijing looking for work. Hired by a messenger company as a courier, he is issued a beautiful new bicycle and promised that—if he's diligent—he can someday own the bike for himself. When it's stolen, he becomes determined to get it back. He finds it in the possession of city boy Tin (Li), who says he purchased it "legitimately" from a flea market and has no intention of returning it. The two repeatedly steal the bike back and forth and gradually develop a bond of reluctant respect, until a bigger problem intrudes on their unusual relationship. Reviewers called it a "sensitive," "modest" tragicomedy that was undoubtedly inspired by De Sica's *The Bicycle Thief.*

*Betelnut Beauty* (2001, Taiwan, Dr) D: Lin Cheng-sheng C: Chang Chen, Sinje Angelica Lee, Tsai Chen-nan, Kao Ming-chun, Kelly Kuo

Dotted throughout Taiwan are roadside stands vending betelnuts, a cultish snack food that offer a mild, euphoric high. The stands are invariably operated by pretty young girls, who simultaneously serve as both vendors and "advertising." Here, Malaysian pop idol Sinje plays Fei-fei, a runaway who takes a job as a betelnut seller after falling in love with Xiao-feng (Chang Chen), a young man recently released from military service. But their peaceful existence is soon threatened by the eruption of a street war between hostile gangs. Reviewers called it a "remarkable" drama, with "spunky" performances by its leads.

*Crouching Tiger, Hidden Dragon* (2000, Taiwan, Ac, Dr, Pd) D: Ang Lee C: Chow Yun Fat, Michelle Yeoh, Zhang Ziyi, Chang Chen, Cheng Pei Pei, Sihung Lung

Li Mubai (Chow), the greatest warrior of the martial world, has decided to end his career, turning his incredible sword, Green Destiny, over to the keeping of an old friend (Lung). Meanwhile, the local governor's daughter, Yu Jiaolong (Zhang), has grown up with a wildly romantic view of the *"jiang hu,"* and covets Green Destiny as her means to leave her suffocating existence. One evening, Green Destiny is stolen by a mysterious figure in black, and Li and his companion Yu Shulien (Yeoh), whom he has long loved but held back from embracing, must track down the weapon before it falls into the wrong hands. The identity of the robber surprises them both: It was stolen by Jiaolong, who, counseled by her nurse, ex-master-thief Jade Fox (Cheng), has decided to embrace a life of adventure. Meanwhile, Jiaolong's former lover, Lo Xiaohu (Chen), is also seeking her out, hoping to steal her away before she is forced into an arranged marriage. Reviewers called it an "astonishing" film that blends "exhilarating combat sequences" and an "epic vision that attains the level of poetry." The film—a loose remake of the first *wuxia* film ever made in Taiwan—turned Zhang Ziyi into an international superstar.

### Devils at the Doorstep (2000, Mainland, Dr) D: Jiang Wen C: Jiang Wen, Jiang Hongbo, Kagawa Teruyuki, Yuen Ding, Cong Zhijun

Actor Jiang Wen follows up his controversial debut, *In the Heat of the Sun,* with this war story about a hapless farmer named Ma Dasan (director Jiang) whose household is the unwilling recipient of two prisoners, transferred to their custody by a retreating Nationalist soldier. One is a Japanese officer (Kagawa); the other is a cowardly Chinese spy (Jiang Hongbo). The family questions the former with the "assistance" of the latter, but the latter manipulates both their questions and the officer's answers, until both are thoroughly confused. Finally, the members of the family confer regarding what to do with their unwanted guests—and make a decision that they will all eventually regret. Reviewers called this "scathing" "black-comic" portrait of the horrible impact of war on the innocent a work of "overwhelming emotional intensity"; the movie, based on a popular novel, has been banned in China.

### Durian Durian (2000, Hong Kong, Dr) D: Fruit Chan C: Qin Hailu, Mak Wai Fan, Mak Suet Man, Biao Xiaoming, Yung Wai Yiu

This film, the first of what director Chan says will be a "Prostitute Trilogy" of movies, takes place in two alternating and contrasting locales—lurid, downtrodden Portland Street in Hong Kong's Mongkok district, and the Mainland's "special economic zone" of Shenzhen. Fan (Mak Wai Fan) is a young girl who lives on Portland Street with her illegal-alien parents. When she witnesses the brutal beating of a pimp (using an unlikely weapon—a spiky durian fruit), she encounters and befriends Yan (Qin), one of the pimp's Mainland whores. Reviewers called it a "richly evocative" work that "shows why 2000 was one of the strongest years ever for Chinese-language cinema."

***From the Queen to the Chief Executive*** (2001, Hong Kong, Dr) D: Herman Yau C: Stephen Tang, Ai Jing, David Li, Sam Wong, Alson Wong

This "bracing" and "disconcerting" social drama based loosely on the real-life plight of a group of juvenile offenders trapped in legal limbo—"detained at the pleasure of Her Majesty the Queen"—who inspire a young woman and a disillusioned councillor to spearhead a petition for their cases to be tried. "Laced with stark, disturbing imagery that could have been pulled from Yau's slasher pics," this film is a "momentous" and "powerful" work. "Unexpectedly, Yau has made one of the most important films of 2001."

***Human Comedy, The*** (2001, Taiwan, Cm, Dr) D: Hung Hung C: Chang Ling-shien, Ethan Chan, Chi-shing Woon, Hsiao Hua-wen

This film by director Hung Hung weaves together four tales loosely based on *The Book of 24 Filial Pieties,* a Confucian classic presenting examples of model behavior by children toward their parents. The storylines—about a salesgirl in a world of her imagination, a young actor rehearsing for a director with terminal AIDS, a couple seeking a new apartment, and a husband risking his life in a thunderstorm for his estranged wife—showcase the tension between selfishness and sacrifice in everyday life. Reviewers called it a "quiet" and "miraculous" portrait of "postmodern Taiwan."

***I Love Beijing*** (2001, Mainland, Dr) D: Ning Ying C: Yu Lei, Zuo Baitao, Tao Hong, Gai Yi, Liu Miao

The third in Ning's "Beijing Trilogy," this film follows a recently divorced cabbie named Dezi as he wanders through the city, making pickups and dropoffs, and interacting with passengers and passersby. "A love song to a city seemingly too busy for love," say reviewers.

***In the Mood for Love*** (2000, Hong Kong, Dr) D: Wong Kar Wai C: Tony Leung Chiu Wai, Maggie Cheung, Rebecca Pan, Chen Lai

A man and a woman, who live next door to each other in a cramped tenement, begin to realize that their respective spouses are having an affair. This throws the two of them together, as they reflect on their partners' infidelity and muse over whether to indulge in one themselves. Reviewers called it "lushly shot," with a "repetitive, dreamlike atmosphere"; "Leung and Cheung have never been better."

***Jiang Hu: The Triad Zone*** (2000, Hong Kong, Ac, Dr) D: Dante Lam C: Tony Leung Kar Fai, Sandra Ng, Anthony Wong, Pang King Chi, Jo Kuk

A "bravura" parody of the Triad world, featuring Tony Leung Kar Fai as Jim Yam, a middle-aged mob boss confronting the arrival of a brutal new generation of punks. Sandra Ng plays his neglected wife, Sophie, who is kidnaped by a vicious rival, even as Yam discovers that he is the target of a mysterious assassin. Symbolic of the film's "artful loopiness" is Anthony Wong's recurring appearances as a despondent Kwan Kung, the God of Warriors (and, by extension, Triads). Reviewers called it "uninhibited and unpredictable"; a "terrific, yet restrained spoof."

***La Brassiere*** (2001, Hong Kong, Cm) D: Patrick Leung C: Lau Ching Wan, Louis Koo, Carina Lau, Gigi Leung, San San Lee

Samantha (Carina Lau), the chief of the Hong Kong division of a Japanese lingerie manufacturer, has been tasked by her Tokyo-based boss with creating the "ultimate bra" by hiring a pair of male designers—under the assumption that women really wear bras for men, so men should know best what they should look like. Reluctantly, she hires Johnny (Lau Ching Wan) and Wayne (Koo), who immediately charm all of her employees, except for Samantha's design chief Lena (Leung), who thinks they know nothing about lingerie, or about women, for that matter. After the boys produce a disastrous first effort, they acknowledge their need to pick up a few pointers—and are forced by Lena to try out the products for themselves. This gives them a fresh perspective on femininity; it also breaks the ice between Johnny and Samantha, and Wayne and Lena. Reviewers called it "witty" and "engagingly mischievous," mocking both chauvinism and feminism in turn. This "remarkably fun" film was one of the biggest hits of 2001.

***Lan Yu*** (2001, Hong Kong, Dr) D: Stanley Kwan C: Hu Jan, Liu Ye, Su Jin, Jin Huatong, Lu Fang

This "soulful" love story is Kwan's adaptation of *Beijing Story,* a work of gay erotica that was anonymously serialized via the Internet (http://www.yifan.net/yihe/novels/beijing/biejing.html). Entrepreneur Chen Handong (Hu) and poverty-stricken student Lan Yu (Liu) have a brief sexual encounter; the former thinks of it as a one-night stand, but the latter falls thoroughly in love. Over the space of months and years, their relationship changes and evolves, as Handong learns what he truly wants and needs. Reviewers called this "matter-of-fact" tale Greater China's "most heartening gay movie yet."

### *Little Cheung* (2000, Hong Kong, Dr) D: Fruit Chan C: Yiu Yuet Ming, Mak Wai Fan, Mak Suet Man, Gary Lai, Robby

In this, the last installment of Chan's "Handover trilogy," the nine-year-old boy of the title befriends a little girl named Fan, who assists him with deliveries for Cheung's father, a take-out cook, while also helping out her illegal-immigrant mother, a dishwasher for the same restaurant. When the Handover arrives, Cheung and Fan are among the many who salute the "return to the motherland" and glory in the fact that Hong Kong is once more in the hands of the Chinese. But neither has considered how reunification will affect the status of Fan and her mother. Reviewers called it a "passionate," "freewheeling" "poetic montage" that "consolidates Chan's status as one of Hong Kong's most interesting directors."

### *Millennium Mambo* (2001, Taiwan, Dr) D: Hou Hsiao-hsien C: Shu Qi, Tuan Chun-hao, Jack Kao, Niu Chen-er, Chen Yi-hsuan

Hou Hsiao-hsien's latest work features "It Girl" Shu Qi as Vicky, a club hostess torn between two men—Hao-hao (Tuan), the obsessive loser she lives with, and Jack (Kao), the older, slightly mysterious gentleman who serves as her escape valve when Hao-hao's suffocating jealousy becomes too much to handle. She decides to give herself a deadline to decide: after the NT$500,000 in her bank account is spent, she'll choose one or the other. Reviewers called it "deceptively intricate and lyrical," though "not one of Hou's great works"; the "cinematography is incredible."

### *Mission, The* (2000, Hong Kong, Ac) D: Johnnie To C: Francis Ng, Anthony Wong, Jackie Lui, Roy Cheung, Lam Suet

Perhaps the most critically acclaimed of Milkyway Image's productions, this ensemble thriller about five gangsters brought together to bodyguard a threatened Triad head has been called "action movie as haiku," with "phenomenal perform-ances" by Hong Kong's greatest character actors. When the youngest member of the quintet, Shin (Lui), begins an ill-advised affair with the Triad's wife, the order goes out to murderous senior gunman Curtis (Wong) to rub him out. But the other henchmen, particularly Roy (Ng), aren't about to let that happen. "A minimalist script lofted by an incredible gathering of talent." "Not to be missed."

### *Needing You* (2000, Hong Kong, Dr) D: Johnnie To, Wai Ka Fai C: Andy Lau, Sammi Cheng, Fiona Leung, Raymond Wong, Hui Siu Hung

A delightful romantic comedy featuring Andy Lau and Sammi Cheng at their peak of charm; what lifts this above even the best middle-market meet-cute fare is the thoroughly self-aware nature of the performances, as Lau plays Wah Siu, a commitment-phobic Lothario sliding uneasily into middle age, and Cheng plays frenetically neurotic Kinki, who is driven to compulsive cleaning at the slightest anxiety. Although Wah initially tries to resolve Kinki's romantic problems through matchmaking, he ultimately realizes that he loves her himself—but now must contend with the fruits of his efforts, a younger rival who happens to be a billionaire. Reviewers call it a "brilliantly well-crafted" confection with "magical chemistry" between the leads. Don't miss Lau's "achingly funny" parody of his own iconic character Wah Dee from 1990's *A Moment of Romance*.

### *Orphan of Anyang, The* (2001, Mainland, Dr) D: Wang Chao C: Zhu Jie, Sun Guilin, Yuen Senyi

This "most auspicious" debut by Wang Chao, Chen Kaige's former assistant director, is about an unemployed factory worker who accepts a prostitute's offer to pay him two hundred yuan per month to raise her baby. Although he has no parenting skills whatsoever, both parties in the transaction are desperate, and the worker is thrust into sudden parenthood. In the process, he and the prostitute begin to turn to each other for emotional support—until the prostitute's brutal pimp, who has discovered that he might be the baby's father, decides that he wants the child for himself. Reviewers called it "fascinating" and "deeply affecting."

### *Platform* (2000, Mainland, Dr) D: Jia Zhangke C: Wang Hongwei, Zhao Tao, Liang Jingdong, Yang Tianyi, Wang Bo

This "scathing" and "blackly humorous" tale of a rural opera company prompted to change with the times has prompted some reviewers to dub Jia China's "most promising" young director. The troupe's four twentysomething members—musician Cui Mingliang (Wang), his on-and-off lover Yin Ruijuan (Zhao), her best friend

Zhong Ping (Yang), and Zhong's boyfriend Zhang Jun (Liang)—have been trained throughout the seventies in the performance of propagandistic "model proletarian operas," but with the end of the Cultural Revolution, these operas no longer have an audience. As the new decade dawns, the quartet of performers decides that they have no choice but to adapt to the era, becoming break-dancing, punked-out rockers. Reviewers called this indie "masterpiece" "perhaps the most important mainland film of the last few years."

### *Shaolin Soccer* (2001, Hong Kong, Ac, Cm) D: Stephen Chiau, Lee Lik Chi C: Stephen Chiau, Ng Man Tat, Vicky Zhao, Patrick Tse, Vincent Kok

A "deliriously brilliant" love poem to the martial arts that broke every box office record in Hong Kong, this film—codirected by and starring Stephen Chiau—is the culmination of the funnyman's lifelong infatuation with kung fu; it is also the sharpest and most uncompromisingly unusual comedy to come out of Hong Kong in years. Chiau plays Sing, a trash collector and former Shaolin disciple whose quixotic dream is to revive the Temple's forgotten skills, which contemporary Chinese have left behind. He experiments with different ways of promoting Shaolin kung fu (including, hilariously, song and dance) before finally running into crippled former soccer ace Golden Leg Fung (Ng), who sees Sing's incredible foot power and proposes the creation of a "Shaolin soccer" team. Sing readily agrees (although his former Shaolin brothers, all in equally pathetic circumstances, are not so easily convinced). But once they're together, the gang's combined skills—from Hooking Leg to Iron Shirt—make them unbeatable, setting them up for a showdown with the "Evil Team" of Ng's villainous former teammate Hung. Meanwhile, Mui (Zhao), a hideously scarred steamed bun vendor with powerful tai chi fists, has responded to Sing's passing kindness with adoration. But Sing has love only for kung fu. Reviewers called the film "Chiau's best ever."

### *Spacked Out* (2001, Hong Kong, Dr) D: Lawrence Ah Mon C: Debbie Tam, Christy Cheung, Angela Au, Maggie Poon, Vanesia Chu

Ah Mon's specialty has been the documentation of alienated street youth; with *Spacked Out,* he explores the lives of contemporary adolescent girls, trapped in a world of disengaged parents, thuggish teachers, plentiful drugs, and freewheeling sex. Cookie (Tam) is just thirteen, but her life already seems as if it's winding down; she's pregnant by an older boy who couldn't care less and doesn't have the money for an abortion. Her father is clueless, and her mother is gone, so she has no one to turn to but her pals Sissy (Cheung), Banana (Au), and Bean-curd (Poon), who have similar problems of their own. Druggy voiceovers and fantasy sequences spiked with surreal images add a "self-consciously arty feel" to this otherwise "intense" and "realistic" portrayal of girls gone wild.

**Suzhou River** (2000, Mainland, Dr) D: Lou Ye C: Zhou Xun, Jia Hong-sheng, Yao Anlian, Nai An

The sophomore effort of director/screenwriter Lou Ye has a "distinctively Hitchcockian playfulness" that follows the unnamed narrator, a freelance videographer (who is never seen onscreen—the story plays itself out subjectively, with the camera standing in for the narrator), as he falls for a mermaid-costumed bar girl named Mei Mei (Zhou). She, meanwhile, tells him a bizarre story, which a motorcycle messenger named Mardar (Jia) told her: Years earlier, Mardar had been assigned to bring a young girl named Moudan to her aunt and fell in love with her in the process. Through an error in judgment, Mardar lost Moudan, and has been seeking her ever since. But Mei Mei is Moudan's identical twin, prompting Mardar to suspect Mei Mei of being his missing love. The story shifts back and forth between perspectives and voices, lending a "vertiginous" feel to the narrative. Reviewers called it "outstanding" and "provocative."

**Time and Tide** (2000, Hong Kong, Ac) D: Tsui Hark C: Nicholas Tse, Wu Bai, Anthony Wong, Cathy Tsui, Candy Lo

Pop star Nicholas Tse plays Tyler, a part-time bartender who ends up sharing an accidental one-nighter with a pretty cop named Jo (Chui). He finds out she's lesbian—and now, pregnant—when Jo's girlfriend shows up with a baseball bat. Tyler decides to do the responsible thing and make some money to support the child. He takes a job as a bodyguard and is assigned to protect a Triad leader whose son-in-law just happens to be a former mercenary named Jack (Wu). When Jack's former unit assassinates Tyler's client, Jack and Tyler must team up to take down Jack's old team. Reviewers called it a "convoluted" but "entertaining" experience, with "relentless action" and "dizzying" stunts.

**Visible Secret** (2001, Hong Kong, Hr, Dr) D: Ann Hui C: Eason Chan, Shu Qi, James Wong, Kara Hui, Anthony Wong

In this return to the supernatural world Hui first visited with *The Spooky Bunch* (1980), Shu Qi plays June, a girl who sees dead people, but only through one eye. Because of this, she usually keeps that eye closed, so as not to experience constant terror. She meets Peter (Chan) in a club, and the two tumble into bed, and then into a relationship. This draws him into her strange world, as he begins to wonder what is real and what is illusion; who is living, and who is dead. Reviewers called this box office hit an "aesthetic masterpiece," with a "palpable atmosphere of eerieness and dread."

**What Time Is It There?** (2001, Taiwan, Dr) D: Tsai Ming-liang C: Lee Kang-shang, Chen Shiang-chi, Lu Yi-cheng, Tian Miao, Cecilia Yip

Tsai's persistent screen stand-in, Lee Kang-sheng, plays Hsiao-kang, a street vendor who sells watches on the sidewalks of Taipei. He lives with his mother (Lu), for whom time stopped at the moment of her husband's death; she persists in imagining that Hsiao-kang's father is still alive, perhaps reincarnated into a fish, cockroach, or other vermin scuttling around the apartment. When a beautiful woman (Chen) asks him for a timepiece that shows the time in both Taipei and Paris, Hsiao-kang sells her his own watch and then becomes obsessed with that distant European city, renting the classic French film *The 400 Blows*, and resetting the apartment's clocks to Paris time. Reviewers called it "precise" and "minimalist," with Tsai's typically "deft absurdist touch."

**Wu Yen** (2001, Hong Kong, Cm, Dr, Pd) D: Johnnie To, Wai Ka Fai C: Sammi Cheng, Anita Mui, Cecilia Cheung

This "strange, but mesmerizing" costume fantasy is an adaptation of a classic opera tale made for Lunar New Year, with all that that entails. Sammi Cheng plays Cheung Mo Yim, a swordswoman whose prophesied fate is to marry the emperor (played by Anita Mui); their destined love is complicated by the fact that a fairy spirit, played by Cecilia Cheung, is intent upon seducing them both—switching sexes as necessary to accomplish her goal. Meanwhile, the other characters aren't above a little cross-dressing as well. Reviewers called this a "live-action cartoon" full of "wild spoofs," "burlesque hijinks," and musical puppet-theater interludes.

***Xiu Xiu, the Sent Down Girl*** (2000, Mainland, Dr) D: Joan Chen C: Lu Lu, Lopsang, Gao Jie, Lu Yue, Li Qianqian

The directing debut of actress Joan Chen tells the tale of Xiu Xiu (Lu), one of millions of urban youths sent to distant, rural parts of China during the Cultural Revolution in order to be "re-educated" through exposure to the peasants. In the case of Xiu Xiu, she ends up in a remote part of Tibet, assigned to learn horse skills from a quiet Tibetan herder named Lao Jin (Lopsang), who is rumored to have been castrated in a battle with enemies. The novelty of her mission wears off, and Xiu Xiu becomes anxious to return home to Chengdu. But months, and then years pass, and no relief team arrives; she soon becomes victimized by a series of passing strangers, who sexually molest her in exchange for promised assistance, which never comes. Reviewers called it a "devastating" and "powerful" work of "tragedy so bleak as to verge on absurdity."

***Yi Yi (A One and a Two)*** (2000, Taiwan, Dr) D: Edward Yang C: Wu Nien-chen, Kelly Lee, Jonathan Chang, Issey Ogata, Elaine Jin

NJ Jian (Wu) is a typical middle-class Taiwanese businessman with a loving wife named Min-min (Jin) and two children, Ting-ting (Lee) and Yang-yang (Chang). Their comfortable existence begins to unravel on the day of Min-min's brother A-di's wedding, when Min-min's mother has a sudden stroke and goes into a coma; the shock from this event precipitates a series of uncharacteristic actions on the part of a family suddenly made aware of mortality. Teenaged Ting-ting awkwardly experiments with romance; Min-min suffers an emotional collapse and goes off to a spiritual retreat; Yang-yang disrupts his class at school; and NJ himself entertains thoughts of an affair with a long-lost ex-girlfriend. Drastic changes loom for all parties, and not all for the better. Reviewers called it an "engaging," "landmark" film.

# Appendices:
# Frequently Asked
# Questions and
# Additional Information

---

**F**or more information and broader links to related references, visit www.OUATIC.com.

## I want to find out more about a specific film, and I can't find it.

*Once Upon a Time in China* hopes to be as comprehensive as possible given the boundaries of this single volume, but it is the unfortunate truth that large sections of Greater China's cinematic story are overlooked or given rather short shrift here, due to the simple fact of lack of space—as well as the availability of other books and resources that do a great job of providing detail on those topics. Fans of specific schools or subgenres—such as martial arts cinema, or Fifth Generation Mainland directors—will find the information here to be mostly an introduction to these areas, as the aim of this book is to provide a cultural and historical context for these films, and not a detailed survey of each topic. Readers will also note that scattered throughout the book's six chapters are short sidebar pieces by *Once Upon a Time in China*'s contributors that digress from the book's strict chronological flow: These provide further detail on important issues, concepts, or phenomena that aren't tied to a strict point in time. Capsule reviews of the most distinctive, influential, or otherwise interesting films of each era are gathered at the end of the book, segregated by era. This set of reviews is far from complete, and, in fact, is winnowed down from over fifteen hundred. The ones that didn't make it into the book, as well as a large amount of additional information on Hong Kong cinema, can be found online at www.OUATIC.com, the book's website.

### Okay, I'm hooked. So where can I find these movies?

The answer is . . . everywhere and nowhere. Hong Kong films, particularly action movies, are widely available in English-language versions at local video stores everywhere, although frequently in a dubbed, repackaged, and oddly retitled format; *Jet Li's The Enforcer,* for example, is actually an English-dubbed *My Father Is a Hero.* High-profile, big-budget Hong Kong movies, like Jackie Chan's works, are even getting theatrical release. The same can be said for works by the most prominent Mainland directors (such as leading Fifth Generation lights like Zhang Yimou and Chen Kaige, and Sixth Generationers like Zhang Yuan), although these are generally distributed only to art-house theaters or on very limited "prestige" circuits. Taiwanese films are the hardest to find of all, with only a handful of films from a smattering of top directors—Edward Yang, Tsai Ming-liang, Hou Hsiao-hsien—available at all.

Even then, all of the above applies only to contemporary films—movies of eighties vintage and beyond. English-translated versions of older films— Mainland and Taiwanese movies from the seventies and earlier, Hong Kong movies from the sixties and earlier—are mostly limited to exquisitely rare festival screenings. Recently, however, this de facto freeze on classic Chinese cinema has experienced a thaw, with the purchase by Celestial Pictures of the rights to distribute the entire Shaw Brothers library—including Shaws' groundbreaking Mandarin films of the fifties and sixties. Celestial is making a good number of classic Shaws films available on DVD in beautifully remastered English-language editions, and has entered into a relationship with Miramax to explore theatrical exploitation of the canon. Visit www.celestialpix.com for updated details.

If you have no luck looking on a local level, there's always the Internet. Dozens of options exist online for the purchase of imported Chinese DVDs, often at discounted prices. Please note, however, that many imported DVDs are region coded. U.S. players are coded to accept Region 1 DVDs only;

DVDs created with Asian markets in mind are coded Region 3, which will not play in Region 1 players. The solutions, such as they are, include purchasing a Region 3 player (available in Chinatown-based electronic stores or, again, online), purchasing a gray-market variable-code or multicode player, or finding code-free—Region 0—DVDs that work on all players. Any good online store will identify the region coding of their product in their film descriptions. Finally, you can also purchase VCDs instead, which are lower quality (about the same as VHS) and have limited or no "extras," but are region-code free by nature and should play in all modern DVD players. One slightly unusual thing about VCDs of Hong Kong origin is that they are often released with dual-language mono tracks—one stereo track will have dialogue in Cantonese, and the other in Mandarin. What comes out of the speaker is a garbled mess . . . unless you turn your balance completely to one or another track. (So much for fancy Surround Sound systems.) It is recommended that you identify which track is the "original" track for the film you're watching and stick with that, even if you don't speak Chinese. The bad dubbing for the alternative track can be a distracting annoyance.

Some online retailers of note:

### YesAsia (www.yesasia.com):
Very good selection of popular Hong Kong and Mainland films on DVD, including a library of classic Mandarin films from Cathay and Shaws; however, most of the classic films and even many of the contemporary ones are Region 3 only.

### Tai Seng (www.taiseng.com):
As the official U.S. distributor for many Hong Kong movies, Tai Seng has the edge on both selection and Region 1/0 offerings; sadly, many current releases are limited to VHS.

### HKFlix (www.hkflix.com) and Poker Industries (www.pokerindustries.com)
Two of the more complete online Hong Kong movie vendors; just about anything you might be looking for should be available here.

**A note about Chinatown retailers:** Every major Chinatown has at least one store advertising VCDs and DVDs for sale—often at what may seem like absurdly cheap prices (six VCDs for twenty dollars, for example). Well, no matter how fancy and professional the packaging may look, much of this product is pirate goods, duplicated fast 'n' cheap in Southeast Asia and shipped around the world for fast disposal—which may or may not stop you from wanting to purchase it, depending on your ethical standards. Practically speaking, these stores are a bonanza as far as selection (though uneven—you may be frustrated to find that one film out of a series of five is simply unavailable anywhere), but the quality of the product is often mediocre to downright bad. If a disc doesn't play or has the wrong movie on it, good luck getting an exchange or return. And while many stores are now organizing their hauls with a little more awareness of the needs of English-only shoppers (even segregating films by actor and director), you won't get much help from sales clerks if you can't find what you want. Also, that the packaging says that a film has English subtitles does not, in fact, guarantee that it does—you'll have to spend $3.99 to find out for sure. Caveat emptor.

## I noticed that the Chinese names in the book are presented in at least three different ways. This is confusing—what gives?

Unfortunately, the reason for this is that the use of English to represent Chinese names is still, in large part, more art than science. In 1958, the Mainland's Communist government developed a system of English transliteration ("romanization") known as "Hanyu Pinyin" (often just Pinyin for short); in 1977, it was adopted by the United Nations as the standard method for romanizing Mandarin, Mainland China's official dialect. Mandarin was also the official language of Taiwan, ruled by the Kuomintang, who had brought with them into exile a romanization system called "Gwoyeu Romatzyh." Invented in 1932, it was complex and ill-equipped for modern terms and usage; however, because the Kuomintang wanted no part of any system generated by the Communists, they replaced Gwoyeu Romatzyh with another standard instead, one then in use by the United States—the "Wade-Giles" system. As a result, the names of individuals primarily associated with the

Mainland are commonly romanized using Pinyin, while those who are primarily associated with Taiwan are romanized using Wade-Giles.

Meanwhile, due to the fact that Hong Kong's primary language has historically been Cantonese, a language that has largely defied standardization, the names of Hong Kong personages are romanized in what can only be called a capricious manner. Scanning through other books and movie sites, you may see the Chinese name Chow Sing Chi, Chiao Sing Chee, or Chau Sing Chi—all of them refer to funnyman Stephen Chiau, and it's tough to say which is the most correct, since Chiau himself apparently doesn't give a damn. *Once Upon a Time in China* attempts to use the most common or most standardized version of Hong Kong stars' Chinese names where possible. Of course, many Hong Kong stars have English names, and in cases where the individual in question uses that name, *Once Upon a Time in China* follows suit, often following the convention of appending it to the Chinese name—for example, Brigitte Lin Ching-hsia. (Things get hairier with stars who have, but do not regularly use, English names, such as "Donald" Chow Yun Fat—and stars who have changed their English names one or more times, such as "Ekin" "Noodle" "Dior" Cheng. In such cases, *Once Upon a Time in China* goes with the most common and/or current usage.)

The silver lining in this chaotic cloud is that it is possible to identify an individual's region of origin based on romanization conventions.

**Mainland China:** Names appear in Pinyin, which is distinctive for using Q for "ch" sounds, X for "sh" sounds, and C for "ts" sounds; surname first, followed by given name, usually consisting of one syllable or two syllables run together—for example, Zheng Zhengqiu, Ruan Lingyu.

**Taiwan:** Names may appear in Wade-Giles or Pinyin, but either way are presented surname first, followed by given name, usually consisting of one syllable or two syllables joined by a hyphen—for example, Lin Ching-hsia, Hou Hsiao-hsien.

**Hong Kong:** Names follow no clear convention, but are presented English name first (if any), followed by surname, followed by the given name as separate syllables—for example, Maggie Cheung Man Yuk, Stephen Chiau Sing Chi, Chow Yun Fat.

## Information available in bookstores and on the Internet

Luckily, there's a plethora of information out there in bookstores and on the Internet. Any of the sites listed here, as well as the OUATIC.com site, will link you to further resources. Consider this just the first step in the journey.

# GREATER CHINESE CINEMA

## Books

*Encyclopedia of Chinese Film* by Yingjin Zhang and Zhiwei Xiao (Routledge, 1998). A bit of an odd duck, this pricey but useful work is marked by both great merits and serious flaws. It is one of the few published reference texts that explores all three cinema industries, and does a solid job of presenting factual, cyclopedic entries on a wide variety of Chinese film topics. However, it largely omits any discussion of contemporary popular film, and its uncompromisingly academic tone may make it of limited use for nonscholarly enthusiasts.

## Websites

**Shelly Kraicer's Chinese Cinemas Page** (http://www.chinese cinemas.org). Kraicer is of a rare breed indeed—an informed and academically rigorous scholar who nevertheless writes with true passion about his subject, which in this case is the three Chinese cinemas. His site offers links to reviews, features, and articles that he's written for a variety of print and online publications and journals. An invaluable port of embarkation for the exploration of Greater Chinese cinema.

**Asian Film Connections** (http://www.usc.edu/isd/archives/asian film/). This site, sponsored and hosted by the University of Southern California, offers a terrific overview not only of Mainland and Taiwanese film, but also of Korean and Japanese cinema, with historical timelines, reviews of key works, and more.

# HONG KONG CINEMA

## Books

*The Hong Kong Filmography (1977–1997): A Complete Reference to 1,100 Films Produced by British Hong Kong Studios,* by John Charles (McFarland & Company, 2000). This huge volume is a must-buy for any true devotee of Hong Kong cinema. It isn't cheap— the *Filmography* is intended as a reference work, and is priced to suit—but it's worth every cent and more. *Once Upon a Time in China* contributor Charles has penned an immense, incisive, and nearly comprehensive compilation of reviews from Hong Kong cinema's most creative and prolific years, and it well deserves an honored place on your bookshelf.

*Great Martial Arts Movies: From Bruce Lee to Jackie Chan and More,* by Ric Meyers (Citadel Press, 2000). Another book by a key *Once Upon a Time in China* contributor, this pop-savvy volume is perhaps the most wide-ranging and inclusive study of the martial arts genre anywhere.

*Hong Kong Cinema: The Extra Dimensions,* by Stephen Teo (British Film Institute, 1998). A terrific historical and scholarly overview by one of Hong Kong's top critics, this book covers the early and contemporary eras of the Hong Kong film industry in a deep yet colorful fashion, and it is written in a tone that isn't too "academic" for an ordinary fan to work through.

*Planet Hong Kong: Popular Cinema and the Art of Entertainment,* by David Bordwell (Harvard University Press, 2000). Though a bit Film Studies–oriented, this is one of the most detailed and comprehensive explorations of the Hong Kong movie industry available, by one of the nation's top cinema scholars.

*The Cinema of Hong Kong: History, Arts, Identity,* by Poshek Fu and David Desser (Cambridge University Press, 2002). More a collection of essays than a linear overview, this is a fascinating "advanced" work for truly dedicated explorers.

*City on Fire*: *Hong Kong Cinema*, by Lisa Oldham Stokes and Michael Hoover (Verso Books, 1999). Another collection of essays, limited somewhat by its emphasis on eighties and nineties works and its preoccupation with the Handover, but still essential reading.

## Websites

**Hong Kong Movie Database** (www.hkmdb.com). The granddaddy of online Hong Kong cinema resources, this handy site offers a convenient tool to search one of the Web's deepest and broadest collections of reviews—each of which includes hyperlinked cast and crew lists, and Mandarin and Cantonese title translations. It's also home to an array of FAQs and other research aids, so it should be any enthusiast's first stop on the Web. Note: The unrelated **Internet Movie Database** (www.imdb.com) has added a decent amount of content on Hong Kong, Taiwan, and Mainland films, and is starting to become much more useful for Chinese film buffs, but still offers no real competition to the comprehensiveness of Hong Kong Movie Database on the Hong Kong cinema front.

**The Illuminated Lantern** (www.illuminatedlantern.com). *Once Upon a Time in China* contributor Peter Nepstad's zine site is a lucid, insightful, and masterfully written collection of themed essays that shed light on topics related to Hong Kong cinema, from Triad films to ghost stories to the influence of religion and philosophy on Chinese film.

**Hong Kong Cinema: View from the Brooklyn Bridge** (www.brns.com). What Brian Nass's site lacks in design polish it more than makes up for in depth, breadth, and quality of writing. Clearly a labor of love, View from the Brooklyn Bridge is home to hundreds of reviews by Nass and *Once Upon a Time in China* contributor Yvonne Teh, as well as a guide to Hong Kong performers that is absolutely startling in its completeness.

**Hong Kong Digital** (www.dighkmovies.com). This is the home of hundreds of archived and regularly updated Hong Kong movie reviews by *Hong Kong Filmography* author (and *Once Upon a Time in China* contributor) John Charles, covering an unimaginably broad swath of the industry's output. Smart, knowledgeable, and seemingly tireless, Charles is the dean of Hong Kong film reviewers on the Web.

**Another Hong Kong Movie Page** (www.kowloonside.com). Tim Youngs's review site, which is somewhat unique in that Youngs, a perceptive and entertaining writer with an enthusiast's joy in the medium, is actually based in Hong Kong and thus has ready access to current theatrical releases.

**Other Hong Kong film review sites of note: HK Film Net** (www.hkfilm.net)—also the home of a very good Hong Kong Movies FAQ; **Kung Fu Cult Cinema** (www.kfccinema.com); **Canton Kid** (www.cantonkid.com); **Dragon's Den UK** (www.dragonsdenuk.com); **Heroic Cinema** (www.heroic-cinema.com) and **Love HK Film** (www.lovehkfilm.com)

**The Special Administrative Region (Hong Kong) Film TOP TEN Home Page** (http://www.geocities.com/Tokyo/Towers/2038) and **Hong Kong Entertainment in Review** (http://www.hkentreview.com). These two sites, run by Jerry Chan and Sanney Leung respectively, provide a prismatic portrait of Hong Kong's pop world, drawn from Hong Kong's tabloids and refreshed weekly. If you want previews of upcoming projects, interviews of and updates on top Canto-stars, and, of course, sizzling gossip, these two sites are your must-click destination.

**Hong Kong Film Critics Society** (http://filmcritics.org.hk) and the **Hong Kong Film Archives** (http://www.lcsd.gov.hk/CE/Cultural Service/HKFA/english/eindex.html). For a more "institutional" perspective on Hong Kong cinema, these two sites (handily available in both Chinese and English) provide reviews, features, interviews, and commentary from Hong Kong's leading body of critics and its official film preservation institution, respectively.

# MAINLAND CHINESE CINEMA

## Books

*Dianying/Electric Shadows: An Account of Films and Film Audience in China*, by Jay Leyda (MIT Press, 1979). First published in 1972, this book was the first Western text ever to provide a survey of Chinese film, although it is less concerned with film criticism (or even the nuts and bolts of the Chinese film industry) than with cinema's role in the PRC's emergent socialist culture. A dry read, but historically interesting as one of the only seen-and-heard accounts of the era.

*China into Film: Frames of Reference in Contemporary Chinese Cinema (Envisioning Asia)*, by Jerome Silbergeld (Reaktion Books, 2000). Probably the most robust and accessible text on modern Mainland Chinese cinema. Though scholarly in tone, it is written with clarity and well leavened with photographs.

## Websites

*Chinese Movie Database* (http://www.dianying.com/en). Created in the mode of HKMDB (and IMDB before it), this site offers a searchable database of information about Mainland film, although it is notably less complete than either of its forbears.

*Chinese Film in the 1930s* (http://xtasy.lib.indiana.edu/iub15). A very nice overview of the golden era of Chinese film, designed with appropriate glamour and elegance.

# TAIWANESE CINEMA

Sadly, there is very little English-language published work dedicated to Taiwanese film. The following websites provide basic introductory material and some links to further resources.

## Websites

**Taiwan Government Information Office** (http://www.gio.gov.tw). The website of the government's information bureau, which offers a general survey of Taiwanese cinema history.

**Taipei Film Archive** (http://www.ctfa.org.tw/e_index_.htm). The home of Taiwan's official film archives, available in both Chinese and English. Unfortunately, the site offers little by way of real content, serving more as a source for event announcements and other bulletins.

# Notes

1. Leyda, Jay, *Dianying: An Account of Films and the Film Audience in China*, Cambridge, Mass., MIT Press, 1972.
2. Kaufman, George S., article for the *New York Tribune*, United States, August 27, 1916.
3. Ibid.
4. Zhiwei Xiao, "Chinese Cinema," in Yingjin Zhang and Zhiwei Xiao, eds., *Encyclopedia of Chinese Film*, New York, Routledge, 1998.
5. Tan Chunfa, "Early Chinese Films: A Historical Page Misread and Ignored for a Long Time," *Dangdai dianying* ("*Contemporary Cinema*"), China, 1995.
6. Du Wenwei, "Xi and Yingxi: The Interaction Between Traditional Theatre and Chinese Cinema," *Screening the Past*, Issue 11, Canada, 2000 (http://www.latrobe.edu.au/screeningthepast/).
7. Zhiwei Xiao, *Encyclopedia of Chinese Film.*
8. Ibid.
9. Shi, Joshua, "Film Stars Light Way for Future Women," *China Daily*, China, June 27, 2000.
10. Mao Zedong, "Pay Serious Attention to *The Life of Wu Hsun*," *People's Daily*, China, May 20, 1951.
11. Zhiwei Xiao, *Encyclopedia of Chinese Film.*
12. *The Columbia Encyclopedia*, Sixth Edition, New York, Columbia University Press, 2001.
13. Lau Shing Hon, ed., "A Study of the Hong Kong Martial Arts Film," Hong Kong, The Urban Council, 1980.
14. As quoted by Desser, David, in "The Kung Fu Craze," *The Cinema of Hong Kong: History, Arts, Identity*, Poshek Fu, David Desser, eds., Cambridge University Press, 2000.
15. Woo, John, comments, from the symposium, "A Get-Together with John Woo," Hong Kong Film Archives, November 2001.
16. Materials for seminar, "Louis Cha and His Martial-Art Novels," Harvard University, September 18, 2001.
17. Teng Sue-feng, "Going His Own Way: Cannes Winner Edward Yang," *Sinorama*, Taiwan, September 8, 2000.

18. Chen Kaige, "China Goes to the Movies," *Time Asia,* September 27, 1999.
19. Codelli, Lorenzo, "Like Father Like Son: Wang Tian Lin and Wong Jing," *Hong Kong Inglese,* (www.spaziocultura.it/gallery/cecudine/fe_2001/ENG/wongjing_intervista_eng.htm), February 2001.
20. Yang, Jeff, interview with Jackie Chan, 1998.
21. Multiple sources, including Oxygen.ie "Cine Masterclass," www.oxygen.ie/cine/cine_mc_woo.php3.
22. Multiple sources, including Dannen, Fredric, and Long, Barry, *Hong Kong Babylon: An Insider's Guide to the Hollywood of the East,* New York, Hyperion/Miramax, 1997.
23. Ibid.
24. Ryor, Kathleen M., "Reflections on the Recent Past in Contemporary Chinese Art," Chinese-Art.com (www.chinese-art.com/Contemporary/volume3issuef/transformations.htm), volume 3, issue 4, 2000.
25. Teng Sue-feng, "Can Grants Save the Taiwan Film Industry?" *Sinorama,* Taiwan, November 1999.
26. Ibid.
27. Teo, Stephen, "Post-'97 Hong Kong Cinema: Crisis and Its After-Effects," *Correspondence: An International Review of Culture & Society,* Issue 9, Council on Foreign Relations, Spring 2002.
28. Short, Stephen, "I Told Kar Wai I Couldn't Move, Couldn't Breathe," Time.com(www.time.com/time/asia/features/interviews/2000/10/11/int.tony_leung.html), October 11, 2000.
29. Kraicer, Shelly, "Interview: Johnnie To and Wai Ka Fai," *Senses of Cinema* (http://www.sensesofcinema.com/contents/01/18/to_and_ka-fai.html), November 2001.
30. Wong, Helene, "Hong Kong Cinema: Two Views," http://www.mic.org.nz/public_html/bigpicture/hongkong.html.

# Acknowledgments

The author would like to gratefully acknowledge all those who love Asian cinema, and who have chosen to share their wit and wisdom on the topic with the world through websites, message boards, mailing lists, and zines. Their passion has reshaped the entertainment industry, transformed the pop landscape, and crafted bright and glittering bridges between cultures.

Thanks also are due to Patty Keung and Celestial Pictures, who provided this book with rare and wonderful photos from the Shaw Brothers' collection, and to Marnix van Wijk of Fortissimo Films, Janet Ma and Nansun Shi of Film Workshop, Jessica Rosner of Kino International, Lammy Li of Golden Network, the Hong Kong and Taiwan Film Archives, and the Hong Kong Film Critics Society, for their contributions to the images found in these pages.

Last, the author would like to offer special thanks to two incredible women, his agent Ling Lucas, for envisioning this book, and his editor, Wendy Walker, for ensuring that it was finally completed.

# About the Contributors

This book is in large part a compilation of the wisdom, effort, and experience of an array of talented, creative individuals—all of whom have been at the forefront of the discovery and dissemination of Asian cinema in the United States through books, websites, message-board postings, and feverish personal evangelism. Any serious enthusiast of Hong Kong, Taiwanese, or Chinese cinema would do well to seek out their incredible canon of work.

## SENIOR CONTRIBUTORS

**Art Black:** In addition to programming Asian film festivals and writing catalog articles, Black has authored historical CD liner notes, served as an entertainment magazine editor and book consultant, and written for countless print and Internet publications. Recently he contributed a chapter on Korean horror films to the collection *Fear Without Frontiers.*

**Grady Hendrix:** Hendrix is one of the founders and programming directors of Subway Cinema (www.subwaycinema.com). A film programming and exhibition collective, Subway Cinema is committed to increasing exposure and appreciation for Asia's popular cinema, which has traditionally been overlooked by American film distributors. It has held ten festivals in the past three years, and won *Time's* award for "Best Movie Website of 2002."

**Ric Meyers:** Meyers is a multiple martial arts hall of fame inductee and the movie columnist for *Inside Kung Fu* and *Asian Cult Cinema* magazines, as well as the author of *Great Martial Arts Movies: From Bruce Lee to Jackie Chan and More.* He has frequently appeared on television as an expert on martial arts cinema, and has provided audio commentary tracks for more than twenty DVDs, including *Once Upon a Time in China, Dragon Inn,* and *Drunken Master.*

**Peter Nepstad:** Nepstad is a freelance writer and editor of *The Illuminated Lantern* (www.illuminatedlantern.com), an online zine devoted to Asian cinema.

**Darryl Pestilence:** Pestilence is an author, critic, and filmmaker whose inimitable opinions on topics ranging far beyond Asian cinema can be read at his weblog, "In Hell There Are No Nightlites" (http://www.angelfire.com/apes/nightlight/index.htm).

## CONTRIBUTORS

**John Charles:** Charles is the associate editor and film reviewer for *Video Watchdog* magazine, and the author of *The Hong Kong Filmography (1977–1997).*

**Andrew Grossman:** Grossman is the editor of *Queer Asian Cinema: Shadows in the Shade,* the first full-length anthology of writing about gay, lesbian, and transgender Asian films. His writings on film and queer issues have also appeared in *Bright Lights Film Journal, Scope: The Film Journal of the University of Nottingham, Senses of Cinema,* and *American Book Review.*

**Linn Haynes:** Haynes is a contributor to many magazines, including *Deep Red* and *Oriental Cinema;* he also writes actors' bios for Crash Cinema's line of kung fu DVDs, and runs the site Sifu Linn's Cave of Kung Fu (http://www.tombofdvd.com). He is currently working on a book on Hong Kong film.

**Matt Levie:** Levie is a film and video editor living in San Francisco whose writings on Chinese cinema can be found in publications like *Bright Lights Film Journal,* among others. He also teaches editing and film theory at the Academy of Art College.

**Gary Morris:** Morris is the editor and publisher of *Bright Lights Film Journal* (http://www.brightlightsfilm.com). The author of a 1985 monograph on Roger Corman, he writes regularly for San Francisco's *SF Weekly* and Portland, Oregon's *Just Out,* among other print and online publications.

**Yvonne Teh:** Teh is a prolific film reviewer whose work can be found under the pen name YTSL on the Web at the comprehensive *Hong Kong Cinema: View from the Brooklyn Bridge* (www.brns.com).

**Curtis Tsui:** Tsui, a producer for the Criterion Collection of DVDs, is a longtime writer on the subject of Asian cinema, contributing to publications ranging from *aMagazine* to *Asian Cult Cinema,* and the online review site DVDAngle.com.

**Caroline Vie-Toussaint:** Vie-Toussaint is one of France's leading media writers and a veteran Cannes Film Festival organizer and judge. Her work has appeared in many of France's top television and movie magazines, while her documentary, *John Woo: A Bullet in the Plate* (in part based on her book, published by Dark Star in 2002) was telecast in Europe during the summer of 2003.

**Photo Editor:** Grady Hendrix

**Photo Researcher** (Beijing): Jonathan S. Levitt

**Webmaster, www.OUATIC.com:** Mark Shih

**Web Graphics, www.OUATIC.com:** Richard Ng

# Index